Virgin Snow

A NOVEL

Moxie Gardiner

NFB Publishing
Buffalo, New York

Printed in the United States of America

Virgin Snow/Gardiner—First Edition

ISBN: 978-1-953610-88-1

>   Title
>   Fiction> Coming-of-Age
>   Fiction> Women's
>   Fiction> Historical
>   Fiction>Book Club

NFB Publishing/Amelia Press
119 Dorchester Road
Buffalo, NY 14213
For more information visit Nfbpublishing.com

Cover art by Arleen Seed.

The author may be contacted at moxiegardiner@gmail.com, or on her website at moxiegardiner.com.

If You Know Someone in Crisis, call or text the 988 Suicide & Crisis Lifeline. The Lifeline provides 24-hour, confidential support to anyone in suicidal crisis or emotional distress. Call 911 in life-threatening situations.

For the people of the West Side of Buffalo,
who inspired this book and still own a piece of my heart,
and for my mother, an angel on earth,
who in no way resembled Big Ange

Part One

The Calling
1968

Chapter One: Call the Priest

Cosi McCarthy made the sign of the cross, took a deep breath, and turned the doorknob to her parents' bedroom. She paused for a second, listening intently for her mother's voice. The Sicilian aunts, her mother's sisters, had trudged through the snowstorm that had shut down Buffalo's streets that evening, to gather in the kitchen at the far end of the apartment's narrow hallway. The low murmurs and smell of espresso suggested that her mother was probably sitting at the table, answering their questions. Cosi slipped inside the bedroom and shut the door.

The airless room reeked of medicine and body odor. Cosi hesitated, staring at the emaciated figure lying motionless beneath the white bedspread. She tiptoed to her father's side and laid a plump hand on his bony one. Johnny McCarthy half-opened his eyes and smiled.

"Daddy?" Cosi whispered.

Her father ran his tongue across his cracked lips. "How's my good girl?"

She held her breath and willed herself not to cry. She focused instead on the white crust in the corners of his mouth, dry as the ashes in the seams of a fireplace, and reached for the glass of water on the nightstand. She dipped a washcloth in it and wiped his lips. "Mama told me not to bother you, but no one will tell me what's happening. How are you feeling?"

Johnny struggled to swallow before he spoke. "I'm fine, sweetheart... don't worry." He gave her a tiny wink. "Go now...before your mother comes back...and we both catch hell."

Cosi glanced over her shoulder at the door, listening again for her mother. She turned back to her father who appeared to be nodding off and felt the tear slide along her nose and down her chin. *Could this be the end?* Her father was only 35 years old, her best friend, and the most important person in her life. She could not imagine life without him. She struggled to choke back her sobs and, fearing she would wake him, stumbled toward the door, and froze. *Were those footsteps?*

Panicked, Cosi opened the closet door, opposite the foot of the bed. She crawled in atop her mother's black shoes and her father's work boots, and crouched beneath the hanging shirts and blouses, trying to slow her breathing, inhaling the cloying admixture of leather, mothballs, and Woolworth's perfume. Leaving the door open a crack, she angled herself so she could see her father lying on the bed and tried not to make a sound.

Seconds later, Big Ange McCarthy burst through the door like a Buffalo snowplow, talking loudly to a second person. Leaning forward, Cosi peered through the crack and spotted the black bag of the family doctor. She held her breath, trying to hear what the doctor was saying.

"Have you called the priest?" Dr. Zanghi was pressing his stethoscope against her father's chest, while her mother paced, the wooden floor creaking beneath her weight.

"Not yet. He's only been like this since this afternoon."

The doctor rummaged through his bag. "He's fading. Make sure he gets his Last Rites."

Big Ange reached up for the thick crucifix on the wall above the bed and set it gently on the nightstand. Every home on the West Side of Buffalo had a cross like this, hollowed out with tiny candles and a vial of holy water tucked inside, the necessary implements for administering the sacraments to the sick or dying. An emergency kit, of sorts, for Catholics on their last legs.

"I got things ready," Big Ange assured him, "but I'm worried Father Mario won't get here in time, on account of the snow." As if to punctuate her concern, the January storm howled and beat a rhythm against the windowpanes.

"Call him now. I can't do anything more than ease your husband's pain." The doctor gave her father a shot and began packing up his things. When he clicked his bag shut, her mother pleaded, "Are you sure, Doctor? Johnny's very tough, you know."

The doctor touched her mother's arm and walked toward the door. Cosi ducked her head under the hanging clothes, barely breathing, as the doctor moved past. He stopped just outside the closet and Cosi could make out his words clearly. "I'll ask your sisters to call Father Mario, and give you time to say goodbye."

"No! I'm not ready."

Dr. Zanghi sighed. "Take your time, then. But you don't have long."

Cosi listened for the closing of the door before she peered through the crack again. Her mother was sitting on the bed, her back to the closet. Big Ange moaned and threw herself on her husband's chest. "Johnny," she pleaded, "Don't die. I love you. I need you."

Cosi heard the anguish in her mother's voice and wanted badly to escape the closet, to offer words of comfort. But she knew her mother all too well. Fear of her mother's temper kept her rooted to the closet floor, and she hesitated long enough to see the bedspread shift and her mother lean back, surprised. Her father was moving.

Cosi put her ear as close to the door as she dared, straining to hear her father's voice.

"Angie..." her father gasped, "I need to tell you something... in case Father Mario doesn't get here. I need to confess a sin...so I can die in peace... and rest in the hands of the Lord."

Her mother began to cry softly. "What is it, Johnny? Tell your Angie."

Her father's breathing was labored, his words coming in short bursts. "It's hard... to say this...I've been unfaithful."

Her mother sat up and took a deep breath. "I knew it," she cried, shaking her head. "I knew all along, you rotten louse." She started weeping in earnest and wiped at her eyes with her apron. "You're a shithead, Johnny, but my hand to God, I swear if you live, I'll forgive you. I *need* you. How am I gonna raise three kids without a husband?"

There was silence before Johnny spoke again. "There's more... your sister Rosa...she came on to me...please forgive me."

Cosi was confused. *What did he just say about Aunt Rosa?*

"My sister?" her mother demanded. "My damn *sister?*"

The rise in Big Ange's voice was a familiar prelude to one of her violent outbursts. Cosi watched her mother push herself off the bed and stomp toward the door. Suddenly, she came into view again, hovering inches over Johnny's face. "You stinking piece of Irish shit," she hissed.

Cosi watched in horror as her mother twisted around, grabbed the heavy plaster Infant of Prague statue sitting on the chest of drawers beside the bed, and held it like a club over her father's head. Johnny simply closed his eyes, resigned to his fate. Her mother screamed, "*sporco bastardo!*" turned, and hurled the statue at the window. The glass shattered and moments later, Cosi felt frigid air creeping beneath the closet door. Again, her mother thrust her face inches from her father's nose. "I curse you and hope your soul rots in hell."

"Angelica…" Johnny wheezed, as Big Ange picked up the Last Rites crucifix, slammed it back up on the wall, and stood, waiting. Cosi watched her father's hand reach, trembling, for her mother's, only to drop back on the bed.

There was a soft knock. "Ange? Is everything all right in there?" It was Aunt Rosa's voice outside the bedroom door.

Big Ange clenched her fists and headed toward the door, but stopped mid-step. The sudden composure in her mother's voice was almost as chilling to Cosi, as the threat of violence.

"Call the priest," said her mother, "and tell him he's too late."

Cosi was barely aware of her mother leaving the bedroom or the screams and moans of her relatives when they heard the news. She lay curled in a fetal position in the closet, shivering and crying, shattered that her father had died with a terrible sin on his soul.

Eventually, she realized she had wet her pants. She slowly pushed open the closet door, satisfied that the room had gone quiet.

All activity had shifted to the kitchen. Still crouching, she scurried to her own bedroom unnoticed. She pulled off her wet clothes, put on her flannel nightgown, peeked down the hall, and breathed a prayer of thanks that the door to the apartment's only bathroom was wide open.

Once she had cleaned herself, Cosi stared at her swollen face in the mirror. What was she supposed to do now? Pretend she didn't know her father was dead? She was a lousy actress—no way she could pull that off.

Her older sister, Little Ange, solved the problem, running past the bathroom screaming "Daddy's dead! Oh my God! My poor Daddy!"

Cosi flung open the bathroom door and found herself face-to-face with her mother. "What happened?" she asked, hoping to look confused.

Big Ange started to speak but Cosi pushed past her. "No!" she cried, doing her best to imitate her sister. "No, Daddy can't be dead!"

Slipping into her room while the wails of her aunts reverberated throughout the apartment, Cosi rummaged through the two shallow drawers that held her clothes. She pulled out her First Communion rosary and struggled to remember the prayers she ordinarily knew by heart. She sat on her bed, numb with sorrow and self-recrimination, and stared at the statue of the Blessed Virgin Mary sitting atop the dresser she shared with Little Ange. Suddenly it occurred to her she had no time to waste. Her father's soul would be judged, and soon. She slid to the floor and knelt in front of the statue, clasping her hands tightly.

"Mary, Mother of Jesus," she whispered, "could you please talk to God right away, about letting my father into Heaven? I know he did something bad, but if it wasn't for the snow, Father Mario would've heard his confession and my dad would be on his way, you know, "upstairs." I don't mean to be disrespectful, but didn't your son Jesus make some mistakes? He's in heaven now, right, so I'm begging you, please have mercy on my father's soul for… whatever he did."

Cosi rested her chin on her knuckles while she waited for some sort of sign, and glanced at the framed snapshot of her family to the left of the statue. It was taken at Ellicott Creek, their favorite picnic spot, two years earlier. It broke her heart to look at her father, tall, russet-haired and healthy at the time, laughing with his arms stretched around the shoulders of his two daughters.

Cosi's older sister, named Angelica after their mother, was still referred to in the family as "Little Ange" though she was no longer little or angelic. At the time the photo was taken, Little Ange had just turned 13 and was already wearing the tight sweaters and heavy makeup that made her popular with the neighborhood boys. Big Ange, then 31, was short, full-figured and hawk-nosed, but pretty in her dark Sicilian way. She stood unsmiling, her hands resting on five-year-old Nino's shoulders. Cosi's little brother's face was expressionless, his eyes averted from the camera. Cosi kissed her finger and pressed it to her father's face, then to Nino's.

Cosi avoided looking at her then-11-year-old self in the picture, standing awkwardly beneath her father's protective arm while trying to cover the swell of her chubby belly with her hands. Although she had turned 13 in December, the photo was a painful reminder that unlike her mother and sister, she was not, and never would be, pretty enough to attract a tall and handsome husband like her dad, or like Joey Catalfano, the older boy next door who looked like a movie star. Cosi's dream was to one day be the mother in a family portrait like this, surrounded by her own loving brood. She looked at her thick, unruly hair and puffy face and wondered, as she often did, why God had made her so ugly.

Little Ange staggered into their bedroom, blubbering theatrically. She glanced at Cosi, who was still on her knees, with a look of disgust. "Get up, you idiot." Little Ange wiped the mascara from under her eyes with a tissue. "It's too late for your stupid prayers."

Cosi got up without a word and crawled into bed. As soon as Little Ange was asleep, she pulled out the diary hidden beneath her mattress, along with the tiny key she kept wedged in a crack between the floorboards near her bed. Unlocking the book, she turned to the page for January 15, 1968.

Dear Joey, she wrote, angling the page toward the light from the street lamp outside her window. *My dad died today and pissed off my mom who cursed him to rot in HELL. I've got to save him. The question is how?*

Chapter Two: Va Fangool

SNOW WAS STILL FALLING THE day after Johnny McCarthy died, and a relentless chill seeped through the uninsulated walls of the McCarthys' second-floor apartment. Cosi sat shivering on her bed with an old quilt wrapped around her shoulders, hoping to write in her diary before her sister showed up.

The little book had been a birthday present from her father, and as with all gifts from him, Cosi treasured it. "Why does it have a lock, Daddy?" she had asked while sitting on the side of his sickbed, fingering the little brass clasp and keyhole.

"So you can keep all your secrets from prying eyes."

She frowned as she smoothed his bedspread. "I don't have any secrets, Daddy."

"Everyone has secrets," her father had said.

Although her birthday was in early December, she had decided to wait until January 1ˢᵗ to begin writing in the "Five-Year Diary." She counted down the days, eager to get started.

On New Year's Day she had filled in the "Year" block with "1968" and paused, chewing on her pencil. There was only enough space for about 25 words a day in the tiny book, so Cosi knew they had better be good ones. An hour later, she had locked the book in frustration. *Dear Diary,* she had finally scribbled, *I don't know what to write about. My life is boring. Diaries are for interesting people, like detectives or astronauts.*

On January 2nd, she had tried again. *Dear Diary, OK I will write something every day because my dad gave me this present and he is very sick in bed.* She brightened, realizing her diary now had a purpose. She would record the miraculous story of how, when her dad got sick, her prayers had made him well. On January 3rd she wrote, *Dear Diary, good news. Dr. Zanghi didn't come today. My prayers are working. Dad is getting better. Thank you, GOD!*

Now, wrapping the quilt more tightly around herself, she flipped through the next few pages to January 8th. That was the day, she remembered, when she had her genius idea. *Dear Joey,* she had penned. *Instead of writing to Dear Diary I decided to write to you because it's more fun to write to a real person, OK?* On January 9th, giggling, she had recorded some details about herself. *Dear Joey, I know you are much older than me but I am mature for my age. I will need to buy a bra soon.* The next day, she poured her heart out. *Dear Joey, the doctor came today and won't tell me anything. I wish I could talk to someone like you instead of crying all day.* The last few pages were a sad chronicle of her father's final days.

As dusk settled on Fargo Avenue, the snow slackened and began to fall softly, like sifted flour. Cosi heard her sister slamming her way through the front door of the apartment, and quickly shoved the diary under her mattress. Today's entry would have to wait.

Cosi tried to shake the feeling she knew was coming, now that it was time to dress for the wake. Without thinking, she reached behind her neck, wrapped a strand of hair around her finger, and began to gnaw on it. Strangely, this always calmed her.

Little Ange threw her coat on the bed and produced a dress covered in thin, clear plastic. Cosi stared, wondering where on earth her sister had gotten it.

"Don't act so surprised," her sister snapped. "I been crying my eyes out over Daddy all day, but that don't mean I'm going to the wake in one of those ugly dresses Mama makes. I went to Norban's and found this one on sale." Little Ange removed the plastic and shot an exasperated look at Cosi. "Well? Get dressed, mopey. And stop chewing your stupid hair."

Cosi was grateful her mother didn't hear her sister's smart-alecky remark. Big Ange took great pride in the clothes she made, including the ones she hand-sewed for the Infant of Prague statue sitting in her bedroom, its head and left hand glued back on after a mysterious accident. Her mother's sewing had come to a halt during the long months of her father's illness, and Cosi wished she had thought ahead like her sister. She had nothing to wear tonight.

Cosi knocked on the thin wall that separated the girls' bedroom from their mother's. "Mama, what should I wear to the wake?"

"Don't matter," came her mother's voice from the other side of the wall. "Just wear something dark to show respect, and don't chew your hair."

Little Ange slipped into the tightly-fitted black cocktail dress and nodded approvingly at herself in the mirror. Cosi rummaged through the narrow closet and grabbed her black and grey plaid school jumper, the darkest piece of clothing she owned. She waited until Little Ange had applied one more layer of mascara and a final coat of red lipstick, before she asked her sister nervously, "How do I look?" Little Ange shook her head. "You are *such* an *embarrassment.*"

The girls waited outside their mother's bedroom door until Big Ange emerged holding Nino's hand. Still carrying the weight from her third pregnancy, she was dressed in thick black stockings, sturdy black shoes, and a long black cotton dress that clung to her many folds. Shutting the door to her room, Big Ange caught the look on Little Ange's face.

"*Stai zitta*, no one cares what a widow wears," she muttered, shooing the family out to the waiting car. She eyed Little Ange's low-cut dress. "You look like a *puttana petita.*"

Big Ange had borrowed money to hold the wake at Bonnano's Funeral Home where the local Mafiosi were rumored to bring their dead. The Mafia, like the weather, was part of the warp and weft of living on the West Side of Buffalo where many households were first- or second-generation Sicilian. Everyone seemed to know someone who knew someone in "the mob," and holding the wake at Bonnano's carried a certain amount of prestige. That said, no one on the Sicilian side of Cosi's family ever spoke of the Mafia, except for Uncle Carm.

"There's no Mafia in Buffalo," Uncle Carm insisted. "That's bullshit made up by Irish cops to make us look bad."

Hearing that, Johnny McCarthy would laugh out loud and fold his arms. He used to love getting into arguments with his Sicilian in-laws. "Oh really, Carm?" Johnny would say. "What about the big FBI raid over at that restaurant down the street? My brother Tommy claims they arrested 32 wise guys. I saw the limousines parked up and down Hampshire Street myself."

Uncle Carm dismissed it with a wave of his hand. "They let 'em all go. No evidence, *capisce?* Which proves my point. The Buffalo cops and the FBI got it in for Sicilians."

Cosi had a lock of hair wrapped around her finger when they entered the funeral home, but when she saw the stiff, unrecognizable figure lying in the coffin, she let it go. That "thing" in the coffin looked nothing like her father, so maybe her father wasn't really dead. Relieved, she reached down for Nino's hand, but he pulled away and wandered off to play with his toys.

A few minutes later, the McCarthys strode in. Three of the four remaining McCarthy brothers—Jimmy, Danny, and the one they called Mack—had come directly from the bar. The fourth, Tommy, left from work, and was still in his police uniform. Cosi's aunts surrounded Big Ange, kissing and hugging and cooing their respects, while the McCarthy uncles went directly to the casket. They wept, placing their large hands upon Johnny's lifeless ones. Uncle Tommy was the first to speak. "Johnny, why couldn't you beat the Big C, you *focker?*"

The Big C? Cancer? No one ever spoke the word, but Cosi knew what the "Big C" was. Now she understood why no one talked to her about it. They were all afraid if they said the word aloud, the terrible disease would find them next. Fear climbed up her spine as she tried to sort out what she had just heard. *How did Daddy get the cancer? Did he catch it from someone? Could I catch it from him?* She stepped quickly away from the casket.

Cosi looked up while her mother's side of the family, the Di Giacomos, silently entered the funeral home. "Nonna" Di Giacomo, Cosi's grandmother, cut to the front of the receiving line, leaning heavily on her black cane. Like Big Ange and Little Ange, Nonna was dressed in black. She always dressed in black, though the year of mourning for her late husband had ended decades ago. The old woman shuffled painfully up to the casket, shook her head, and then bit her hand when she looked inside. Everyone knew she hated her son-in-law.

Big Ange's three sisters and their husbands waited patiently in line to pay their respects. Francesca, the oldest sister, and her husband Carm, stepped up after Nonna. Aunt Franny, whose salt-and-pepper hair was always pulled into a severe bun, was a more pious version of Cosi's mother. She presented Big Ange with a Mass card. "I already prayed the first day of the Novena for him, Ange. Eight more to go. I'm going to the Lewiston shrine on Sunday so I can pray direct to the Virgin Mother."

Big Ange kissed Franny's cheek and patted her hand. "Thanks Franny. I'm gonna need the Virgin's help."

Rosalia, the sister who was a year younger than Big Ange, and her husband Benny, moved next to the head of the line. Cosi held her breath. Aunt Rosa looked beautiful in a fitted suit, her glossy black hair done up in a beehive, her make-up expertly applied. Big Ange and Rosa had long despised each other, and Cosi was very worried that this might be the time and place her mother's hatred would finally explode. But when Rosa came up, Big Ange simply looked away and muttered in a flat voice, "Thanks for coming."

With the slightest shift of her eyes, Big Ange watched Rosa move toward Johnny's body. Cosi saw her aunt sob and grab the edge of the casket, rocking back and forth, while her mother looked away and greeted the next guest. Cosi exhaled nervously. This was not like her mother.

Mariella, the youngest of the sisters, was sobbing loudly as she stepped up with Uncle Tony. Everyone loved Aunt "Mari," the only member of the Di Giacomo family, they all agreed, who had a tender heart. All Cosi could see when she looked at her aunt, though, was the large mole on the tip of her chin. Cosi tried to avoid staring, but her eyes jumped to it like iron filings to a magnet.

"Ange, anything you need, you tell me." Aunt Mari blew her nose into a dainty lace handkerchief and shoved it inside the sleeve of her dress. "I made baked ziti. I'll bring it over."

The funeral home was overflowing now with mourners, and Cosi could see the McCarthys congregating in a tight knot on one side of the viewing room, joking and making small talk with her father's co-workers from the steel mill. On the other side, she could see her Sicilian uncles and neighbors gesturing with their hands and cursing in Sicilian, while casting sidelong glances at the men across the room. The long history of physical violence between the Irish and Sicilians who vied for jobs in Buffalo's factories and along its waterfront always made Cosi uneasy when the two sides of her family came together. At weddings and funerals, where emotions ran hot and tempers flared easily, the men would occasionally express their feelings by pounding each other with their fists.

All eyes turned when Father Mario, pastor of Saint Michael the Archangel Church, entered the room. The male mourners surrounded him, hoping for a chance to talk to the man who absolved them of their sins and took instructions directly from God. Several women pressed toward the priest, admiring his bedroom eyes and perfect hair, and Aunt Mari sighed, "*Madonne*, Rosa, why did God have to take the one guy in the neighborhood who looks like Cary Grant and make him a priest?"

The crowd parted briefly so Father Mario could walk directly up to Big Ange. He picked up her hands and held them while he spoke, and Cosi could see her mother's face softening in his presence. The priest then turned to Little Ange, who quickly arranged her face to look both devout and mournfully attractive, inhaling and sighing as she answered his questions.

Cosi froze when she heard Father Mario ask about her and Nino. Unlike her sister, she was terrified of all the priests at Saint Michael's, convinced they remembered the sins she confessed and could see inside her blemished soul. Big Ange pointed to Nino playing under the casket, and then to Cosi, who was trying to make herself small behind a large spray of flowers. The priest headed toward her, and Cosi felt her heart flip.

Dear Lord, what should I say? Should I tell him about Daddy's dying confession and how he begged for forgiveness, but that Mama cursed him to Hell instead? Should I ask him to pray for Daddy's soul? Cosi could barely breathe now, as she reached for her hair. *If I tell him all that, he'll ask how I know. I'll have to confess how I hid in the closet and heard Daddy's secret.* Her bladder throbbed and she eyed the ladies' room, hoping she could make a run for it.

Father Mario put his hand on her shoulder. "How are you, my child?"

"I…I'm fine, I guess," Cosi croaked, looking at the floor. "I mean, my dad's dead and all so I'm not really fine but I …" Uncle Carm walked up and interrupted her.

"Hey Father, how you doin'?" Uncle Carm stepped in front of Cosi. He was of the firm opinion that nieces never had anything important to say. "I saw the story in the paper about the Pope, saying we should end the war in Vietnam." Father Mario hesitated and Uncle Carm continued. "What I wanna know, is the Pope saying all Catholics should be against the war?"

Heads turned. For the first time, Cosi noticed Mr. and Mrs. Catalfano, her next door neighbors, edging closer to Father Mario to listen. Her heart thumping, Cosi scanned the room, hoping to spot their son Joey. The Sicilian and Irish uncles also overheard the question and shoved their way closer to hear the priest's answer.

"President Kennedy was *for* the war, and he was a great President and a good Catholic, God rest his soul," offered Uncle Jimmy McCarthy.

"It's not quite as simple as that…" began Father Mario.

Mr. Catalfano interrupted him. "Father, does that mean my Joey, who's gonna be a soldier and go to Vietnam…is he doing something wrong in the eyes of the Church?"

Cosi gasped and covered her mouth. *Joey is going to Vietnam?*

"Of course, he's not doing something wrong!" shouted Uncle Mack with his brothers standing shoulder-to-shoulder behind him. "Your son'll be fightin' the godless Communists. That's the most important thing in the eyes of the Church, right Father?"

Uncle Tony spoke up, looking uncomfortable. "My son Dominic is a conscientious objector so he's staying outta the war. The Pope says people should follow their conscience."

"Your son is a gutless coward, pure and simple," Uncle Danny retorted.

"Who you calling a coward, you stupid mick?" demanded Uncle Tony. He slammed his left fist into the crease of his right elbow and raised his right fist in Uncle Danny's face, a gesture the neighborhood called the Italian salute. "*Va fangool.*" Uncle Tony spat on the floor.

Cosi eased farther behind the floral displays to get out of the line of fire. Uncle Danny shoved Uncle Tony and flipped him the bird. "Go *feck* yerself, you *feckin'* greaseball."

Uncle Tony lunged at Uncle Danny and within seconds, the two were rolling around the floor in their best suits and ties. The Sicilians rushed to Uncle Tony's defense and threw punches at any Irishman they could reach. Cosi's Irish uncles and the steelworkers enthusiastically joined the melee, pushing, punching, biting and cursing any and all of Big Ange's Sicilian relatives.

Father Mario tried to get between the combatants but Uncle Tommy the cop pulled him to the side. "Let 'em fight, Father," he advised. "They need to get it outta their systems."

Cosi ran crying to her mother, who was shrieking at everyone to stop. Someone hit Uncle Carm squarely in the jaw and sent him flying backwards into her father's casket. There was a collective gasp as the casket lurched, tipped over in semi-slow motion, and crashed to the floor on its side. Big Ange moaned, slumped sideways, and fell heavily to the floor. Cosi ran and knelt next to her, sobbing, "Mama, wake up, don't die on me too, Mama, don't die!" Little Ange pulled her mother's head into her lap and cursed her uncles. "Assholes! See what you done!"

Aunt Mari rushed to her sister with smelling salts. When she came around, Big Ange took one look at the toppled casket and cried, "Where's Nino?" A great hush descended over the room as Father Mario, Aunt Mari, and several others walked cautiously toward the casket.

Aunt Mari slipped her arm under Father Mario's and hugged it to her breast. "Oh my God, I'm afraid to look." Tiptoeing around behind the fallen casket, they heard Nino's voice. He was not under the casket, but kneeling on all fours nearly face-to-face with his dead father.

"Daddy?" Nino rocked from side to side.

Big Ange hurried over to scoop him into her arms. *"Meschino,* it's OK," she purred.

"Daddy?" Nino repeated again, his eyes blank. "Daddy?"

Dear Joey, Cosi wrote in her diary that night. *I heard at my dad's wake you're going to Vietnam. PLEASE DON'T GO. You could die there and I can't take another funeral.*

Chapter Three: The Evil Eye and the Virgin's Visit

The mourners at Johnny McCarthy's funeral the next morning were not prepared for the thaw. The packed church was stifling and people were shedding their heavy winter coats.

"*Dominus vobiscum*," Father Mario intoned.

"*Et cum spiritu tuo*," replied the congregation. The parishioners of Saint Michael's still wanted their funeral Masses conducted in Latin; the Vatican's new rules be damned.

Perspiring under her many layers, Cosi stared at the casket and fingered the little cloth scapular that hung from her neck. Father Mario had given one to every child in her class and told them they would be spared the fires of Hell if they always wore it. Why hadn't she thought to put her scapular over her father's head when he lay dying?

After Mass, the long funeral cortege sloshed through the city streets, slowly making its way to Forest Lawn Cemetery. Uncle Mack, being single, offered to drive Cosi's family in his new Buick Le Sabre. The McCarthys were proud of Uncle Mack's college degree and his well-paying job at Marine Midland Bank. "Mack's the smart one," her father used to boast. "And it never hurts to have someone in the family who can put his hands on a few quid."

The route to the cemetery went past the foreboding state psychiatric hospital, its dark maroon Gothic buildings walled off from the street by a black wrought iron fence. In the distance, Cosi could see patients on the porches behind heavy steel screens, pacing like caged animals, she thought sadly. Her mother and all her superstitious Sicilian relatives were convinced the patients were under the evil spells of *streghe* and demons, and everyone in the Buick made the sign of the cross as they drove by.

At the cemetery, Cosi felt dizzy while she stood contemplating the gaping pit. Mercifully, the burial ceremony was short. Big Ange went to the casket, made the sign of the cross, kissed the red rose the funeral director handed her, and placed it carefully on top. When she turned away, a long, animal-like moan came from some place deep inside her. The mourners stared and Uncle Mack tried to draw her into a hug, but she pushed him aside.

"Take me home," she croaked. She clutched Nino's hand and headed for the car.

"Wait." Uncle Mack grabbed her arm and spun her around. "Everyone in the church basement will be waiting for you to start eating. Do you want them to just stand there starving? Pull yourself together, woman. You have an obligation."

Big Ange found a handkerchief in her purse, wiped her eyes and blew her nose loudly. Uncle Mack pulled out a wrinkled pack of cigarettes and lit one, handing it to her. She inhaled, coughed, and handed it back. "Obligation? All I got now are stinking obligations." She coughed again and sighed. "OK, I'll go. But I'm not talking to nobody."

An obscene amount of food awaited them at the funeral luncheon. The aunts and other parishioners had put together an enormous Irish-Italian buffet, with dozens of dishes arranged between the corned beef and cabbage at one end of the long table, and pans of lasagna at the other. In the corner, her Irish uncles pulled chairs together, smoked cigars, and told stories about her father. Someone brought out a photo album and Cosi saw that even as a boy her father was good-looking, with a lopsided smile and wavy hair that reminded people of Elvis. Even the hard hat her father wore at the steel mill had the singer's nickname — "The Pelvis" — written on it.

Cosi's mind drifted back to the horrible, confusing scene in her parents' bedroom. What had her father actually done with Aunt Rosa? Why would her mother, who told her father on his deathbed that she loved him, curse him a minute later? This wasn't how the Holy Sacrament of Matrimony was supposed to work. She felt a headache coming on, and a chance whiff of cigar smoke sent her running to the ladies' room. After vomiting twice, Cosi stumbled back to the dining area. Seeing Cosi's colorless face, Big Ange turned to Uncle Mack. "*Now* can we go?"

Cosi clung to her mother's arm on the way to the car, the pounding in her head so intense she could barely open her eyes. Her uncle was going on and on about Senator Robert Kennedy, who was soon to give a speech at the University of Buffalo. Cosi held her hands over her ears. *Can everyone just please shut up?* But Uncle Mack kept up the chatter. "Now Bobby Kennedy…there's an Irishman who'd give LBJ a run for his money."

Big Ange ignored him while she walked, scanning the parking lot. Little Ange grabbed her uncle's arm, suddenly excited. "I hope he does run. I think Bobby's dreamy. If he stops at UB to give a speech, I'm going."

Big Ange slapped the back of Little Ange's head. "No daughter of mine's going to UB. The place is fulla communiss and hippies."

Little Ange laughed, "What do you know about college, Mama?"

"I know girls have no business being there." Big Ange helped Cosi into the back seat and added, "No husband wants a wife who's smarter than he is."

"Is that what you're worried about? I'm not gonna *go* to college. I just wanna get a good look at Bobby Kennedy. I'm going to secretarial school to learn typing, you know that. The only way to get outta this stinking hellhole is to be a good secretary and marry a rich businessman."

"Now you're talking sense."

Once she had settled Cosi next to her in the big back seat, Big Ange continued to stare out the window. Cosi lifted her head from her mother's shoulder just in time to see Aunt Rosa picking her way through the slushy ruts. When Aunt Rosa was near their car, Big Ange slowly moved her hand to the bottom of the window, folded down her two middle fingers and pointed her index and baby fingers at her sister. She twitched her hand. Cosi knew immediately it was the *fare la corna*. Her mother was secretly cursing Aunt Rosa with the *malocchio*—the evil eye.

Cosi felt too sick to care and barely remembered Uncle Mack carrying her up to the apartment. At some point during the miserable night that followed,

Cosi awoke with a start, remembering her forgotten diary. It hurt her pounding head to try to write in the dim light from the street lamp, but she was worried she might not survive the night.

To Whom It May Concern, she wrote. *If I die and you find this diary, please DO NOT show it to JOEY CATALFANO!!*

Dr. Zanghi was on the phone with her mother the next morning.

"She's burning up," Cosi heard her mother say. Big Ange was standing in the living room, the extension cord on the kitchen wall phone pulled to its full length. "But she won't let me put the thermometer you-know-where."

Cosi lay in her bed, her twisted sheets soaked with sweat. She had thrown up repeatedly during the night, and her mother looked worried when she had brought the weak tea with sugar and a piece of dry toast that ended up all over her blanket.

"OK. I'll tell her you said she has to..." Big Ange put the receiver down and marched into Cosi's bedroom with the rectal thermometer and a jar of Vaseline.

Cosi wailed. Her mother had not seen her bottom since she was a baby. Reluctantly she rolled onto her side and pressed her burning face against the cool side of the pillow while her mother briskly went about her business.

"It's 105.2" muttered her mother, looking at the offending instrument before returning to the phone. A minute later she was back, sitting on Cosi's bed.

"Dr. Zanghi told me there's a bad flu bug going around this year. It's very contagious, he says. They're even telling the hospitals not to let sick people into the emergency rooms. He wants you to stay in bed and drink liquids. I'll bring some washcloths to try to get your fever down. Your sister's gonna have to sleep on the couch."

After her mother wiped her fiery face with a cold washcloth, Cosi looked up at her, grateful for this small kindness. Big Ange pulled the blankets up to Cosi's chin and put a plastic wastebasket next to the bed. "In case you gotta puke again."

Cosi had no idea how much time had passed when she next awoke. Her bedroom was dark, with only the weak light of the street lamp casting shadows across her sister's empty bed. The hammering in her head continued as she looked at the dim outlines of her dresser, the mirror, her sister's posters, the white statue of the Blessed Virgin Mary.

Whenever she moved, her stomach lurched. She tried to lie still, focusing her eyes on the shiny porcelain replica of the Virgin Mother, its long white shawl covered with tiny roses. She began to recite the "Hail Mary" and felt her eyes grow heavy. Maybe sleep would come at last.

The statue turned its head and looked at her. Cosi choked back a scream. Petrified, she pulled the blanket over her head and tried to breathe. *Dear God, is She here to tell me I'm about to die?* She clawed at her chest, searching for her scapular. "I love you, Jesus," she whispered into the blanket, and waited to find out what it was like to be dead.

Nothing happened. *Well, if I am dead, that didn't hurt too much.* She inched the covers back from her head and saw the statue, bathed in the soft light of the streetlamp, still looking at her. Then it spoke:

"My child, do not be afraid. It is not your time to come to Heaven. Your father committed a mortal sin and died without absolution. You must sacrifice your life to save his soul and save your family from the consequences of his actions. If you do this, God will forgive."

Cosi tried to respond but no words came. She pinched herself three times and pulled the hair at the nape of her neck as hard as she could. *This isn't real,* she told herself. *This is a dream.* She laid her hand over her rapidly beating heart and quickly rolled to face the wall. When she mustered the courage to look once more, the statue gleamed, frozen and white.

Her fever broke the next morning. She spent the next several days in a stupor, too frightened to say anything, but the vision tormented her. Had it really happened? One thing was certain: she did not die that night, just as the Virgin Mother said. She struggled to remember the Virgin's words, but the only ones that stuck in her head were "you must sacrifice your life."

What did *that* mean? Jesus sacrificed *his* life and died a hideous death. Surely, Jesus' mother did not want her to do that. Maybe she wasn't supposed to die at all, and "sacrifice" meant giving up earthly pleasures or dedicating her life to helping others. How was she to know?

Cosi knew she needed to hear from the Blessed Virgin again, but the thought terrified her. What if she didn't like the Holy Mother's answer? Saying no to a command from the Virgin Mary was not an option, so for several nights she lay awake, face turned to the wall, hoping to find another way to learn what fate had in store for her.

Of one thing she felt certain. The Visit—and that message—was likely to change her life forever. Miracles had a way of doing that …whether you liked it or not.

"MAMA," COSI began one afternoon while her mother shaped meatballs in the kitchen. "Do you think the Virgin Mary really visits kids, like the ones at Lourdes and Fatima?"

"Are you kidding me? She's too busy up in Heaven, taking care of all those useless men. She probably has to cook for everyone up there…" Big Ange paused and *BAM!* Her hand slammed down, flattening one of the meatballs. Cosi eased silently out of the kitchen.

It had been weeks since the "Visit" and Cosi needed to talk to *someone.* Her dad was the one she had always gone to with questions, and her mother, at least for now, seemed like a poor substitute. Little Ange, she knew, would laugh in her face. There was only one other person she even considered asking. Aunt Franny went regularly to the Lady of Fatima Shrine in Lewiston, 20 miles north of Buffalo, to pray. If anyone would know if the "Visit" was real, it would be Aunt Franny. Cosi would ask her after Sunday dinner at Nonna's.

Cosi enjoyed the weekly dinners with the Di Giacomo family almost as much as the wild gatherings of the McCarthy clan. Nonna, Uncle Carm, Aunt Franny, and their son Vito lived together in an upstairs flat on West Avenue. In the apartment directly below them lived Uncle Tony, Aunt Mari and her cousins, Dominic and Alessia. Down the street lived Uncle Benny and Aunt Rosa. Cosi's family lived the farthest away—one block up and two blocks over on Fargo Avenue near Niagara Street. The Di Giacomo women would never consider living farther than walking distance from each other. None of them had a car or knew how to drive, and they loved to gather frequently for coffee and gossip, like crows flocking to a dumpster.

It seemed that everyone in Cosi's crowded West Side neighborhood was related in one way or another. Thousands of Sicilians, like her grandparents, had come to Buffalo from Sicily's small, impoverished mountain villages like Montemaggiore Belsito and Valledolmo. They found rooms or flats near the Niagara River where earlier waves of Sicilian immigrants had settled, especially in one notorious section known as "The Hooks."

Cosi had been inside every house on her block at one time or another. The houses were crammed so close together you could hear the neighbors snoring on either side. She grew up playing kickball and Red Rover in the street with neighborhood kids whose mothers would invite her in to drink Kool-Aid or eat freshly baked cookies. Some days she amused herself with a secret game, trying to guess which house in the neighborhood she would live in one day with her own husband and many children.

Walking into Nonna's tiny apartment, Cosi could smell the bread in the oven and a huge pot of sauce bubbling away on the stove. Cosi prayed it was meatballs dancing merrily under the lid this week, not tripe or pig's feet, which Nonna sometimes slipped in.

This Sunday, the meal seemed to drag on. Cosi twisted her hair impatiently while her uncles commiserated about the Buffalo Bills' lousy record. Her aunts, sitting at the other end of the table, debated whether Loblaw's or Super Duper had better deals that week. Cosi pushed a piece of tripe under her napkin and waited until Aunt Franny finished her coffee.

"Can we talk alone, Aunt Franny?"

Her aunt stared in surprise. The unspoken rule was that children were to shut up and learn from their elders at the dinner table, not have private, one-on-one conversations. Cosi reddened, but Aunt Franny followed her out to the back hall, folded her arms, and waited.

Cosi took a deep breath. "Aunt Franny, I know this will sound crazy, but I think the Blessed Virgin came to visit me."

"What?" Her aunt narrowed her eyes and looked angry. "This is not something to joke about. What did she say to you?"

"Well…she said I wasn't going to die from the flu because I needed to do something first. She said I might have to… sacrifice my life," Cosi hesitated. Now was not the time to bring up her father's sin.

"What was she wearing?" Aunt Franny demanded.

"She was dressed all in white, and there was a light shining on her," Cosi whispered.

Her aunt grabbed her by the shoulders and searched her face. She shook her, looked at her again, and suddenly erupted, *"Madre di Dio!* You heard from Our Lady of Fatima? Are you sure?" she shouted, shaking Cosi once again to see if she could frighten any deception out of her. "If you are lying, that is a mortal sin, and I must slap you."

"I think…I'm sure." Cosi was frightened now. "I mean, I was in bed looking at the white statue of Our Lady and she talked to me. She saved my life. It's why I'm still here."

Cosi watched her aunt's face pivot from doubt to awe. "Our Lady of Fatima visited you!" She dropped to her knees, took her niece's hands, and began to pray the Hail Mary aloud. When she got to the part, "blessed art thou among women," she looked meaningfully at her niece. "Holy Mary, Mother of God, pray for us sinners," they intoned together, "now and at the hour of our death, Amen."

Aunt Franny rushed back to the dining room with Cosi in tow and interrupted the arguments over sports and supermarkets. "There has been a miracle! Cosi was visited by the Blessed Virgin Mary!" There were bewildered gasps and murmurs as the relatives stared, first at Franny, then at Cosi. Finally, they turned to Big Ange for an explanation. Big Ange shrugged.

"I got no idea what she's talking about. What can I say? She's got a wild imagination…."

Aunt Franny cut her off. *"I'm* the first one she's told. Our Lady visited our little Cositina while she was sick in bed. The Blessed Mother spared her life."

Cosi could see the skepticism on the faces of her relatives, especially her mother's, but she was also relieved. At least Aunt Franny believed her. After much shouting and hand-waving, the adults decided there was only one thing to do — talk to Father Mario.

After Mass the next Sunday, the four Di Giacomo sisters brought Cosi to the rectory at Saint Michael's. "Father," Big Ange began, trying to arrange herself more comfortably on the hard wooden chair. "We had a certain unusual thing happen to my Cositina here," she nodded in Cosi's direction.

"She heard from the Mother of God," blurted Aunt Franny, making the sign of the cross.

"She *thinks* the Virgin Mary talked to her while she was lying in bed, out of her head with a high fever," Big Ange retorted, to make sure Father Mario was aware of all the circumstances. "She hasn't heard from the Holy Mother since."

"We just need to know if there is something special we should do, like go to a shrine or say special prayers to the Blessed Virgin," Aunt Franny explained.

"Or maybe let the Pope know," suggested Aunt Mari.

"Cosi's not sure what she's supposed to do next," sighed Big Ange. "She thinks God wants her to die but she's not sure how. Why would God want a little girl to die, I ask you? I'm afraid my daughter might do something very stupid, Father."

Cosi shifted uncomfortably in her chair. Father Mario made a little steeple with his hands and looked at her. "Tell me about it in your own words, my child."

Cosi told the priest what she remembered of that night. The light shining on the statue. The head turning. The words spoken to her. "She said I wouldn't die of the flu" Cosi offered, looking steadily at the floor, "but she wants me to sacrifice my life."

Father Mario nodded thoughtfully. When Cosi finished, he sat quietly, eyes closed. Finally, he bowed his head. "Let us pray." The Di Giacomo sisters bowed their heads and Cosi quickly followed suit. "Heavenly Father, we ask you to provide us with your divine guidance on the spiritual path that you wish your child, Cositina McCarthy, to follow. Share with us your wisdom, we beseech you, so that we may steer her down the path you have determined is her destiny. In the name of the Father, Son, and Holy Spirit."

"Amen," they responded in unison. Big Ange and her sisters looked at Father Mario.

"It may take a while before we hear back," said the priest.

"How long?" asked Big Ange, tapping her foot.

"God works on his own timetable."

Big Ange rolled her eyes and leaned forward. "Father, tell me something. Isn't it possible Cosi got the calling to be a Catholic sister? Couldn't that be what the Blessed Virgin meant?"

Father Mario rubbed his chin. "I suppose it's possible."

Cosi stiffened, horrified at the thought. Become a *nun*? Nuns were mean, horrible women who lived with other nuns. She wanted a husband and lots of children. She started to protest but Big Ange slapped her hands down on her knees and stood up, knocking over her chair.

"It's settled then!" she erupted. "My Cosi's gonna become a nun." Big Ange clasped her hands together and looked heavenward. "Thank you, God, for making something special outta her." She flung her arm around her daughter and hurried her toward the door.

"Well, I'm glad we got that straight," Big Ange told her sisters as they filed out of the rectory. "I made a pie. Who wants to come over?"

Dear Joey, Cosi wrote in her diary that night. *I am doomed. Sacrificing my life is bad enough. Becoming a nun? That's worse than death.*

CHAPTER FOUR: SAINTS AND SCHOLARSHIPS

THE SNOWBANKS ALONG FARGO Avenue, gritty and pockmarked like a kid with bad acne, were an eyesore by the time March arrived. Cosi, holding Nino by the hand, climbed carefully over the blackened mound blocking their driveway to get to Uncle Mack's car. Uncle Mack reached up and, wedging his hands under Nino's armpits, lifted him easily into the back seat. He did the same for Cosi, grunting as he struggled not to drop her.

"You're getting to be a big girl. Are you sure you want to go to the parade?"

"Yes. Nino loves it."

When her father was alive, he would wake them early to beat the crowd lining the St. Patrick's Day parade route downtown. There they would stand in the bone-chilling cold for hours, waiting for the cavalcade to begin. Her father would give them each a small sip from his flask and the burning liquid would make Cosi choke, although she liked the way it warmed her insides. She always felt sorry for the majorettes in their skimpy uniforms, especially when Little Ange laughed and heckled the ones with the reddest legs.

Big Ange used to go along with the Saint Patrick's Day traditions, but this morning Cosi found her mother sitting in her bathrobe, drinking coffee and watching "Dialing for Dollars." When the phone rang, Cosi heard her mother say, "You can take them if you want, Mack. I'm not going anywhere."

An hour into the parade, Uncle Mack shouted, "Keep an eye out kids, your Uncle Jimmy should be coming soon." Mack lifted Nino onto his shoulders and tried to steady Cosi as she strained on her tiptoes to look for Uncle Jimmy, marching with the other politicians from the Irish First Ward.

"Uncle Jimmy, over here," screamed Cosi over the din of the South Park High School marching band. Uncle Jimmy waved as he went by, and kept waving until he was out of sight, to no one in particular, Cosi realized.

"Can we wait for Tommy, or are you too cold?" Uncle Mack had his shoulders hunched under Nino's weight and his hands shoved deep into his pockets.

Cosi looked up at Nino who was staring at nothing. "We're fine, I think."

Uncle Tommy and his fellow police officers from the Second Precinct followed shortly after, little puffs of moist air preceding them as they marched. Many wore white and green wool scarves over their uniforms to display the Irish colors. Cosi spotted her uncle immediately, his limp a dead give-away, and waved. Uncle Tommy smiled at them as he walked by.

"Want to go to Uncle Tommy's for hot chocolate after the parade?"

Cosi looked at her boots. "I guess so."

"Don't be sad now. Your Daddy would want you to have fun today."

"OK," she said finally, looking up at Uncle Mack, who was drinking from her father's old flask. "But only for hot chocolate."

Every house in the old First Ward was festooned with St. Patrick's Day decorations, and Uncle Tommy's house was no exception. Several officers were sitting in the living room looking at a scrapbook of old newspaper clippings spread out on the coffee table, shots of whiskey lined up nearby.

"Look at this one, Donny," said Uncle Tommy. "Remember Slick Martin?"

"Remember? How could I forget, mate? He was the wanker who shot you in the hip during the hold-up, right? A real maggot, that one."

"Yeah, that's him. See this article? He got what was coming to him a few years later."

"Stabbed in the back 14 times or something, right? Guess we weren't the only ones who hated that git." They all laughed. Cosi, who had been sitting quietly, sucked in her breath.

"They say the young guy who stabbed him was mental. Old Slick never saw it coming. Tell you the truth, I'm glad the kid got away with it."

"What happened to him, the kid?" Cosi began to gnaw at a lock of her hair.

Uncle Tommy pulled her next to him, hugging her to his ribs. "Now don't you worry, sweetheart. They caught the guy who killed Slick. He's not loose on the streets or nothing. They locked him up in the nut house and threw away the key." Uncle Tommy turned to his buddies and whispered, "She's got a wild imagination, this one. She thinks the Virgin Mary wants her to die, so she's afraid of everything."

It was getting dark when Uncle Mack dropped them off at home. Cosi was relieved to see her mother in the kitchen, fully dressed and making spaghetti. They ate quietly and, shortly after dinner, Big Ange announced she was going to bed.

Cosi was watching television with Nino sleeping on her lap, when she heard a strange sound coming from her mother's bedroom. She gently lifted Nino, tiptoed to the room, and opened the door slightly, enough to see the broken window still covered with plywood and her mother lying on the bed, her face buried in her father's coat.

"Are you OK, Mama?"

Her mother made no effort to wipe her face. "When you say your prayers tonight, thank the Blessed Virgin for deciding you're gonna be a nun. You'll be married to Jesus, and he won't break your heart."

Cosi quietly shut the bedroom door and leaned with her back against it. *Can't you tell, Mama, that my heart is already broken?* Her father was dead, along with her dreams of having a house, a husband, and children. Being married to Jesus would not fix that.

For the Di Giacomo family, the only religious holiday in March that mattered was the Feast of Saint Joseph on March 19th. Many of the Catholic schools in Buffalo closed in honor of the Virgin Mary's earthly husband, who also happened to be the patron saint of Sicily. Families would host a large "Saint Joseph's Table" in their homes and sometimes invite neighbors.

This year it was Uncle Tony and Aunt Mari who would host. Cosi kicked off her boots in the front hall and shoved her hands deep in her pockets in her latest attempt to break her hair-chewing habit. It would be the first time her family came to the feast without bringing a dish. Her mother said nothing, but Cosi could feel her shame as they walked in empty-handed.

The past two months had been a struggle in the McCarthy household. Cosi's father had made enough money at the steel plant to pay the bills and put food on the table, but her mother soon discovered that the family savings account held the children's First Communion money, and nothing more. Big Ange had no idea what to do, since she had never had a job or managed money in her life. She spent the first two weeks after Johnny's death trying to find the checkbook. Uncle Mack had come to the rescue, offering to help her apply for widow's benefits.

"Your benefit, as a widow with three children, comes to a little over $5,000 a year," he said when he hung up the phone after a long conversation with Erie County Social Services.

"*Madonne*," said Big Ange. "$5,000! We're rich!"

"Well, no. With his overtime pay at the steel plant, Johnny was taking home nearly $10,000 a year. You'll have to live on half of that. Your mortgage is over $300 a month, which means you'll have less than $1,400 left, or about 100 bucks a month. Break that down further, and you got about $25 a week to spend on utilities, food, clothing, the kids' tuition and everything else."

Big Ange pressed her palms to her temples. "You're hurting my head with all these numbers. How my gonna raise a family on $25 a week?"

"You can always go on welfare."

"Never! I will *not* go on welfare and shame us all." She folded her arms across her ample chest and stared at the ceiling. "I'm the bread winner now. I'll figure something out."

Cosi took one look at Aunt Mari's groaning table and quickly forgot her mother's distress, brightening at the sight of *calamari*, shrimp *scampi, pasta con le sarde*, and mussels *marinara*. There were vegetables in abundance, including breaded cauliflower, stuffed artichokes, and a large *antipasto* with everything from stuffed eggs to *caponata*—the sweet and spicy eggplant salad that was one of Cosi's favorites. She immediately looked for the altar dedicated to Saint Joseph, and found, nestled among the votive candles and lilies, her favorite desserts—*sfinge, cannoli, pizzelles,* and the sesame seed cookies they called *giuggiuleni.* She would have some of each, even if Little Ange got on her case.

Aunt Mari sidled up to Cosi and whispered. "You will be the Virgin Mother this year. Nino will be the boy Jesus, and my Dominic will be Saint Joseph."

Cosi looked at her in surprise. Little Ange, the oldest niece, always played the role of the Virgin Mary. Her sister loved sitting at the separate "saints table" where the three "special guests" were served first. When Aunt Mari showed Cosi to her seat, Little Ange gave Cosi the finger and mouthed "I hate you."

While she enjoyed the special treatment, Cosi found she missed hearing the dinner conversation at the main table. Her uncles were arguing about something that sounded important. She leaned forward to catch the gist of it.

"I hear they're gonna start busing at Grover," Uncle Tony, a graduate of Grover Cleveland High School, complained to Uncle Carm. "You can bet there's gonna be trouble."

"Sheesh! Tell me why they gotta do that?" demanded Uncle Carm, slamming his hand on the table. "It's like cramming the Irish and Italians into the same neighborhood, all due respect," he said, avoiding Big Ange's glare. "Each should stick with his own kind."

Cosi could not understand this kind of talk, which she had heard before. Why did her family dislike black people so much? Slick Martin had shot Uncle Tommy, and yes, Slick was black. But her family knew more people shot by their own friends and family members than by black people.

She remembered the first time a black family tried to move into their West Side neighborhood. The father, mother, and young son lived in an apartment above the corner grocery store. By all accounts, they were a working-class family like everyone else, no different from the Holy Family, Cosi thought, just looking for a safe place to stay. She sickened at the memory of the family moving out after someone threw eggs at their windows and wrote the "N" word on their door.

"If there's gonna be trouble at Grover," Big Ange huffed, "then my kids ain't going there. We gotta keep Cosi and Little Ange in Catholic school."

Cosi sat up. *Did Mama just say I could go to Catholic high school next fall?* Little Ange was already a sophomore at Bishop McMahon, but as the bills mounted up over the past two months, Big Ange started dropping hints her oldest daughter might need to transfer to a public high school. Cosi knew how much this pained her mother. Being able to send the kids to Catholic school was a source of pride for all the West Side families who could afford it.

The men pushed back from the Saint Joseph's table and rubbed their swollen stomachs while the women served coffee. Cosi immediately went to her mother's side.

"Mama, can we really go to Catholic high school next year?"

Her mother closed her eyes and rubbed the bridge of her nose with her thumb and forefinger. "We'll see."

Cosi knew her mother believed her primary job now, was to protect her daughters' virginity, something Big Ange herself had failed to do. Little Ange's unexpected debut was the reason Big Ange ended up with Johnny McCarthy in the first place. "Your virginity is the only thing you got worth anything," her mother told them repeatedly. "Put it in a safe and lock it up." An all-girls Catholic school was as good as a chastity belt, in Big Ange's view.

Cosi couldn't care less what her mother's reasons were. She had been hoping to go to Holy Martyrs Academy since starting first grade at Saint Michael's. The principal had told Big Ange that Cosi might one day be eligible for a scholarship to the prestigious high school. There were only three ways to get into Holy Martyrs—by being rich, very smart, or preparing to enter the convent. Cosi decided to talk to Sister Mary Mark after school the next day.

"Yes?" said Sister Mary Mark curtly, not looking up when Cosi edged into her office.

"It's me, Sister. Cositina McCarthy."

"Oh, Cositina come in," Sister Mary Mark stretched her thin lips into what passed for a smile. "Father Mario told me you now have a special relationship with the Virgin Mary. You should feel honored."

"Yes, Sister." Cosi puffed up a bit. "My mother thinks the Blessed Virgin wants me to become a nun, so I'm wondering if you think I could get a scholarship to Holy Martyrs."

"Oh? The Virgin Mother told you to become a nun?"

"Well, not exactly." Cosi blushed. "She said I wouldn't die from a fever because I had a special purpose."

"I see. And you assume that special purpose is to become a nun?"

"Well…I'm not sure, Sister." Cosi was flustered. She must not lie to a nun. She paused, then brightened. "But if I go to Holy Martyrs and get a spiritual advisor, I'm sure I'll find out."

"Do you *want* to become a sister in our Order? Or a cloistered nun? Do you understand the difference?" Sister Mary Mark stared at Cosi until she squirmed. "Taking your vows is a very serious commitment. You need to be sure this is what God wants. I would like you to talk to a spiritual advisor *before* you decide to go to Holy Martyrs Academy. I have already spoken to Sister Valentine and she has offered to become your mentor. If you still want to go to Holy Martyrs after talking to her, come and see me again."

Cosi was elated. Sister Valentine, the new second-grade teacher, was easily the most popular nun at Saint Michael's. She was young, pretty, and for a nun, quite hip. Like the rest of the school's pre-pubescent teens, Cosi found her fascinating. Rumors swirled around the school that Sister Valentine was in love with Father Mario, had long blonde hair hidden beneath her habit, and from time-to-time, snuck out of the convent to have a night on the town.

"Thank you, Sister Mary Mark, thank you so much," Cosi gushed, unsure if she should hug her principal or shake her hand. "I'll talk to Sister Valentine tomorrow."

Sister Mary Mark started to say something and Cosi thought she saw a hint of sadness in her principal's eyes. Sister Mary Mark quickly looked away and busied herself with the stack of papers sitting on her desk.

Dear Joey, Cosi wrote, *things are looking up. If I can get into Holy Martyrs they'll know I'm not good nun material and that will be that!*

CHAPTER FIVE: RADICAL NUNS AND SEXUAL REVOLUTIONS

W HEN COSI KNOCKED ON the door of the second-grade classroom, Sister Valentine was busy drawing something on the board with colored chalk.

"Hello! You're Cositina McCarthy, aren't you?" Sister Valentine grinned. "Come in."

Cosi looked around the room, unsure what to say. Should she begin with the visit of the Blessed Virgin, or go straight to the point about needing a scholarship to Holy Martyrs?

"They call me Cosi. What are you drawing on the board?" she asked, stalling.

"They're symbols of peace and unity." Sister Valentine continued to draw while she spoke. "The dove with an olive branch is the traditional symbol of Christianity. This one is a crane, a peace symbol in Japan, and next is the one associated with peace protests here in the United States. This one is the Bahai star, which symbolizes the unity of God, religion, and humankind."

Cosi looked at her, surprised. "Why do you care about all that stuff?"

"We Sisters need to be attuned to the challenges we face in the world of today," said Sister Valentine, "not just the words in our Daily Missal." She winked at Cosi and smiled again, showing her perfect white teeth. "What you see isn't for my second graders. It's for my seventh-grade catechism class. My students need to know about things like the "rights of man," so-called 'just wars,' and why all religions should be tolerant of each other's beliefs." She put down the chalk and turned to Cosi. "So, what can I help you with today?"

"Sister Mary Mark said I should talk to you about becoming a nun. My mother thinks I got the Calling, but the Blessed Virgin wasn't very clear about what she wants me to do."

"Ah, yes, I heard about the Visitation. Come here and sit down. Let's have a little chat."

Cosi sat in one of the too-small chairs behind a too-small desk, while Sister Valentine sat next to her, looking perfectly comfortable.

"Let's begin with a few basic questions. Why do you believe in God?"

Cosi looked warily at her. *Is this a test?* "I believe in God, the Father Almighty, Creator of heaven and earth. I believe in Jesus Christ, his only Son…" Cosi began reciting the Apostle's Creed.

"No," interrupted Sister Valentine, "I'm not asking you what you memorized from the catechism. I am asking why *you* believe in God. Why do you think there is a God?"

Cosi was startled. *How can a nun even ask such a thing?* "Of course, there's a God. Only communists and atheists don't believe in God."

Sister Valentine sighed. "Okay, but how many people in this world are Christians or Jews or Muslims simply because they inherited their beliefs from their parents? How many people have given any real thought to why they believe in God?"

A warm flush crept up Cosi's neck. She was not expecting this.

Sister Valentine reached over and squeezed Cosi's hand. "I am not asking this to embarrass you. Before you become a Catholic Sister and commit your life to God, you need to fully understand what you are getting into. Your faith must be very strong. Look deep into your soul and question everything. That's the only way you can make an informed decision, and not have regrets later."

Cosi's face fell. She had to send her application to Holy Martyrs within the next 30 days. She could feel her scholarship slipping away.

"I understand, Sister," she said, looking at the floor. She got up to go.

"You're not giving up that easily, are you?" Sister Valentine cocked an eyebrow. "Let me hear your rebuttal."

Cosi looked lost. "My rebuttal?"

"Yes. What do you have to say for yourself. Be honest."

Is she kidding? Arguing with some nuns would get you three sharp raps across the knuckles with a wooden ruler. Cosi tried to pull her thoughts together.

"OK, I admit I haven't thought about the things you're talking about. But if I can go to a good religious high school, with smart teachers, they can help me figure it out." Cosi crossed her fingers, hoping again this was a convincing argument.

Sister Valentine laughed. "Not bad, but you need work on your debating tactics if you ever want to win arguments. Will you agree to read the things I ask you to read this summer? Will you start to volunteer in the community as soon as possible? And will you join the debate team next year to sharpen your mind?" Sister Valentine stood up. "If you agree, I will strongly recommend that Holy Martyrs accept your application and award you a scholarship."

Cosi was confused. So now Sister Valentine *wanted* her to go to Holy Martyrs? She felt like she was riding the Wild Mouse at Crystal Beach, her head whipping left and right when she hit the sharp turns.

"Yes, Sister. I will read the books you give me, join the debate team, and volunteer in the community. I promise," she said, crossing her heart.

"Good. Now make sure your application gets there on time. Let Sister Mary Mark know we have had this talk. I'll do the rest. And here," Sister Valentine handed Cosi a slim book. "Start with this. It isn't long or difficult to read. After you've finished, come back and see me."

Cosi looked down at the paperback. On the cover was a statue of the Buddha, and the book was entitled, *Siddhartha*. She had a feeling this would be nothing like her Nancy Drew mysteries.

"Thank you, Sister." Cosi shoved the book in her book bag and hurried out of the room, eager to escape before Sister Valentine changed her mind.

Cosi walked home slowly, absorbed in her thoughts, ignoring Minnie the crossing guard when she waved her cheery hello. Everywhere children were playing outside on this mild, 45-degree day. Mothers threw open the windows of their apartments to let out the stale winter air and hang throw rugs and blankets on windowsills. The dirty snowbanks were small bumps now, and steady rivulets ran into the gutters and formed oily puddles in the potholes.

Cosi kicked at a lump of melting snow. If only her father was alive to explain this bewildering conversation with Sister Valentine. He, like all her relatives, blamed most of the world's troubles on the Second Vatican Council, which attempted to modernize the Catholic religion and make it more understandable for its followers. Johnny McCarthy declared the Council's final decisions "the dog's bollocks," and would no doubt have disapproved of Sister Valentine and all her radical ideas.

Distracted, Cosi walked upstairs and into the apartment. A screaming Little Ange pushed by her. "Oh, I can't friggin' believe you, Mama! You are the squarest person on earth!"

Little Ange stomped into the bedroom and slammed the door. Cosi walked into the kitchen where her mother was sitting at the table, making her grocery list. It was obvious she was struggling with her temper. Big Ange looked up and bellowed after her oldest daughter, "I *said* you are too young to go to Toronto with a boy. Get that through your thick skull."

"I hate you and your stupid rules!" came a muffled voice from down the hall. "Get that through *your* thick skull! You're the only person on the planet who hasn't heard of the goddamn sexual revolution!" They could hear Little Ange throwing things as she raged behind the bedroom door.

Big Ange bit her hand to stop herself from cursing and finally looked at Cosi standing in the kitchen doorway. "I swear to God she'll be the death of me one day." Big Ange rubbed her forehead with the heel of her hand. "Be a good girl and go to the store, OK?" She handed Cosi a list of items and a $10 bill without looking at her. "Make it stretch."

Cosi took the money. "Mama..." she began and thought better of it. Her mother had shut her eyes and rested her chin on her folded hands. Cosi would tell her about the scholarship later.

On her way to the Super Duper, she thought about Little Ange's comment. *A sexual revolution? What does my sister know about S-E-X?* Although Cosi was in eighth grade, the subject was never formally discussed in school. She did remember a time though, shortly after her First Communion, when a neighborhood boy told a group of kids how his brother had "put his pony in his girlfriend's barn." Cosi, though clueless, had giggled along with everyone else, but when she heard the boy's parents had whipped him with a belt, she was petrified. Obviously, being involved in such a discussion must be a mortal sin.

She remembered trembling when she went to her next confession. "In the future, try to keep your thoughts pure," Father Mario had said to the frightened seven-year-old. "For your penance say three Hail Mary's and the Act of Contrition." Cosi left grateful that God was so forgiving, and vowed to avoid all future discussions of ponies and barns.

Outside the Super Duper, she avoided looking at the West Side Public Library, sitting in the shadow of the supermarket. She knew it would draw her into its bosom like a loving granny, for she adored the little library with its musty smells and silent aisles. It inspired the same kind of awe and reverence as Saint Michael's Church. But she would have to endure the wrath of her mother if she came home late with the groceries.

She hesitated at the door of the supermarket. Perhaps she had a few moments to check the library's card catalogue for "sexual revolution." She hurried in past the cranky old librarian and looked to see if anyone was peering over her shoulder as she rifled through the card catalogue.

There were no cards for books with the words "sexual revolution" in the title, but she found two cards with the word "sexual." They were by a man named Alfred Kinsey, one called *Sexual Behavior in the Human Male*, the other, *Sexual Behavior in the Human Female*. Navigating her way quickly to the appropriate section of the shelves, she found the book about male "behavior," looked quickly through it, then immediately slammed it shut. *How can they have books like this in a public library! Surely, these books are on the <u>Catholic Church's Index Librorum Prohibitorum.</u>* She hurried out, wishing she could unsee what she just saw. She had a funny, tingling sensation in her underpants and worried about her next visit to the confessional.

She ran to the grocery store, pulled out her mother's shopping list, and tried to focus. Five-pound bag of flour, dozen eggs, milk, margarine, two small cans of Contadina tomato paste, onion, garlic bulb, a small jar of Miracle Whip, Quaker Oats, and a pound of sliced *capicola*. She would have to stop at Zarcone's Meat Market to buy that last item.

Cosi watched anxiously as the cashier rang up her items. "That'll be $10.30."

"That can't be," said Cosi. "I totaled it up in my head. Can I see the receipt?"

The cashier rolled her eyes and pulled the receipt out of the cash register. A woman in line behind Cosi folded her arms and shook her head.

"The eggs are on sale for 49 cents and not 69 cents" Cosi pointed out, "and the Miracle Whip is only 79 cents and not 99 cents." The cashier called her manager.

"She's right," said the manager, going over the receipt. "Give her a credit for those."

"The new total is $9.90," said the irritated cashier. "Bag it yourself."

It was cold now that the sun had set, and the wind whipped her hair as she rushed home. There wasn't enough money left for the *capicola,* and she sighed, relieved she had an excuse to skip Zarcone's and get home before her mother got mad. Counting pennies and enduring humiliation at the checkout counter were something people without fathers had to get used to, she told herself. Silently she handed her mother the groceries and the dime. Her mother promptly dropped the dime into the empty Quaker Oats box she kept hidden behind a large bottle of cod liver oil, where Little Ange would never find it.

CHAPTER SIX: SAFETY, SECURITY, AND THE WORLD'S LARGEST ROSARY

Buffalo was abuzz. Cosi ran home from school on April Fools' Day, having learned President Johnson announced the night before that he would not run again, clearing the way for Senator Robert Kennedy of New York to run for President on the Democratic ticket. When she told Little Ange, her sister squealed with joy, did a little dance, and decided it was time to become an involved citizen.

Two days later, Little Ange hung out at the local Democratic campaign headquarters after school, brought home a large poster of the senator's face, and hung it on her bedroom wall. She handed out "Sock it to 'em, Bobby" campaign pins to her family and friends. Her mother shook her head and threw hers in a drawer. "A single mother's got no time for politics," she told her irritated daughter.

On the 4th of April, Little Ange turned on the TV. "Senator Kennedy is giving a campaign speech in Indianapolis tonight," she said, imperiously. "We need to watch the news."

That's a first, thought Cosi. Since when had her sister ever shown interest in the news?

Cosi watched Little Ange adjust the rabbit ears antenna, trying to reduce the static on the black-and-white screen. The picture was still fuzzy when Walter Cronkite looked up from his papers and into the camera. "Good Evening. Dr. Martin Luther King, the apostle of nonviolence and the civil rights movement, has been shot to death in Memphis, Tennessee."

The sisters looked at each other. Little Ange grabbed the rabbit ears again, trying to improve the sound. Cosi knelt in front of the screen to hear better.

"Governor Buford Ellington has called out 4,000 National Guardsmen. And police report that the murder has touched off sporadic acts of violence in a negro section of the city...." Walter Cronkite continued, pressing a sound piece to his ear.

"Holy shit. We're in for it now," said Little Ange.

The next evening, they sat rapt in front of the TV, switching among the three channels, listening as broadcasters reported on the news as it came over the wires. There was a clip of a somber Robert Kennedy on the back of a flatbed truck in Indianapolis, where he announced Dr. King's assassination to a mostly black audience in a poor part of the city. People screamed and cried when the Senator broke the news, while he tried to compose himself and said he felt their pain. He reminded them of his brother's assassination, still fresh in everyone's mind.

"What we need in the United States is not division," he told the crowd, appealing for calm. "What we need in the United States is not violence or lawlessness; but love and wisdom, and compassion toward one another, and a feeling of justice toward those who still suffer within our country, whether they be white, or they be black."

"He's gonna be our next President, I can feel it," Cosi murmured. "He'll stop all this violence." Her mother and sister stood silently behind her, for once not arguing. With a shake of her head, Big Ange reached down and switched off the television.

"Let's eat," she said. "God knows we'll need our strength."

Tensions flared in the poorer sections of Buffalo, as in many cities around the country, and not for the first time. The year before, all of Buffalo was on edge when riots broke out across a broad swath of the impoverished East Side, one of 159 riots that exploded across the country during "The Long Hot Summer of 1967." For five days angry crowds smashed cars and broke windows. Uncle Tommy and many other police officers were called to try to stop the mayhem, and Cosi's whole family, even the Di Giacomos, prayed for his safety. Newspapers reported the number of injured each day as the violence threatened to spill over to other parts of the city. Dr. King had come to Buffalo to call for peace, just five months before his murder.

Cosi could sense her mother's growing anxiety. The latest riots just added to the long list of worries for her family. Their West Side neighborhood had always been tight-knit and the people here looked out for each other. But signs of decay had already begun to seep into the neighborhood. Every now and then, a member of the "non-existent" local Mafia was found shot to death in a restaurant or car. Brazen robberies and physical assaults were on the rise. Street gangs that called themselves "frats" vandalized buildings, terrorized neighborhoods, fought each other for turf, and increasingly roamed the streets with impunity. Rapes and sexual assaults were frequent, but discussed only in whispers amongst the women. Her mother began to believe that dangers lurked everywhere and she was powerless to protect her family.

"Buy a gun," advised Granny Archer, the McCarthys' other next-door neighbor. Granny grew up in Ohio's Appalachian foothills, where she learned to "shoot the tit off a squirrel when I was just a young'un." Her recently departed husband had dragged her to Buffalo when he got a job at the Trico plant making windshield wipers. She had never adjusted to the "big city."

Big Ange's fears though, went far beyond safety. She had few skills to support her family financially and taking a job as a cashier or waitress was out of the question. The school system at the time labeled Nino "mentally retarded." Big Ange declared that until the school system wised up, Nino would stay home with her.

They still owned their house—for now. Because it was a "double," with separate upstairs and downstairs apartments like many in the inner city, Cosi's family rented out the lower apartment. Uncle Danny McCarthy, Aunt Joanie, and their five children lived below them. Her cousins were poor and often dirty, and their flat smelled of unwashed diapers and un-spayed dogs. When Uncle Danny could not come up with the rent money, her father would let it go. Her mother was not so generous.

"You're a right big pain in the hole, Ange," Uncle Danny snapped, when she had gone downstairs on the first of April to ask him for the rent.

"I gotta feed my children." Big Ange looked him in the eye, unsmiling.

"What you need to do," snarled Uncle Danny, "is find a new sucker to marry."

"Maybe, but until I do, you need to pay up or I'm gonna find a new renter." Big Ange stomped up the stairs, empty-handed and furious. "*Cazzo*," she muttered under her breath, "I'll show him who calls the shots around here."

Big Ange knew these were empty threats, for she had few options. What little money she had was running out. Now it was the week before Easter, and she had to tell her daughters there was not enough money for new Easter clothes. Little Ange was livid.

"If you don't get a job soon, I will." She glared at her mother, hands on hips, ready for battle. "I have a friend who makes good money selling pot, and he says it's no hassle with all the potheads living around here."

Big Ange picked up an empty saucepan and threw it at her daughter, who easily stepped aside. "*Puttana!* She screamed. "I won't have a drug dealer living under my roof!"

"Don't worry, Mama," Little Ange sneered. "If I ever make any money, I won't be living in this friggin' dump!"

On Good Friday, Big Ange headed off to church to pray her rosary along the Stations of the Cross. Cosi knew her mother was looking for Divine financial inspiration. "God's gotta give me something to go on," she told Cosi, pinning her black lace mantilla to her hair.

Big Ange returned with a smile on her face and called her three children into the kitchen. "God answered my prayers and gave me a plan. I'm gonna start my own business and call it 'Big Ange's Infant of Prague Shop.'" The girls nodded approvingly.

On the West Side, every home had at least one Infant of Prague figurine. It represented Jesus as a boy (the "infant" part was a misnomer), and the statue could be large or very small, depending on the family's income and level of devotion. What made this religious icon different from others was the elaborate garments it wore, often of silk and lace, sometimes studded with gemstones, and embroidered in gold thread.

"Instead of making robes for free, I'm gonna make 'em and sell 'em to other families. But I'm gonna need your help making our garage into a shop. I can work there while you're at school, and keep Nino with me."

"Oh Ma, there are rats in there!" Little Ange laughed. "Who's gonna shop in that dump?"

"Also" said Big Ange, ignoring her daughter, "I'm gonna ask your Uncle Mack if he'll teach me how to drive." At this, both girls gasped. Their mother had never shown the slightest interest in driving.

Cosi remembered the ad she had seen on her mother's dresser for the Universal Gym on Sheridan Drive. "Celebrating our Second Big Year in Buffalo. Less than 83 cents per visit!" Her mother would need to drive if she was planning to go to a gym. Cosi scratched her head. *Why would she care about losing weight now?* She was going to ask but thought better of it. She and her mother had an unspoken understanding: I'll ignore your weight problem if you ignore mine.

ONE beautiful morning in May, when the scent of the lilac trees in the Catalfano's backyard wafted through the neighborhood, Uncle Carm drove over to the McCarthys' apartment with Aunt Franny to take Cosi to the Lewiston shrine. Winter was finally, truly over and everyone in Buffalo sighed in collective relief. Uncle Carm drove all the way to Lewiston with the car windows open. It was nearly fifty-five degrees—t-shirt weather in Buffalo.

While her aunt looked for Father Ryan, the Barnabite Father in charge of the shrine, Cosi wandered through the halls of the round basilica, stopping to look at the photographs of the three shepherd children who believed they had seen the Blessed Virgin in Fatima, Portugal. Cosi read the Virgin's simple message to them: *"If people do what I tell you, many souls will be saved and there will be peace."* That Visitation had happened during World War I, and the message to those children had been pretty clear. Aunt Franny was now talking quietly to Father Ryan, and they both glanced at Cosi as she pretended to study the stained-glass windows.

"Come with me, Cositina," said Father Ryan after the two adults had finished talking. She followed him up two flights of stairs to the top of the dome, where they could see the grounds of the shrine and surrounding hills. "Look down," he said. "What do you see?"

She looked where Father Ryan pointed, unsure at first of what she was supposed to see. Then it came to her. At the front of the basilica lay a heart-shaped pool surrounded by lights, at the end of which was a beautiful marble cross. "It's a giant rosary," she murmured.

"The largest outdoor rosary in the world," Father Ryan confirmed. "The pool is meant to represent the Virgin Mary's Immaculate Heart. I understand you have a special relationship with the Virgin Mother?"

"Yes, Father, I do."

"Then you must carry the same message as the children of Fatima. We will only have peace in Vietnam if the faithful offer up prayers and make sacrifices. Now bow your head and I will give my blessing."

Cosi bowed her head. *Holy Cow, that's it!* she thought, looking gratefully at Father Ryan.

Dear Joey, today I learned my special purpose is to end the Vietnam war. A pretty big job, but worth it, if you don't have to go.

CHAPTER SEVEN: GRADUATION AND THE BLUE NUNS

ON JUNE 1ST, THE MORNING her eighth-grade class was to graduate from Saint Michael's, Cosi looked frantically through the *West Side Times*. She finally found the newspaper's article on her graduating class, buried on page eight, and smiled. She was on the honor roll, had won an award for her essay on "Buffalo, the City of Good Neighbors," and saw her name on the list of students going to Catholic high schools in the fall.

Her mother had stopped making the Infant of Prague garments to work on Cosi's graduation dress. "It turned out good." Big Ange eyed the length of the skirt. "You been growing so much your old dresses would've shown off things that shouldn't be seen in church."

Cosi was happy. She had grown three inches taller in the past six months and her body was starting to change. She knew some of the girls in her class, church ceremony or no, would be wearing the mini-skirts that were now all the rage, but she wasn't going to argue with her mother. It was enough for her mother to tolerate Little Ange teasing and gathering Cosi's hair in an up-do, and allowing her to wear pink lipstick for the first time.

Cosi looked in the mirror to admire her hair and examine her face, which seemed different somehow. She had the same wide eyes and fat lower lip, but her face seemed longer, more oval-shaped now, and with her hair done up, she looked, well, almost grown up.

"You're gettin' to be a fine bit o' skirt," called Uncle Danny from his folding chair on the lower porch, when Cosi and her family came out the front door. "Pretty blue eyes and gettin' tall, just like your Daddy."

Big Ange gave him a contemptuous look. "*Porco misero*," she said, loud enough for him to hear, and looked at Cosi as if seeing her for the first time.

Big Ange mumbled a quick prayer and hurried her brood toward the church. "Remind me to have your Aunt Franny take you to see the movie about Saint Maria Goretti," she told Cosi, stopping to catch her breath.

What's it about?" asked Cosi.

"You'll see."

When they arrived at the church, Cosi spotted Sister Valentine talking to a group of students and waved shyly. To her surprise, Sister Valentine immediately came over.

"Good morning, Mrs. McCarthy. That's a fine girl you've got there."

"I was thanking God for that very thing this morning." Big Ange eyed Sister Valentine. She had heard of her reputation.

"I wonder if you would let Cosi work at the school this summer. She could help me prepare for summer-school classes."

"Oh?" Big Ange feigned surprise. "I was hoping she could earn a little babysitting money this summer, to help out at home."

"Of course, I wouldn't want volunteer work to interfere with a paying job, but if she can spare some time in the mornings, the school would deeply appreciate it. And I know Cosi really appreciates that scholarship." Sister Valentine smiled.

Cosi held her breath, sure her mother would ruin everything. Finally, after looking Sister Valentine up and down again, Big Ange reluctantly nodded her head.

"OK, but only in the mornings, when she won't have real work."

After the graduation ceremony, groups of kids clustered together outside the church, hugging and crying, promising to keep in touch. Cosi stood alone, pretending to look at her diploma, while her mother talked to Sister Mary Mark. Tina Mortadella, one of the more popular girls in her class, walked over in her red mini-skirt and white boots, an entourage in tow.

"Hey Cosi," Tina smiled sweetly. "Are you having a graduation party at your house?"

"No, I didn't want one." Cosi shrugged, hoping she sounded convincing.

"Of course, she's having a party," interrupted Big Ange, sizing up the situation.

Cosi looked at her mother. Her aunts were coming over for coffee and doughnuts, the only party her mother could afford.

"Great." Tina glanced at her posse. "Can we come?"

Big Ange looked at the smiling faces. "Sure, you can come."

They trotted off giggling and Big Ange bent down and whispered to Cosi, "We can afford to buy an extra dozen doughnuts, so you can finally have friends over to the house. Besides, we got something to celebrate—the first future nun in the family!"

Word of the Visitation had gotten around the eighth-grade class. Cosi watched as Tina told her friends there was a party at the McCarthy house where "the so-called miracle happened."

"Little Ange," barked her mother, "run over to Balistreri's and buy another dozen doughnuts. And stop at the market and buy a can of frozen orange juice."

No sooner had Cosi and her mother walked into their flat when the guests began to arrive. Nonna came in with Aunt Franny, and Aunt Rosa and Aunt Mari were right behind. The aunts looked at each other, bewildered, when the doorbell rang again, and Aunt Mari went to answer it.

"Well, what do we have here?" she said as she looked out over a sea of faces.

"We're here for the party!"

Two dozen kids rushed in like a swarm of locusts, moving first to the kitchen in search of food, then throughout the house looking for clues to the miracle. Cosi was horrified. Why did all these kids show up? Where was her sister with the extra doughnuts and orange juice? Why were people going into her bedroom? She rushed in behind Tina and her gang who were examining the room like homicide detectives. They looked up at Little Ange's poster of Bobby Kennedy, along with posters of the Beatles, the Rolling Stones, and the musical "Hair."

"Gawd," scoffed Tina, "what kind of square likes the Beatles better than Gary Puckett and the Union Gap?" She sauntered around Cosi's side of the room, looking up at the crucifix on the wall and the tiny First Communion rosary on the dresser. She stopped in front of the statue of the Virgin Mary.

"Is *this* the statue that talked to you? Make her talk again so we can see it."

Cosi felt her face burning. "It doesn't work like that."

"Ha! I thought so. I knew it didn't really happen. Cosi just wants to make herself look important, when everyone knows she's a big fat loser." The other girls laughed.

"Let's get outta this dump." Tina took one last contemptuous look around. "Some party. They don't even have any food." She marched off triumphantly, her acolytes right behind her. When the boys saw the girls leaving, they followed like puppies. When Little Ange finally ambled through the door, nearly everyone was gone. She plopped the doughnuts and orange juice on the table and sneered, "Why did we waste the money? I knew no one would come."

Cosi fled out the back door, down the steps, and into the backyard. When she reached the narrow alley behind the dilapidated garage, she stood among the empty beer bottles and urine-soaked cigarette butts and began to sob. Not only was she a joke at school, but her sister would now torment her about how unpopular she really was. Cosi could hear her mother calling from the upstairs window. She sat on her haunches and began to pray.

"Dear Virgin Mother," she looked heavenward through her tears, *"why did you do this to me? Everyone hates me and thinks I'm a liar."* She scanned the sky. *"You did visit me, didn't you? If so, please come back. My mother wants me to become a nun, but I'm not sure that's what you really want from me. If you do, please give me a sign."* She wiped her nose on the sleeve of her dress. She stopped sniffling and waited.

An hour passed. Cosi noticed a run starting in her panty hose, right above the knee. She licked a finger and dabbed where the run ended, trying to get it to stop, but it kept climbing up her thigh. Her mind drifted to the conversation she had with Sister Valentine back in May, after she finished *Siddhartha*.

"Sister, I read the book," Cosi recalled telling her, but I didn't understand all of it."

"I didn't expect you to understand it all," Sister Valentine had responded as she stacked second-grade spelling books. "The idea was to expose you to something new and get you thinking. That's my job as your spiritual advisor."

Cosi had persisted. "So, am I like Siddhartha? He didn't know what his purpose was in the beginning. Is that why you gave me this book?"

She recalled the look Sister Valentine gave her when she answered the question, saying, "I gave you this book because you have four years of high school ahead of you." The Sister had then put her fingers under Cosi's chin and lifted it, looking directly into her eyes. "You have a lot to learn and think about before making a lifelong commitment."

Cosi had asked one final question: "Sister, did it take you long to make your decision? Are you happy you're a nun?"

To which Sister Valentine had replied, "That is a conversation for another day."

Squatting in the garbage-strewn alley behind her garage, Cosi's mind returned to the present. She thought about how desperately she wanted to tell Sister Valentine the truth—that she *wanted* to take a different path, to get married and have children. But a visit from the Virgin Mary, telling you what you had to do in life? *That* was something special and rare. Did she really have a choice about her future?

Cosi stood up to stretch her legs and noticed an odd-looking bottle with a blue label, all but buried in a pile of more familiar brown ones. She went over and pulled it out. It was an empty Blue Nun wine bottle. She looked at the cartoonish nuns on the German label, their sly grins seeming to say, "You prayed for a sign. Now you got one."

She dropped the bottle and hung her head. She took a deep breath, brushed off her dress, and clasped her hands together. *Holy Mary, Mother of God, thank you for letting me know. I might not like it, but now I know what I'm supposed to do.* She wiped the pink lipstick from her mouth with the back of her hand, and headed up to the apartment.

Chapter Eight: A Summer of Sorrow, Soldiers, and Swimming

On the Monday after graduation, Cosi ran out the back door of her apartment and down the worn wooden steps to the concrete stoop at the bottom, just as dawn was breaking. She was at peace now. She planned to get up early to watch the sunrise every morning because summer in Buffalo was a precious thing, and she did not want to miss a minute of it.

From her vantage point on the stoop, she could see the first rays spreading behind the garage. She hugged herself in the chill air and luxuriated in the thought of two months' freedom from school. Her work with Sister Valentine did not start until mid-June and she planned to spend her summer days at the neighborhood swimming pool, reading and relaxing by the clear blue water.

She had spent the weekend praying and working hard at accepting her fate. If she was destined to become a Sister of St. Luke, she would start acting like one. She began to make vows she believed were very nun-like. She would say the rosary every day to end the Vietnam War. She would try to meet someone black and poor, and befriend them. She would be kind and gentle with little children, especially Nino, and she would raise money to feed the hungry around the world. She would fish returnable bottles out of the trash, and put the money she earned from claiming the deposit in the collection box at church.

When she put her first coins in the poor box after Sunday Mass, her mother raised an eyebrow. "Who's poorer than we are?" Cosi shrugged. Her mother had a point.

It was still early in June when Cosi came home from school at lunchtime to find Little Ange lying across her bed, weeping hysterically.

"They shot him! They shot Bobby!' she screamed into her mattress.

"Bobby? Bobby who?"

"Bobby Kennedy, you moron! My Bobby!"

Cosi was stunned. "What? Is he OK?"

"No! He's in a coma. They think he's gonna die!"

"What's this world coming to?" Big Ange asked her sisters, who sat huddled in the kitchen around the coffee pot, having come over as soon as they heard the news. Cosi sat quietly at the table, thankful the aunts were tolerating her presence. She needed answers. Why were all these good people, famous people, getting shot? President Kennedy, Dr. King, and now Senator Kennedy. Why was God letting this happen?

"Benny thinks it's the communiss, like that *stugatz* who killed President Kennedy," said Aunt Rosa, wiping her nose with a paper napkin. She had been sick with a number of strange illnesses this year.

"They already caught the killer." Big Ange poured more coffee. "Some foreigner. Got some grudge against the US of A. Why do foreigners live here if they gotta grudge, I ask you?"

She handed Aunt Rosa a handkerchief, one she had not yet ironed. "You need to take better care of yourself, Rosa. Seems like you're always sick these days." Cosi saw her mother's smug, sideways glance and knew what she was thinking — Aunt Rosa's illnesses were proof the *malocchio* she cursed her sister with was working.

The next morning, they saw the terrible headlines that the Senator had died of his wounds. On her way to church, Cosi passed Uncle Danny and Aunt Joanie, sitting amidst the clutter on their front porch, smoking.

"You know it was the Mafia who killed 'im," Cosi heard Uncle Danny telling his wife. "They hate any Irishman making something of hisself."

"He was a looker." Aunt Joanie shook her head sadly. "I would've voted for him."

"Now that just goes to show why women shoulda never got the vote." Uncle Danny spat irritably on the floor. "Only an eejit would vote for a guy 'cause he's a looker."

"So why would you vote for him?"

"Cause he's Irish, of course."

THE sun finally gained enough purchase by early July to warm the frigid waters of the neighborhood swimming pool. Cosi grabbed her one-piece bathing suit and headed down Massachusetts Avenue, stopping at Ganci's Groceries to buy a baloney bomber and a bottle of Wink. She hurried on, sweating after the nine-block walk, eager to dive in and enjoy the sudden hush that came with swimming underwater. She quickly undressed, squeezed into her bathing suit, and running from the locker room without stopping, jumped directly into the pool. She gasped from the shock of the cold water and jumped up and down, rubbing her shoulders.

"Hey Cosi," she heard someone call.

Cosi turned to see Gabriella Mortadella, Tina's older sister, swimming toward her. *Dear God*, Cosi thought, *she's heard about my horrible graduation party.* She turned to swim away.

"Hey wait, don't you remember me? I'm Gabby." The girl grinned in a friendly way. "I hear you're going to Holy Martyrs in September. I started going there last year."

Cosi nodded, suspicious. She had no idea why Gabby, a popular, older girl she barely knew, would want to talk to her. Was this another trick?

"If you like, I can be your sponsor when you start in September," Gabby continued when Cosi said nothing. "All of the sophomores try to help out the new freshmen."

"OK." Cosi was still wary. She was almost afraid to look at this girl with the sparkling brown eyes, long black hair, and two-piece bathing suit that highlighted her curves. Cosi glanced down at her own, too small, green polka-dotted swimsuit, and sunk lower into the water.

After an awkward silence, Gabby tried again. "Well, see you around, OK?" She started to swim away then turned to add, "Oh, and ignore my bratty sister, will you? She's a head case."

Cosi couldn't help but smile. "Yeah, well, my sister's a jerk too."

Gabby laughed. "I know your sister. She was in my class at Saint Michael's. She treated the rest of us like dog turds."

Cosi giggled a little too loudly. "I thought I was the only one she treated like that." Gabby waved and swam back to a group of kids waiting for her in the shallow end.

Cosi watched to see if any of them would turn to look at her, certain she was the butt of some mean joke. She was getting used to being an object of derision, but no one in Gabby's group looked over. Gabby and another teenage girl climbed up on the shoulders of two boys, dripping thighs held tight against the boys' ears. The girls began pushing each other as hard as they could to knock each other off, laughing and screaming as they did. Cosi watched, wishing she could be a part of something like that, just once, before she became a nun.

THE next time Cosi saw the same group at the pool, Gabby invited her to join them. "C'mon, we need another person for the chicken fight."

Cosi started to protest when a boy dove underwater, pushed his head between her legs, and came up laughing and sputtering, with Cosi on his shoulders. The boy staggered a bit and she was mortified. She also got that funny feeling down there, the one that told her this must be a sin of some sort, but once they got started and the focus seemed to be on knocking each other over, she told herself it was just a game. Nothing to worry about.

She used all her weight to push against the smaller, lighter girls and they went down easily. When she and the boy were the last team standing, he fell back slowly until he was under water and picked her up gently over his head. When he came up, he grinned at her. The sun reflected off his dark eyes and perfect white teeth.

"I'm Jack. You're pretty good at this," Jack told her.

Gabby swam over and hugged her. "You're a natural!"

Cosi beamed. She could not believe her luck—she was finally making friends. Cool friends, including a fine-looking boy who laughed like her father. She would also have Gabby looking out for her when she started school in September.

Unfortunately, her luck that summer didn't extend to making money for the family. She had few babysitting jobs—Little Ange was always a neighbor's first choice because she was older and considered more responsible—and her sister jumped at every chance to babysit because she had a new boyfriend who snuck in when the parents were gone.

Little Ange showed Cosi a fresh new hickey one morning. "If you tell Mama, I'll cut all your hair off while you're sleeping." Cosi was used to her sister's threats and had long ago stopped caring what she did with boys. She assumed Little Ange had committed so many mortal sins she was already doomed to eternal damnation, and Cosi had no intention of saving *her* soul.

Much more troubling to Cosi was the fact that she could not stop thinking about Jack and his long, wet hair between her thighs. Try as she might, she could not push these impure thoughts from her mind. She knew almost nothing about sex, other than it was sinful, but still, she thought she needed another look at those books in the library. She wanted to know why she was having feelings in places she barely knew existed, and how she could stop them.

It did not help when Uncle Danny's oldest son, Rory, would sit with his friends on the front steps of their shared house, and embarrass her with nasty comments.

"Hey Cosi," Rory called as she hurried down the steps in her shorts and bathing suit one hot August afternoon, "anybody get their hands on those cantaloupes yet?" Cosi's face turned pink as she threaded her way through Rory and his buddies.

"I like the way that ass jiggles," said one, appreciatively.

"I'd be happy to pop that cherry," quipped another, and they all guffawed.

When Cosi reached the bottom of the stairs, she stopped abruptly. The door of Mr. Catalfano's station wagon swung open and Joey emerged from the back seat. She had heard he was coming home for one last leave before heading off to Vietnam, and now she was almost face-to-face with him as he stood in his Army uniform, tall and regal as a Greek god, placing his hat carefully on his head before he closed the car door.

Joey looked at Cosi's red face, then at Rory and his friends, and said in a deep, even voice, "Cut that shit out. She's just a kid." The boys stopped talking and Cosi stood, unable to move or speak, as Joey made his way up his front steps, arm-in-arm with his parents.

She always knew there was something different about Joey. Not only in the way he looked and spoke, but in the respect he commanded. Joey did not cop a cool, tough-guy attitude like other teenage boys in her neighborhood. He had a quiet seriousness, coupled with a muscular frame, that made even the members of BETA, one of the West Side's toughest frats, steer clear of him.

Ever since she was a little girl, Joey had looked out for her. Once, when she was five and he nearly 11, he carried her all the way home after she fell off her bike and twisted her knee. She looked at him now and saw the kind of man she had always hoped to marry. She sighed. When he looked at her, he still saw the little girl next door with the hurt knee.

Mrs. Catalfano was worried sick when Joey turned 18. His draft number was pretty low, almost guaranteeing he would be going to Vietnam. But Cosi knew that didn't matter to Joey. Mr. Catalfano had been a soldier who fought at the Battle of the Bulge during World War II, and later in Korea when Joey was a baby. Joey idolized his father. He didn't wait to be drafted.

When the Catalfano's were getting ready to take Joey to the basic training bus back in February, Cosi hid. The last thing she wanted was Joey to see her crying over something she couldn't explain. Once he was gone, she would watch Mr. Catalfano chain smoking on his front porch, pacing back and forth, running his fingers through his short gray hair. There were ominous news reports coming out of Vietnam that month about something called the Tet Offensive, and the list of American soldiers killed or wounded kept growing longer. People had begun to whisper that the war would not be over anytime soon.

All through the winter and spring while Joey finished his training, Cosi saw his mother sitting alone in church with her rosary. Cosi had wondered then how Joey's mother would go on living if something happened to her only child. Cosi could see the toll it was taking on everyone she knew, pitting friends and family members against each other. Vietnam was a country she had barely heard of before the angry brawl at her father's wake. Now, after his last brief home leave, Joey would be headed there, despite the prayers of those who loved him.

She arrived at Sister Valentine's door in tears the next morning. "Sister, if you were God and had the power to fix the worst problem in the world today, would it be the Vietnam War?"

Sister Valentine looked thoughtful. "That's a tough one. The war in Vietnam is terrible, but is it worse than the nuclear missiles the US and the Soviet Union have pointed at each other? Worse than the poverty and misery black people suffer in our ghettoes every day? Worse than all the children starving in Biafra and other war-torn countries around the world...?"

"You're not helping me," interrupted Cosi. "The Virgin Mary wants me to do something important. To *save* people. What can I do to stop the war and bring the soldiers home?"

Sister Valentine sighed. "You're too young to worry now about tackling the world's toughest problems. I do appreciate your passion though, and I promise to give your question serious thought. For now, you need to focus on high school. You'll be surprised how tough the transition will be. In addition to your studies, you need to be ready for many hours of volunteer work in the second semester. I have some ideas for you, but be advised. Whatever you take on will be harder than you think."

Cosi tried to hide her impatience. "I know that, Sister. Nothing has been easy so far."

That night, Cosi sat staring at her diary, wondering how much more of her soul she should bare in the little book.

Dear Joey, she wrote, *please don't die. Wait for me to grow up so I can tell you how much I love you, without you laughing at me.*

Chapter Nine: Holy Martyrs and the Infant of Prague Shop

JUST BEFORE SCHOOL STARTED, Cosi began collecting soap for the poor people in South Vietnam, a program she had read about in the newspapers. She went door-to-door asking neighbors for leftover bits of soap, and with her bottle deposit money, sent packages of the bits to a US Army unit in Saigon. She hoped Joey would be impressed. She told him about it in her weekly letters along with chatty little tidbits on new TV shows and movies. She checked her mailbox each day, hoping for a return letter with news from Vietnam. He never wrote back.

One Saturday morning while her mother was grocery shopping, Cosi sat with Nino in front of the TV, eating cereal. When Nino's favorite cartoon, *The Road Runner,* came on, he rocked back and forth with excitement.

"Beep-beep!"

"Beep-beep!" Cosi responded.

She looked lovingly at her little brother. Nothing made her angrier than the neighborhood kids who made fun of him. He was just a little boy who had a hard time connecting with people. She knew he would never be like other boys, would never grow up and get a job, or live on his own. He rocked back and forth, transfixed by the cartoon characters on the screen, and she wondered what would happen to Nino if she entered the convent. Would her mother be able to care for him when she herself grew old?

"Maybe I need to sacrifice my life for you," Cosi whispered in his ear. "I will always take care of you, Nino. I promise."

"Beep-beep!" said Nino.

SUMMER drew to a gentle close. Cosi wandered out after dinner one Saturday to take up her evening post. Their house had an upper front porch, in addition to the lower one outside of Uncle Danny's flat. The house faced west, toward the Niagara River, and though Cosi could not see it from where she sat, she liked to imagine the setting sun slanting on the swiftly flowing water. She settled into an old cane rocking chair, rested her feet on the iron porch railing, and waited.

As the dusk began to settle, Cosi could see the red glow of her neighbors' cigarettes while they sat on their porches and exchanged stories. Groups of teenage boys gathered on the street corners to tease and shove and comment on the girls who strolled by. Windows opened to cool the houses down for bedtime, and the sandflies from the river began their nightly pinging on the window screens. Mothers stood on their porches, calling children who were now in trouble for not being home before dark, while alley cats yowled for their supper.

Cosi felt it then. The first pang of what she later learned was called melancholy. Summer was nearly over and high school was just around the corner. Why did she feel so sad? Maybe because high school seemed like a giant step toward adulthood, and the days when she could retreat into her mystery books, or play with her paper dolls, were gone forever.

She tried to shake off the feeling. There was a better way to look at the end of summer, she told herself. She was going to her dream school, Holy Martyrs Academy, and things were better at home. Her mother had learned to drive and made enough Infant of Prague outfits to open her new shop in the backyard. Somehow, she had scraped enough money together to send Cosi and Little Ange to Catholic high schools.

How she managed it was something of a mystery. Earlier that summer, Cosi and Little Ange swept out the filthy garage and Mr. Palumbo, a sign painter who lived down the street, made a small sign that read "Big Ange's Infant of Prague Shop" to hang above the door.

"There." Big Ange craned her neck to see if people would see her new shop from the front sidewalk. "Now all we need are customers."

On her first day of business, Big Ange went out to the garage and sat inside with her new cash lockbox. She had several of her best garments displayed on statues donated by members of her family, clustered together near the garage's side window. Big Ange's own Infant of Prague statue, the one with the glued-on head and hand, sat in the window as well.

When she grew tired of sitting in her shop, Big Ange would wander out with Nino for a short walk, or to pull weeds from around the tomato plants that grew with surprising vigor in a small patch of dirt beneath the garage window. At five o'clock on the dot, she hung a "Closed" sign on the garage door and went upstairs to make dinner.

By mid-August, only a handful of customers had bought garments. One evening, Cosi watched her mother open her lockbox and carefully count the money. Big Ange shook her head in disgust. "*Merda.* Thirty damn dollars." She slammed the lid shut.

"What about the money we made babysitting?" Cosi asked nervously.

Big Ange pulled out the bank passbook that recorded their savings. "Your sister made $54.75. At least that's what she tells me. You made a whopping $14.50. That ain't enough to pay even Little Ange's first bill at Bishop McMahon. Thank God you got that scholarship, but I got no idea how much your books will cost."

"What about that check we started getting after Daddy died?"

"That barely covers the mortgage, utilities, and food."

Little Ange walked into the kitchen in a halter top and cut-off jeans, smelling like her boyfriend's Old Spice aftershave.

"Bad news," said Big Ange. "We got no money to send you to Bishop McMahon."

"Are you *effing* kidding me?" Little Ange burst out, immediately furious. "I made more money babysitting than you made with your stupid outfits, and I can't go back to Bishop McMahon? You are one lousy excuse for a mother!"

Big Ange slapped her daughter's head. "Shut your face. I'm in no mood for your smart mouth." Little Ange spit on the floor, and Cosi fled from the screaming match that followed.

Two days later, Cosi's frantic prayers to the Virgin Mary seemed to pay off. She was watching Nino play on the front lawn when Mr. Schiavonni, a neighbor from down the block, walked into the backyard and stopped at the Infant of Prague Shop. Her mother came out to greet him with an odd look on her face. Mr. Schiavonni was "dressed to the nines" as her mother would say, with a handkerchief in his lapel pocket and a white fedora on his head.

Cosi strained to hear what they were saying but could only make out words like "business" and "investment" while Mr. Schiavonni waved his hands and talked rapidly to her mother. They walked around the outside of the shop, went inside, came out again. He turned to leave and Cosi saw a strange look on his face, the kind her mother had whenever she held "aces around" in her pinochle hand. He gave her mother a little wave and walked quickly away.

Later that evening, while tearing apart a head of lettuce for their dinner salad, Cosi asked nonchalantly, "Mama, what did Mr. Schiavonni want?"

"Oh, he just asked if I wanted some business advice, in order to get the shop going." Big Ange looked intently at a long zucchini she was peeling. "He says his corner stores are doing real good, and he's learned a few tricks of the trade. He wants to help us. I told him, sure, I was interested. So, what does he do? He pulls out his wallet and gives me what he calls 'seed money.' It's what you gotta have if you wanna be in business, according to Mr. Bigshot Businessman Schiavonni."

"Seed money? What does that mean, Mama?"

Big Ange took a deep breath. "It means you can stop worrying. I'm gonna use the money to pay for your books and Little Ange's tuition."

Cosi jumped up and hugged her. "Thank you, Mama, thank you! I love you! I'm going to make you real proud of me."

Her mother shrugged her off. "Enough. When I finally got a nun in the family, then I will be proud. Now go check on your brother."

Cosi turned to leave, but stopped. "When do you have to give the 'seed money' back?"

Big Ange pulled an onion out of the vegetable drawer. She took a cleaver and, with one heavy whack, sliced it in two. "Mr. Schiavonni said it was a loan.

I'm supposed to start paying him back when I sell more Infant of Prague robes."

She avoided Cosi's eyes and sighed. "Let's just hope he's a patient man."

Chapter Ten: A Sea of Penguins

Cosi looked for Gabby Mortadella the minute she stepped off the bus at Holy Martyrs. In front of the school was a vast sea of girls in black dresses with white collars and cuffs like hers. She waded into the noisy crowd, friends shrieking with delight when they found each other, hugging as if it had been years, not three months, since the last term ended. Cosi was soon able to pick out the freshmen, who stood by themselves, unsure of where to go and what to do.

"Hey Cosi!" she heard a voice from somewhere in the crowd, "over here."

To Cosi's immense relief, Gabby pushed her way through the jumble and grabbed her arm. "Follow me," she said, pulling her toward the front steps.

Cosi looked up at the old red brick building that served as the Mother House for the Sisters of Saint Luke, as well as the all-girls high school. It was the place where novices, teachers, and elderly Sisters in the order all lived. Gabby quickly explained to Cosi that the school was located on the first two floors, and the locker rooms and student lounge were in the basement. The upper floors were strictly off-limits to students.

"Where am I supposed to go now?" Cosi had a lock of hair twirled around her finger.

"Follow everyone else!"

A bell rang in the hallway. Cosi watched what had to be hundreds of girls streaming in the same direction, sorting themselves by class in the school auditorium. She looked for the freshmen and took a seat next to a girl with long red braids.

"Hi, I'm Amanda Burns," whispered the girl, shaking Cosi's hand. Cosi gave her a nervous smile. "Cositina McCarthy."

A large nun began tapping on the lectern. "Good morning students, and welcome back to Holy Martyrs Academy. For those who are new here, I am Sister Matthew, your principal. Before we begin, let me welcome Father Jawalski to the podium to lead us in prayer."

After prayers, Sister Matthew introduced the teachers. Most looked friendly enough, but one in particular, Sister Agatha, the math teacher, worried Cosi. She had the same pinched face as the kindergarten teacher back at Saint Michael's who spanked Nino for not paying attention in class. Cosi had not forgotten that nun. She decided to avoid Sister Agatha.

She was quite curious about the gym teacher. Mrs. Bannerman was a lay teacher, not a nun, who told the gathered students, "Just call me Coach." She was tall, muscular, had salt-and-pepper hair, and a rowdy laugh. Cosi liked her immediately. She decided to violate her lifelong rule of avoiding exercise at all cost and take at least one gym class.

Her homeroom teacher handed her a class schedule and she quickly learned that freshmen had little say in what subjects they would take. Her entrance exam scores placed her in advanced English, Science, and Math classes. Much to her dismay, Sister Agatha would be her Algebra II teacher, but she perked up when she saw her first period was gym class. Cosi hurried happily to the gym where the girls dressed quickly in their shorts and t-shirts and sat on the floor.

"Good morning, Ladies!" boomed Coach Bannerman. "Stand up and let me get a look at you! The girls jumped to their feet and stood in a crooked line, all knees and elbows, while Coach walked up and down. She shook her head and muttered, looking them over.

"You're a sorry looking lot, but that's going to change. Your mamas probably told you it's OK to be girly. Well not here!" she barked. "Drop down and give me 10!"

The girls looked at each other, bewildered.

"Drop down and give me 10 push-ups!" she yelled, louder this time. Cosi had never done a push-up in her life, and neither, judging by the confusion, had most of the other girls.

"Let me demonstrate." Coach dropped to the floor and executed 25 swift, ramrod-straight push-ups. "Now you try it, and do your best! That's it, butts down, heads straight!" She walked from girl to girl, telling them how to hold in their stomachs, how to bend their arms. "OK, that'll do for now. You will get better, I promise. Now let's do 10 laps and call it a day."

When the girls rounded their second lap around the gym, Cosi, red-faced and sweating, could not breathe. She stopped and bent over, holding her knees, thinking she might vomit. Coach looked the other way, pretending not to see her.

In English class, Cosi could still feel the sweat soaking the back of her uniform and did not cool down until Home Economics. When the bell rang for lunch, she searched for Gabby among what seemed like dozens of tables in the cafeteria. She found her sitting with a group of girls, talking excitedly. Cosi hesitated, but Gabby looked up and waved her over.

"Hey everyone, this is Cosi McCarthy, a friend from my neighborhood. She's a freshman, so be nice to her," said Gabby, eyeing a mischievous-looking girl named Roberta.

Cosi blushed. Gabby had described her as a friend! Grinning, she opened her brown paper lunch bag, removed her sandwich and apple, and made the sign of the cross to say grace. Roberta rolled her eyes and put her finger down her throat.

Gabby whispered, "Don't do that Cosi. Everyone will think you're weird."

Cosi was shocked. "You don't say grace?"

"Just don't be so obvious," Gabby continued under her breath, as Roberta stood up and pretended to bless everyone at the table. "It's OK to pray, just don't do it in front of people. Keep it private, if you know what I mean."

Cosi wondered how many more mistakes she would make before this day was over. French class seemed to go well but her final class of the day was Algebra II. Sister Agatha stood, arms folded across her non-existent bosom while the girls filed in, waiting until everyone was seated and silent. She walked up and down the aisles between the desks, looking carefully at each girl, sniffing for fear and trepidation as if they were rotten fruit.

"I don't tolerate any foolishness in my class," she stated, pacing her words with her steps, "nor do I tolerate tardiness, slothfulness, vanity, disrespect, flightiness, dull-wittedness, or giggling. In short, you are here to learn math, and math you *will* learn. Do I make myself clear?"

"Yes, Sister Agatha," said the girls in unison.

"Good. I will make an example of the first person who steps out of line, so you should all say a little prayer that you are not the first. Turn to page 14 in your textbook."

Cosi hunched over and tried to make herself small. She was in the middle of a silent prayer to the Blessed Virgin when Sister Agatha loomed over her.

"What is your name, Miss?

"Cositina McCarthy, Sister" Cosi whispered.

"Well, Miss McCarthy, please tell the class the name of the father of modern algebra."

Cosi began to sweat again. She did not know the answer. "Pythagoras?"

"Right country, wrong Greek." Sister Agatha marched briskly up to the blackboard. "The answer is Diophantus." She wrote it furiously in white chalk, underlining it twice. "Did you *read* the first chapter of your book before you came to class today, Miss McCarthy?"

"No Sister," said Cosi, "I didn't get my book until this morning."

"That is no excuse!" shouted Sister Agatha bringing her wooden pointer down hard on her desk. "Remember what I said about stepping out of line? Being unprepared for class and making excuses is completely unacceptable. I will see you after class, Miss McCarthy."

Cosi walked out of Holy Martyrs at a few minutes after 5 p.m., fighting back tears. She had never had a problem with even the strictest teachers at Saint Michael's, and now, on the first day of high school, she was already in trouble. Sister Agatha made her write "Diophantus is the Father of Modern Algebra" fifty times and, afterwards, clean all the chalkboards.

While she was wiping the board, Sister Agatha had stood, hands on hips, staring at Cosi's feet. "What on earth are those?"

Cosi looked down. "They're called Keds, Sister... a kind of sneaker."

"I know what they are. They are completely inappropriate to wear with your school uniform. I don't want to see them on you again."

Cosi looked down at the cheap white cloth shoes. "I'm sorry, Sister. My mother can only afford to buy us one pair of shoes. I'll need these for gym class."

"If you can't afford to dress properly," said Sister Agatha, narrowing her eyes, "you shouldn't be coming to this school."

Humiliated, Cosi got off the bus at Saint Michael's instead of going home. Sister Valentine was at her desk going through papers. She stopped when she saw Cosi's face.

"What's wrong?"

Cosi burst into tears. She told Sister Valentine about nearly throwing up in gym class, embarrassing herself in front of the older girls at lunch, and her run-in with Sister Agatha. "She hates me and said I don't belong at Holy Martyrs," Cosi sniffled. "Maybe she's right."

Sister Valentine grabbed several tissues and handed them to Cosi. "Listen. Stop worrying. Do your work and lay low around Sister Agatha. I happen to know her."

Sister Valentine looked out the window, focusing on something off in the distance. "Sister Agatha's not interested in changing with the times. She is set it her ways. And unfortunately, there are Sisters who are good at being Sisters, but not very good at being human beings." Her face softened. "Did you join the debate team?"

"Not yet. I plan to, next week."

"Good. That might come in handy. Have you thought about your charitable work?"

"Yes, Sister, but sending soap to Vietnam and putting coins in the collection box isn't enough. I want to do something that makes a difference. I heard you marched in a protest."

Sister Valentine looked surprised. "Oh, you did, did you? Do you really think you're ready for something like that?" Cosi nodded emphatically.

Her spiritual mentor sighed. "I suppose it's as good a time as any to find out if you're up to the challenges our Order faces today. Once you have settled in at school, we'll go on a little field trip. I'll take you to see some people who could really use your help."

Chapter Eleven: The Steel Mill
and the Priority List

O N A BRITTLE SATURDAY at the end of November, when ice was forming on Lake Erie and bitter gusts of wind made it difficult to walk, Cosi stood with Sister Valentine in front of Saint Michael's Church. They were waiting for Mr. Battista, a retired parishioner, who always seemed to be hovering about. Today he had offered to drive them to Our Lady of Victory Basilica in Lackawanna. "The field trip we talked about," Sister Valentine told Cosi.

Driving south over the Skyway Bridge, Cosi could feel her palms tingling inside her mittens as the car climbed steadily upward, soaring high above the Buffalo River. From the top she could see Lake Erie ahead and, turning to look behind her, the narrowing of the lake into the swiftly-flowing Niagara River. Although the height of the Skyway made her dizzy and the cold wind stung her face, she hung out the window to see what she could of Buffalo's industrial waterfront, and of Canada, across the lake to the west. She grinned as the heavenly aroma of Cheerios baking at the nearby General Mills plant, tickled her nose.

The car began to descend and Cosi could see the vast sprawl of the steel plant on both sides of the road. When her father was alive, he would occasionally drive the family to the complex and park outside its gates. They would walk up to the chain-link fence and gawk at the enormous buildings that seemed to stretch for miles.

"Did you ever see the like of it kids?" Johnny would ask, swelling with pride. "You're looking at the biggest steel-making operation in the world! We helped win World War II right here, making millions of tons of steel for ships and tanks. Yes kids, your dad works at one of the most important plants in the world." She felt an ache when she thought of his eyes sparkling, talking about the plant like it was one of the Seven Wonders of the World.

Mr. Battista turned on Fuhrmann Boulevard and across Tifft Street toward South Park Avenue. Cosi turned to Sister Valentine, who was shuffling papers on her lap.

"What will we be doing at the basilica, Sister?"

"I want you to meet some people and listen to what they have to say. Maybe you'll find your 'special purpose' in helping them out."

The car pulled up in front of one of the most beautiful churches Cosi had ever seen. Made entirely of white marble but dulled by soot from the nearby factories, it had a grand entrance framed by colonnades on either side. Atop the colonnades were sculptures of groups of children, the group on the left colonnade led by a nun, while a similar group of children surrounded a priest on the right. It occurred to Cosi that this church was the creation of the famous Father Baker, and it was he, cast in marble, leading the children atop the right colonnade.

Being "sent to Father Baker's" was a threat held over the head of every misbehaving child in Buffalo, especially adolescent boys. She spotted a plaque explaining that Father Baker, who died years before, had founded not only a home for orphaned boys, but also an infants' home, a hospital, several schools, and this basilica. Would she do volunteer work here?

"Come and see the inside," said Sister Valentine, glancing furtively over her shoulder and opening the door. Cosi had no idea what to expect. Orphaned children? She twisted her hair and stepped inside.

A slender black nun rushed down the aisle and up to Sister Valentine, throwing her arms around her with a tight squeeze. "I'm so glad you've come! Hurry now. I tried to get them to wait for you, but they've already started."

Sister Valentine quickened her pace. "Cosi, this is Sister Theresa, a good friend of mine." Sister Theresa glanced at Cosi and shot a questioning look at Sister Valentine, who gave a barely perceptible shake of her head. Sister Theresa seemed to understand and smiled.

"Nice to meet you, Cosi. Are you joining us today?"

"Not just yet," said Sister Valentine, brusquely. "Wait here a minute, Cosi. Look around the basilica. There's a lot to see."

The two Sisters hurried off and Cosi looked around the cavernous interior. It was almost too much to take in. Paintings of saints and angels adorned the vaulted dome, painted blue like the sky. She wandered off to the left and found the Grotto Shrine of Our Lady of Lourdes, honoring the Virgin Mary's appearance to St. Bernadette. *I seem to remember that no one believed her either,* thought Cosi, looking at young Bernadette's statue. She lit two small votive candles, one for her father and one for Joey, and knelt to pray.

Cosi remembered the reason Father Baker started his infants' home. When the priest learned about all the tiny human bones found during routine dredging of the Erie Canal, he created a haven for unmarried women and their unwanted children. Cosi had been outraged when she first heard the story. *What kind of mother would drown her baby?* Now she wondered if the prostitutes and poor women who had lived along the canal really had a choice, or if disease and starvation had killed their little ones *before* they were thrown in the water.

Sister Valentine reappeared, out of breath, and motioned Cosi to join her. They hurried out the rear door of the basilica toward a nondescript building two blocks away. They rushed down a short flight of steps to a steel basement door, and when Sister Valentine opened it, Cosi stopped short. There, sitting on folding chairs in an unheated room, were thirty or more black men, along with Sister Theresa. Everyone stood when they entered the room.

"Please, no need to stand up. Let me introduce you to Cosi McCarthy, the girl I mentioned. She is thinking of joining our order, and I want her to learn about the problems you are facing. Cosi, take a seat next to Wilbur over there."

Cosi sat next to an elderly man who smiled at her. She smiled back, and, looking around the circle, continued to smile, trying to put herself at ease. She had never been in a room with so many black people before. She noticed a scowling young man on the other side of the room, wearing a black beret and staring at her. She looked away and sat on her hands to keep them from shaking.

"Well, Sister, I ain't seeing no changes. They still give us the worst jobs. We work in the coke ovens or the blast furnaces, the hottest and dirtiest jobs. When we ask why, they say it's because the black man can stand the heat better than white people—and that ain't right." An angry murmur ran through the crowd.

"So," said Sister Valentine, "we must continue to press them to rectify the situation. We must demand that the Attorney General order a right of transfer for any Negro who was discriminated against prior to the ruling, and give first priority for any new vacancy…"

"That's all bullshit," said the scowling man Cosi had noticed earlier, getting to his feet and addressing the others. "You think we're gonna get anywhere working with a government run by the white man? This ain't just about the steel plant. What about the slums we live in? What about no jobs, or jobs where we don't even make enough to reach the poverty level? What about our kids going to run-down, overcrowded, segregated schools? What the hell is the Attorney General gonna do about all that?"

Cosi saw men nodding their heads. She squirmed in her seat.

"I listened to Dr. King when he spoke here last November." Sister Valentine moved closer to Sister Theresa. "He talked about every one of those things and called for a massive action program to bring social justice to the nation. I believe if we follow his program…"

"Oh yeah," the man in the beret cut in, "and look what happened to him! How did all that 'non-violence' work out for him, huh? All bullshit! The Black Panthers, they the only ones talking sense. Look at their Ten Point Program. That's what we should be talking about here, not this other shit." He began distributing leaflets around the room.

Sister Theresa took two long strides and grabbed the leaflets. They struggled until the young man let go and sat glowering in his seat.

"This isn't the time, Marcus!" Sister Theresa shouted, eyes flashing. "You're disrupting the meeting and you're not helping. You know the Panthers have a reputation for violence. All this neighborhood has to do is get wind that we're working with the Panthers, and they will shut us down faster than you can say 'Huey Newton.' Now," she said, taking a deep breath and smoothing her wimple, "let's get back to business."

Cosi listened open-mouthed as the men talked about their treatment at the steel plant. Surely, this could not be the same place her father worked, she thought. Her father would have done something. Yet, she heard story after story of supervisors and clerks rejecting employment applications if they knew the applicant was black. They talked about a "Priority List" of white applicants who would have their paperwork rapidly processed to get the best jobs.

"No black man has even been *on* the Priority List," said Wilbur.

When the meeting was over, Sister Valentine put her arm around Cosi's shoulder and hurried her toward the door. "Mr. Battista will be here with the car soon. We need to move." Cosi noticed Marcus talking to some of the younger men, clustered out of earshot in a corner.

Running back with Cosi toward the basilica at full speed, Sister Valentine had her long skirt hoisted, her veil flapping in the wind. Once inside, they hurried down the aisle of the empty church toward the front door. Outside, they saw Mr. Battista in his car, engine running.

"Good field trip, Sister?" asked Mr. Battista. "I always loved this place."

"Oh, I think Cosi learned quite a bit," said Sister Valentine. She gave Cosi the same little shake of the head that, Cosi now realized, meant not to tell him anything. Cosi was so upset by what she had heard, she wouldn't know what to say anyway. Her father had never mentioned any of this, and she was ashamed.

The next morning, a little before the Bills football game, Cosi went downstairs hoping to catch Uncle Danny while he was sober. She found him sitting on his recliner, Bills sweatshirt stretched taut across his belly, a bottle of Genesee Cream Ale in his hand. His sons sat sprawled on the floor around him, the air heavy with the smells of sweat and testosterone.

"Uncle Danny, did any black men work with you and Daddy at the steel plant?"

"What?" Uncle Danny was squinting at the TV. They were showing the

Bills' record for the season to date, one of the worst in their history. "Losers!" screamed Uncle Danny. "*Feckin* gobshites! Get yer arses in gear this week!"

Cosi waited until the yelling stopped. "Did any black men work with you and Daddy?"

Her uncle finally looked at her. "Yeah, we worked with 'em. If you wanna call it work." He chuckled. "Mostly they just stood around, leanin' on their brooms."

"Well, did you know they were being horribly mistreated? Given only the worst jobs?"

"Whaddya bothering me about girl? They don't get good jobs 'cause they don't do good work!" He leaned forward, elbows on knees, waiting for the Bills to come out on the field. Cosi sat quietly for a few moments, thinking. She felt sick to her stomach.

"Uncle Danny, did you ever hear of something called the Priority List?"

"The List? Sure. That's how me and your dad got our jobs."

"But...did you know that list was only for white people?"

Uncle Danny took a swig of beer. "Leave me alone now. Game's about to start."

On the Sunday after Thanksgiving, Cosi stood in the back of Saint Michael's Church looking for Sister Valentine. Spotting her walking slowly up the aisle, deep in conversation with Sister Mary Mark, Cosi waited until they got nearer and said, "Good morning, Sister. Can I walk with you back to the convent?"

"Sure, Cosi." Sister Valentine said something to Sister Mary Mark, who nodded and walked ahead. "What's on your mind?"

"I've been thinking about that meeting. Why are *you* going to meetings with black people from the steel plant? They're not from our parish and they don't seem to like white people very much. Why did you bring me there?"

Sister Valentine looked straight ahead, rubbing her arms under her wool shawl to keep warm as they walked through the lightly falling snow. She hesitated in front of the convent, but said, "Let's keep walking." They walked a couple more blocks when she turned to look Cosi in the eye. "Can I tell you something in confidence? Something you can't discuss with anyone?"

Cosi's eyes widened. "You mean, like a secret?"

"Yes. You see, many parishioners at Saint Michael's would be upset if they knew I was going to those meetings. They have old-fashioned ideas about what Sisters like us should be doing. They think we should pray, do charitable works, teach their children—and that's it. Being a social activist is not acceptable. Sister Mary Mark worries that if people here know I go to those meetings, they'll want me transferred."

Cosi winced. "Because you meet with black people?"

"No, it's more complicated than that. Look Cosi, if you're going to enter the convent, you need to understand how much things have changed. Some of us believe our calling is to get involved, to fight against racial discrimination, to protest against the war, and demand changes in our political system. We can't go back to the way things were. You need to know this."

Cosi was stunned. What would her mother say if she knew? "Do you still go to marches and protests and everything?"

"Yes, sometimes. I marched with Dr. King in one of the Selma-to-Montgomery protests. Sister Theresa and I were both there. They tear-gassed us, spat on us, and jeered at us along with others who marched that day. That's when I made up my mind to keep fighting for justice."

"So, being a teacher and working with little kids, that's not an option anymore?"

"If your conscience allows you to do that. My conscience tells me what happened to those men at the steel plant was wrong. I must get involved." Sister Valentine paused. "Your father worked at the steel mill. Don't you feel an obligation to help those men?"

Cosi did not know what to say. Yes, she felt sorry for those men—and the poor people in Vietnam, and young soldiers like Joey fighting overseas, and her mother and Nino and all the unwanted babies in rivers. Her head was spinning. How was she supposed to know what the Virgin wanted her to do? There were too many things wrong with the world.

Dear Joey, who knew that becoming a nun these days would be downright dangerous? Maybe the Virgin Mary knew, all along.

CHAPTER TWELVE: A MARTYRED VIRGIN AND SNOW SAUSAGES

ON THE FIRST OF December, Cosi and Little Ange went up into the attic to retrieve the Christmas decorations. They strung fat, colored lights along the railing of the upstairs porch and put an artificial wreath on the front door. Their father had always insisted they get a real tree, which this year meant their mother would have to wait until Christmas Eve when she could buy one at half price from the few remaining in the Super Duper parking lot.

On December 8th, Cosi's fourteenth birthday, the aunts came to the apartment bearing gifts. They had spent the morning at Mass celebrating the Feast of the Immaculate Conception— a Holy Day of Obligation—honoring the conception of the Blessed Virgin Mary.

"We should have recognized it as a sign," Aunt Franny told her sisters while they drank their *Medaglia d'Oro* espresso at the kitchen table. "We should have known Cosi would be a favorite of the Virgin Mother, on account of being born on her Holy Day." Aunt Franny presented Cosi with her first long, black mantilla, "because you're almost a woman now."

Aunt Mari gave Cosi a silver charm bracelet with a tiny cross. Aunt Rosa gave her a blue sweater "to match your pretty eyes." Big Ange gave Cosi two tickets to the movie theater. "There's a movie you need to see, now you're 14. Aunt Franny's gonna take you."

Aunt Franny dutifully arrived the next evening. Cosi overheard her mother saying to her aunt, "Make sure you answer any questions she might have about you-know-what." Aunt Franny nodded, and they were out the door.

Settling into their seats, Cosi could see only a few other shapes in the rows ahead of them. The movie was in Italian and she had to read the subtitles in order to understand what was going on. Apparently, eleven-year-old Maria Goretti was a poor girl who lived with her large family and another family in Italy. She seemed very religious. Was she going to become a nun?

Cosi watched carefully. The black-and-white film flickered, showing Maria babysitting for her little sister. A neighbor, Alessandro, was working in the barnyard, watching Maria in a furtive way that made it seem like he was waiting until she was alone. Cosi held her breath when Alessandro snuck into the house.

Alessandro was creepy and reminded Cosi of Rory and his friends. She watched as Alessandro dragged Maria into a darkened room and threatened her with a knife. Maria cowered against the wall, crying and saying what he wanted her to do was a mortal sin. When she said she would rather die than do what he wanted, he threw her to the floor and stabbed her repeatedly.

Cosi sat up in her chair, horrified. The actor who played Alessandro, shirt open, chest slick with sweat, somehow made his eyes bulge when he brought down the knife each time. At the end of the movie, the written epilogue said Maria Goretti, who later became Saint Maria Goretti, had forgiven Alessandro for stabbing her as she lay dying. Shaken, Cosi turned to her aunt when the lights came on.

"Is that what I'm supposed to do if a boy wants to kiss or touch me?"

"Yes." Aunt Franny looked directly in her eyes. "That is the point. A girl must never, ever let a boy touch her in *that* way," she nodded at the movie screen, "until she is married. But thanks to God, as a nun you will never have to put up with this."

"But what if the boy is bigger or stronger than I am, like Alessandro was, and he forces me to, you know, do something like *that*?"

"Then you must be prepared to sacrifice your life, rather than have a mortal sin on your soul," said Aunt Franny, matter-of-factly. Cosi searched her aunt's face. *So that's what Mama wanted me to learn? That I should be prepared to die if a boy tries to go too far with me?*

Cosi and her aunt started to walk home as the snow began to fall. Grant Street was decorated for Christmas, wreaths hanging from every street lamp, shoppers hurrying past with bags bulging with toys bought at Woolworth's and Kresge's. They walked by Smith's Drugstore at Grant and Ferry and could hear the sounds of the piano and young tap-dancers in the Betty Rogers Dance Studio, practicing their shuffle-ball-changes up on the second floor.

"I don't understand any of this, Aunt Franny."

"What don't you understand, *cara?*"

"Now that I'm 14, Mama says I'm supposed to learn about you-know-what. Is that movie what I need to know about S-E-X?" Aunt Franny drew in her breath, but Cosi continued. "I mean, I don't understand it. If sex is wrong, if we're supposed to die rather than have sex with a boy, why is it OK to have sex after you're married? What's the difference?"

Her aunt examined the Christmas decorations with new interest. Cosi stopped walking and waited until her aunt finally looked at her. Aunt Franny sighed.

"Well, when you get married, which is a sacrament, you are married before God. That means you have God's permission to have…uh…relations, so you can make babies. Making babies is OK in the eyes of God if you're married. Making babies when you're not is a sin."

"So, if I'm married, I can have sex as much as I want, as long as I'm trying to make a baby? How will I know if I'm making a baby? Can I feel it right away? What happens if a baby doesn't grow in me, like poor Aunt Rosa? Is that a sin in the eyes of God?"

"You're talking too loud now. Be quiet."

"No, I won't be quiet! Mama said it was time for me to learn. My parents had three children. Did they only have sex three times? Did you and Uncle Carm only have sex twice?"

Aunt Franny grabbed her by the ear and began dragging her down Grant Street. "That's enough!" she said angrily. "You ask too many silly questions. You need to spend your time preparing to be a Bride of Christ. You don't need to know all these other things."

Her pride wounded, Cosi pried her aunt's fingers from her ear and let her walk ahead. She was never going to get answers from Aunt Franny. She made up her mind to visit the West Side Library again and find those Kinsey sex books.

Dear Joey, if you ever wanted to kiss me, I would let you. Just promise me you won't go too far.

ON Christmas Eve, Little Ange and Cosi dragged a half-frozen tree out of the trunk of Johnny's old Ford Falcon, up the linoleum-covered stairs, and into their apartment, leaving a trail of melting snow and pine needles in their wake. Cosi was thrilled when her mother said they could stay up past midnight to welcome Jesus' birthday, grill some meat, and "break the fast" they had all been observing during Advent. At dinner, they had the traditional "feast of the seven fishes," though all they could afford was pasta with canned clam sauce.

"Seven clams on each plate," said Big Ange. "Close enough,"

As the hour approached, neighbors began to drag out their charcoal grills. Later, after attending midnight mass, they would return to cook spicy Italian sausages to signal an end to the six-week fast. Cosi knew her parents, like others in the neighborhood, usually observed this ritual long after the children were in bed. This Christmas Eve, the first without her husband, Big Ange would let the girls participate.

Cosi decorated the tree with her mother while Nino slept and Little Ange stood in the driveway, attempting to light the charcoal briquettes in the rusting grill. The snow was falling in big wet flakes, making the charcoal difficult to light.

"This is *effing* stupid, Mama" called Little Ange several times from the driveway.

Cosi, in her nightgown, winter coat, and rubber boots, came out with an umbrella. She held it over her sister while Little Ange squirted more lighter fluid and tried again. Before long, the coals were burning brightly. Big Ange came down with a string of sausages, bought earlier that day from Zarcone's, then went back up to fry onions and green peppers while the girls stood under the umbrella and watched the meat sizzle.

The night seemed magical to Cosi. The softly falling snow, the companionable heat of the coals, and the delightful aroma wafting from the grill, wrapped her in a warm cocoon of love, neighborhood, and family. She stepped outside the umbrella, closed her eyes and let the flakes tickle her cheeks.

"Hey," said Little Ange, looking at her watch. "It's Christmas. Wanna smoke a joint to celebrate?"

"Are you crazy?" Cosi hissed.

Their mother appeared out of nowhere, holding a plate of warm rolls filled with the fried vegetables. Little Ange shot her sister a warning but Cosi knew better than to say anything. The snow slowed to a few flakes and Big Ange stuck the string of sausages with a long fork and neatly cut off two for each of them, nestling them carefully in the buns. She had also brought down three small glasses of Whiskey Sours, topped with maraschino cherries, and stood silently for a moment, looking at the glowing briquettes. She handed Cosi the plate of sausages, turned her face to the dark sky, and held up her glass.

"*Salud,*" she said, "and Merry Christmas, Johnny, wherever you are. Our little Cositina, you will be proud to know, is on her way to becoming a nun. Little Ange is, well, what you'd expect. Nino is doing OK and I am making a little money. We're trying our best down here, so if you do see God, please ask him to make next year a better one for the McCarthy family."

Little Ange drank her Whiskey Sour in one gulp, handed Cosi her sausages, and walked down the snowy street to smoke her Christmas joint.

Dear Joey, Merry Christmas. I hope you're OK. All I want for Christmas is for you to come home in one piece.

Part Two

Temptation
1969

Chapter Thirteen: Crack the Whip

Cosi climbed the hall stairs clutching a bag of groceries, her fingers numb from walking home in the January cold. She shouldered her way through the apartment door and heard the telephone ringing in the kitchen.

Little Ange rushed out of her room. "It's for me." She grabbed the receiver from her mother's hand and dodged the inevitable slap.

"Hello," breathed Little Ange into the mouthpiece. She paused, frowning. "Here." She handed it to Cosi, dangling the receiver from its cord. "It's for you."

Surprised, Cosi took the phone.

"Hi!" It was Gabby. "We're going ice skating tomorrow at Front Park. Wanna come?"

The temperature was supposed to be a brisk five degrees on Saturday, and colder by the river, but Cosi did not hesitate. "Sure!" She looked quickly at her mother. Big Ange stood silently with folded arms, lifting her chin at the phone, her way of asking, "Who is that?"

Cosi mouthed the words, "My friend."

Big Ange cocked an eyebrow and turned to finish scrubbing her pots.

Like everyone in Buffalo, Cosi had learned to ice skate when she was small. There was always a neighborhood father who flooded his yard with a garden hose when temperatures fell below freezing, and she and the other kids on the block would bring their skates. The surface of this makeshift rink was usually uneven from occasional snow melts, clumps of unmown grass, frozen dog crap, and forgotten toys, so Cosi learned early how to swerve, stop, and maneuver around objects. She got new skates for Christmas every few years but eventually lost interest in backyard skating. This, however, was an invitation to go to a real skating rink. With friends.

Cosi frowned. "I don't think my skates fit anymore."

"You can rent some. Come on. It's really fun."

Cosi looked at her mother. "Can I go ice skating, Mama? I'll be going with an older girl from school, Gabby Mortadella. She'll keep an eye on me."

"Hmmph" said Big Ange, scrubbing her pot more vigorously. "You shouldn't be going to a place like that. You, a girl who's gonna be a nun. I skated at Front Park when I was a teenager. I know what goes on there. Kids go to flirt and feel each other up. Not ice skate."

"I'm not going there to flirt! I just want to go ice skating. Please, Mama?"

"We'll see."

Gabby knocked at the door the next morning and Cosi invited her in. Big Ange looked at Gabby, hands on hips, unsmiling.

"Good morning Mrs. McCarthy," chirped Gabby. "What a lovely home you have here." She looked around, smiling, ignoring the worn sofa and threadbare rugs.

"Good morning, Gabriella," said Big Ange, her tone as cold as ice chips. "I know your family from church. I hope you and your sister were raised to be good Catholic girls who know how to behave themselves around boys."

"Oh yes, Mrs. McCarthy. We know how to behave. 'Keep your eyes open and your legs closed.' That's what we were taught."

"Hmmph," said Big Ange. "You learned that from your mother, did you?" They faced each other, waiting for the other to blink. Gabby widened her smile.

"May I try a piece of your *panettone*, Mrs. McCarthy? I just love *panettone*." Gabby eyed the week-old Christmas cake on the counter. Big Ange, still suspicious, cut her a slice and set it on the table. Gabby sat down without hesitation and dug in.

"So, you're going to Front Park to skate," said Big Ange after a long silence, warming a little to the girl who was eating her cake with such enthusiasm. "You gonna be careful walking through that park? A lotta perverts hang out there."

"We'll be careful," responded Gabby. "We know a pervert when we see one."

Big Ange sighed and carried Gabby's empty plate to the sink.

The girls were out the door and bounding down the front steps before Big Ange could say no. "Wow, you did it. You're amazing, Gabby!"

They were chatting happily, leaning into the stiff wind from the river while walking briskly down Niagara Street, when Gabby stopped in front of a house, ran up the steps, and rang the doorbell. Cosi immediately recognized Jack, the boy who carried her on his shoulders at the swimming pool. She flushed deeply, but Jack seemed not to notice.

"Hi Gab, I'll grab my skates and be right with you. Who's this?" he asked, smiling.

"This is Cosi. You two met last summer at the pool."

"Oh yeah, sure." He squinted at Cosi while he wrapped a scarf around his neck. "You got taller or something. Are you sure you're going to be warm enough like that?"

Cosi thought her pounding heart might split her parka open. Jack looked even more handsome in his navy pea coat and ski cap than he did in his bathing suit. She had on her usual odd assortment of hand-me-downs — coat, hat, gloves, and boots — but Jack was right to be concerned. She had no scarf.

"Here," he offered, "you can borrow one of mine." He wrapped a long scarf gently around her neck. "There," Jack patted the scarf when he finished, and pulled her hood over her head. He trotted down the steps with Gabby, and while the two walked ahead and talked about the new Beatles *White Album*, Cosi tried to calm her nerves. She would get to skate with Jack!

When they arrived at the rink, Cosi was surprised to see how many people were crammed into the warm shed on this cold afternoon. There were at least a dozen benches full of bundled-up kids lacing their skates, while other kids chased each other around, trying to balance on narrow blades as they wobble-ran across the rubberized flooring. Cosi inhaled the smells of wet leather, disinfectant spray, and hot chocolate while she laced up her skates and took deep breaths.

"Let's go." Gabby grabbed Cosi's mittened hand. "They're about to play crack the whip."

Cosi hesitated before she entered the rink. Although sure of herself on skates, she wanted to size up the other skaters. She did not want to make any social blunders, not with Jack around. There were half a dozen teenage boys zooming in, out, and around the other skaters like hummingbirds, doing loops around the pretty girls, and spraying ice when they stopped. Around the sides of the rink, other skaters looked as if it was their first time on ice, hugging the rails and shuffling their feet along. In the middle of the rink, a long snakelike line of boys and girls started to form, the more practiced skaters laughing and grabbing hands as they whisked by.

"Come on!" Gabby pulled Cosi onto the ice and skated quickly to the end of the line.

The skaters initially formed a straight line, all headed in the same direction, when the first boy turned quickly, jerking the line in a different direction. As the centrifugal force built up, Cosi tried to hold on to Gabby's hand, but in a flash found herself spinning off toward the side of the rink, holding only a glove.

"Good one!" Gabby squealed. She snatched Cosi's hand again and they headed back to the line, but after a while, Cosi figured out how to anticipate which way the whip would crack and became bored with the game. She was heading back to the shed to warm up when Jack came skating over.

"Skate with me awhile?" He took Cosi's hand, guiding her around the rink. He clowned around, sometimes skating backwards and pulling her to him, sometimes grabbing a mitten and taunting her to chase him. So elated was she that she had Jack's undivided attention, she barely noticed it was getting dark and the rink was closing.

The snow crunched loudly underfoot on the long, cold walk home. The streetlights came on, bathing the neighborhood in white gold. Far too quickly for Cosi, the three arrived in front of Jack's house. He ran up his front steps and turned around.

"Hey Cosi, see you around some time, OK?"

"Wait," stammered Cosi, surprised by her forwardness. "You forgot your scarf." He looked in her eyes while he unwrapped it from her neck, kissed her red nose, and went inside.

Lying in bed that night, Cosi felt the strangest sensations coursing through her body, as if electric eels were swimming through every part of her. She could not stop thinking about Jack and it frightened her. These were not feelings a future nun should have. She threw back her covers, got out of bed, and dropped to her knees, praying the "Our Father," with special emphasis on the final verse, "*and lead us not into temptation….*"

The next morning Cosi looked carefully at her face in the bathroom mirror. Why hadn't Jack recognized her? Yes, she had grown taller over the past year and was losing the chubbiness in her face. Maybe she was prettier now? She looked down at her belly and the handful of fat she could still grab in each hand and groaned, realizing her coat had covered that. *Oh well. Who would care if a nun is fat?*

The thrill of skating with Jack lingered all Sunday. Cosi thought of him while vacuuming her bedroom floor, humming while she bent to get under the beds, and noticed a thick yellow book beneath Little Ange's. Curious, since her sister never read anything but magazines, Cosi knelt down and retrieved it. She stared at the title, *Everything You Always Wanted to Know About Sex (But Were Afraid to Ask)*. She gasped, put the book back under the bed, and ran to the bathroom to wash her hands.

Try as she might to erase the book from her mind, it kept calling to her. She sat on her bed and argued with herself. Here she was, 14 years old, and knew little about sex, other than it could get you in trouble or even killed, like Saint Maria Goretti, or get you damned to Hell, like her father. She was too embarrassed to ask Sister Valentine. Maybe this book would have some answers. She pulled it out again and saw the author was a doctor, "David Reuben, M.D." *It's a medical book*, she told herself. *How sinful can that be?*

Cosi opened the cover with the tips of her index finger and thumb, flipped to the table of contents, and took a deep breath. There were chapters entitled "Male Sex Organs" and "Female Sex Organs," and chapters with words she had never heard before, like masturbation, impotence, intercourse, frigidity, menopause. She noted the book was hundreds of pages long, closed it, and slid it back under the bed. If her sister caught her, Cosi would never hear the end of it.

Dear Joey, I know I shouldn't ask you, but doesn't everyone need to know <u>*something*</u> *about sex, even nuns?* She hesitated, wondering if she should write or even think the next words. *Have you had sex?*

CHAPTER FOURTEEN: TEMPTING FATE

Cosi GOT UP LATE the following Monday morning and missed the usual city bus she took to school. She was standing at the bus stop in her school uniform, her bare knees exposed and turning red from the cold, when she heard her name. It was Gabby, running with her hand holding down her hat, her scarf flying and boots wobbling, trying not to slip on the icy sidewalk. Cosi saw the bus turn the corner, heading toward their stop, and called to Gabby to hurry.

"Tell him to wait for me," shouted Gabby, dropping two of her books in the snow and turning back for them. The bus pulled up and the door opened. Cosi looked back to see Gabby now only a few houses away.

"Could you please wait for my friend?" Cosi pleaded, showing the unfamiliar driver her bus pass. The bus driver looked out his door.

"She's late every morning," said the bus driver, shaking his head.

"Thanks, Myron," Gabby grinned, breathless, as she climbed on the bus. "I owe you."

"You owe me more than one, sweetheart," the driver muttered, shutting the door.

Gabby sat down with a whoosh and brushed the snow from her books. "I really thought I was going to miss it this time."

"I never catch this bus." Cosi chewed her hair nervously. "I think we're gonna be late."

"Naw, we'll get there just as the bell rings. Throw your coat in the hallway and bring it to your locker later. That's what I do." Cosi looked at her watch. How she wished she could be as cool as Gabby!

"Did you have a good time skating with Jack?" Gabby casually changed the subject.

"Sure," Cosi fiddled with her books, trying to appear nonchalant.

"Far out. I think dating Jack would be good for you."

Cosi blinked. "What? You know I can't date anyone. I'm gonna be a nun."

"Oh, don't be a ninny. Just because you're *gonna* be a nun doesn't mean you have to act like one now. Enjoy your teenage years, then 'get thee to a nunnery' and do your penance. At least you'll know what life is all about, unlike the old bats who live in the Mother House."

Cosi considered this. "No, my mother would never let me date. She fights with my sister all the time about her boyfriends. She would have a heart attack if I started dating."

"Well, does she have to know?"

"Keep a secret from my mother? Are you kidding?" Cosi shook her head. "I don't mind Jack giving me a skating lesson or two, but that's it."

"OK," Gabby shrugged. "Suit yourself. I thought you should know Jack's interested."

They sat in silence while the bus grumbled through the snowy streets. Gabby smeared Chapstick on her lips, and suddenly brightened, remembering something. "Hey, Meatball is having a birthday party at his house next Saturday night. Wanna come?"

Cosi vaguely knew Michael Meteri, fondly known in the neighborhood as Meatball. He was several years older than Gabby and one of the most popular kids in the neighborhood, for reasons Cosi did not quite understand.

"Well sure." Cosi didn't want to admit that the only party she had ever been to with kids her own age was her own pathetic graduation party. "Do I need to bring a gift?"

Gabby chuckled. "It's not that kind of party. If your Mom gives you any trouble, you just let me know. I know how to handle her now."

Cosi was sweating as she dropped her coat outside the door of algebra class and hurried inside. Sister Agatha barely glanced at her as she rushed to her seat and opened her math book just before the bell rang. She exhaled, relieved, but noticed no one else had their books open. She had forgotten there was a quiz this morning.

She thought she saw a smirk on Sister Agatha's thin lips when, at the end of class, she handed back the quiz with a red "D+" at the top. "See me after class, Miss McCarthy."

She barely listened as Sister Agatha lectured her on the need to study harder than the rest of the class. "I'm afraid you're at a real disadvantage, intellectually," Sister Agatha said, at what Cosi feared was the beginning of a long rant. Cosi surreptitiously glanced at her watch again. She was supposed to stop by the guidance office this morning to sign up for her first volunteer job, keeping her earlier promise to Sister Valentine. She sighed and waited patiently for the end of her math teacher's latest rebuke.

When Cosi finally arrived at the office, she found a long line of girls ahead of her. She looked at the sign-up roster and was disappointed to see the best volunteer jobs—those working with children—were gone. Only two opportunities remained on the list: reading to the elderly nuns on the top floor of the school, and visiting patients at the psychiatric hospital. Cosi stopped to consult Sister Valentine after school. "Which do you think I should choose?"

"I know which will be more of a challenge. Working with psychiatric patients is very demanding. Our sweet, elderly sisters, on the other hand, would welcome your visits."

"OK then, I'll read to the old sisters," said Cosi, looking at the icicles dripping outside the classroom window, secretly relieved she would not have to work at the hospital. She hesitated then, trying to decide whether to broach the subject that was really bothering her.

"Sister, there's something I've been meaning to ask you. When you were young…younger, I mean…did you ever like a boy?"

Cosi thought she caught a hint of a smile on her mentor's face. "I was in love once."

"Really?"

"Yes. A long time ago, but I remember the feeling." There was a pause, then a chuckle. "My advice for you is to follow your heart. Falling in love and getting married instead of entering the convent wouldn't be the worst thing in the world, would it?"

"Oh yes, Sister. It would be. The only reason my mother loves me now, is because I'm going to become a nun."

"You know that can't possibly be true," said Sister Valentine, her voice softening. "I'm sure your mother loves you and she just doesn't know how to show it."

Cosi shook her head. "I'm sorry, Sister. You don't know my mother."

Cosi counted down the days until Meatball's party, and nearly fainted when her mother agreed she could go. "You walk there with Gabby. You sing, blow out the candles, eat cake, and come home. No birthday party should take longer than one hour."

"Yes, Mama."

"Tell Mrs. Meteri I said hello, and that I got some new fabrics for the Infants."

"I will Mama," Cosi quickly agreed, remembering now that Mrs. Meteri was one of her mother's best customers.

When Cosi arrived at the Mortadellas' house, Gabby took one look at the way she was dressed and dragged her to the bedroom. "You can't go any-where looking like that."

Gabby went to the dresser and started pulling out clothes. "You're a little bit different size than me but these might fit. Try them on." Gabby held up a pair of bell bottom jeans and a turtleneck sweater she had just bought from a hip new store in Allentown called the Town Squire. "Here. Wear these. You'll look fabulous!"

Cosi pulled on the jeans, sweater, and a leather belt with a large metal buckle and looked at herself in the mirror. "Oh, my goodness." Cosi turned in front of the mirror, shocked by how the tight clothes accentuated her breasts and hips. "I can't go anywhere looking like this."

"Of course, you can," said Gabby, hanging a peace symbol necklace around Cosi's neck. "This way you'll fit in and people won't think you're some goofball."

They were half a block away from the Meteris' house when Cosi heard the music. Drawing closer, she could see windows opened to the freezing January night. The house was full of people and she started to panic.

"Gabby I can't…"

"Come on." Gabby took her hand and squeezed. "I'll introduce you to everyone." They walked through the front door and a cloud of thick smoke enveloped them. They plunged into a room with wall-to-wall kids and music so loud the floor vibrated.

"Let's go find Meatball," yelled Gabby over the crowd.

Cosi followed closely as Gabby pushed her way through the crowd to the back of the house. They found Meatball sitting on the bed in his darkened room along with five or six girls. He was smoking some sort of pipe in the glow of an orange and yellow lava lamp.

"Hey Gabby, come on in, take a toke." Meatball offered her the odd-looking contraption. "I just got this bitchin' new bong for my birthday. Hey, who's the little Lolita?"

"You know Cosi McCarthy, don't you Meatball?" Gabby asked, taking the device. "Cosi's my good friend from school." Gabby put the bong to her mouth and inhaled deeply.

"Cosi, oh sure. Come on in," said Meatball. "Make yourselves comfortable, ladies."

Meatball's long curly brown hair fell below well his shoulders, flowing uninterrupted into his curly brown beard and moustache. In the middle of this halo of hair, two round cheeks and a pair of red-rimmed, half-closed eyes poked out. His arms encircled an enormous stomach, lovingly rubbed by two hippie-looking girls, as if he was the Buddha of Buffalo.

Gabby exhaled a large amount of smoke. "Thanks Meatball, but we're gonna walk around and check out the scene for a while. Cosi's new to all this."

"Far out," said Meatball, pulling one of the girls onto his stomach and blowing smoke into her nostrils while she inhaled.

Cosi headed angrily towards the front door. She passed another bedroom and caught a glimpse of several couples in various stages of undress. She looked away and turned to Gabby. "Why did you bring me here?" she hissed, her face a deep magenta.

"What's wrong?" Gabby looked hurt. "Cosi, look, I know you don't do drugs, have sex, or drink. But can't we just hang out here, listen to music, and talk to people? These are my friends, and I want you to be my friend too. I'm not going to make you do anything you don't want to do, and neither will they. Please, Cosi. Don't make me choose between you and them."

They stood looking at each other, and Cosi finally relented. Of course, she did not want to lose her best friend. Her only friend. Besides, she had to admit she really liked the music, and she felt a strange excitement being here, despite herself.

"Come on, let's go find you a non-alcoholic beverage," said Gabby, throwing an arm around Cosi's shoulders.

In the kitchen, Cosi was surprised to find her cousin Dominic, Aunt Mari's son, standing amidst a group of guys, arguing vehemently about something. "Cosi? What are you doing here?" asked Dominic, his eyes only briefly leaving the debate.

"I'm here with my friend Gabby," said Cosi, under her breath, "And Mama knows I'm here, so no need to report anything to her."

"Aw, it's cool, cuz," said Dominic, taking a swig of beer. Cosi stood on tiptoe to get a look at the teenager with the long, dirty-blond hair who was clearly the center of attention.

The blond guy was speaking in a soft voice. "No, a conscientious objector doesn't have to refuse to serve solely on the basis of religious beliefs. It can also be on the basis of moral principle. Either way, the objector must demonstrate a sincere, long-standing objection if he hopes to get an exemption. You can't simply claim an objection because you don't want to go."

"Well, I think you're all a bunch of chicken-shit yellow bellies," said a red-faced kid Cosi did not recognize. "You make up some bullshit excuse because you're afraid you'll get shot."

The blond kid was unperturbed. He seemed to hold the crowd in his hands, answering questions, even angry ones, with ease.

"You're entitled to believe what you want," he said calmly, "but some of us believe this is an immoral and unjust war. And if we went ahead and fought, believing it was wrong, just to ensure public approbation—*that* would be the act of cowardice."

Approbation? Who talks like that? Cosi wondered. *No one from this neighborhood.*

"You suck," said the red-faced kid before turning away and stomping out of the kitchen. The blond guy walked over to the refrigerator and pulled out a beer. "Would you like one?" he said to Cosi. She realized she was the only one still staring at him.

"Uh, no, that is, well, actually I'd like some pop, if there is any," said Cosi.

"Hmm," he said, rummaging through the bottles, "how about a ginger ale?"

"Perfect," said Cosi gratefully, taking the bottle from him.

"My name is Marty Paczinski, by the way." He pushed a lock of hair from his eyes.

He's Polish, Cosi thought. That explains why I've never seen him before. With his long hair and beard, sweet-sad eyes, and angular face, she thought he looked a bit like a blond Jesus.

"I'm Cosi McCarthy," she said, extending her hand.

He took it and kissed it. "Nice to meet you, Cosi McCarthy," he said, holding her hand. She felt faint. This guy was like something out of a fairytale.

She noticed he seemed to be staring at her turtleneck sweater and was sure he could see butterflies beating wings inside her chest.

"I like your necklace." He nodded at the peace symbol and took a sip from the bottle.

"Thank you. I'm sorry…I didn't mean to stare at you earlier," she said, flustered, not sure where to look. "It sounded like you were talking about something important."

"Hi Marty!" Gabby strolled into the kitchen, deliberately bumping her hip against his. "I see you two found each other."

"You know each other?" Cosi and Marty asked Gabby at the same time. They laughed.

"Cosi and I go to Holy Martyrs together," Gabby explained, "and we're good friends. Cosi, Marty and I have gone to some peace rallies together."

Dominic joined them. "Hey man, you hitting on my little cousin?"

"She doesn't look little to me."

"She's only a freshman, so behave."

"Well then she needs someone to protect her from this lascivious crowd," laughed Marty. He took her arm and walked her through the stoned-out dancers, calling "Let the lady pass," until they were out the back door and in the yard. They sat down on the steps. Cosi was shivering but Marty seemed oblivious to the cold.

"Look at the stars." He pointed. "There's Orion and there's Orion's belt. Orion dominates the winter sky. That bright white star at the lower right of his belt? That's Rigel, which forms his knee, and if you look to the upper left of his belt, you'll find Betelgeuse. And over there are Orion's two dogs—Canis Major and Canis Minor... and then over there..."

Cosi listened dreamily as Marty continued his tour of the night sky. She forgot about the cold, the party, and her awkwardness. She had never met anyone like Marty—eloquent, funny, and interested in something other than hockey and football. She wondered how old he was. She felt she could listen to him talk forever.

"What were you talking about in there...about an objection?" she asked.

"I think the war in Vietnam is morally wrong," Marty explained. "I don't want to be drafted, based on that moral objection. When I turn 18, I'll refuse to go to Vietnam."

"How old are you?" she asked, surprised he was not already 18.

"I'm 16," he said, eyeing her curiously. "You?"

"I...I'm 15," she said, immediately regretting her lie. They sat in silence for a while.

He leaned back on his elbows. "And you? Can I assume from your necklace that you're against the war?"

"Well, I say the rosary every day and pray to end the war. I also collect soap for the Vietnamese people," she said, suddenly feeling childish. She hesitated to mention Joey. She couldn't bear the thought of someone criticizing him.

Marty searched her eyes. "Hey, would you ever consider coming to one of our end-the-draft rallies? We try to keep them peaceful. You can more learn about the war and why we want to educate guys before they are drafted. What do you say?"

Cosi knew what her mother would say, but she also knew she liked being around Marty Paczinski. Maybe they could work together to end the war in Vietnam.

"Well, I have to check with my mother, but I'd like to go.

"Give me your number and I'll call you when we're planning another rally." Marty pulled out a little black notebook. "Don't worry. It's not full of girls' telephone numbers." He smiled. "It's just a calendar with some note pages."

Gabby came down the back steps just as Cosi finished giving Marty her phone number. "Hey you two, time to break it up. I promised Cosi's mother she'd be home by 10."

"I'll call you," shouted Marty, as Cosi and Gabby hurried out of the backyard.

All the way home, Cosi smiled. "Uh, oh," said Gabby. "Is it possible that a future nun has a crush on Marty?"

"Stop that." Cosi gently punched her friend's shoulder. She looked at the rows of softly lit houses along Fargo Avenue, then up at the stars and the dark night sky. She could not recall a Buffalo night quite as exquisite as this one.

"Can't say I blame you," Gabby laughed. "Marty is one sexy guy."

Later that night, as soon as Little Ange was snoring, Cosi crawled under her sister's bed and retrieved the big yellow book. It was time to learn what sex was all about.

Dear Joey. I'm reading this book and oh, my face is red. The things people do in the bedroom! Yuck! Maybe I better become a nun.

CHAPTER FIFTEEN: SOCIAL CLIMBERS, FEMINISTS, AND POINTY BRAS

"I'M NOT SURPRISED YOU'RE having a hard time," Sister Agatha was saying, while Cosi swiped at the blackboard with a wet cloth. "You shouldn't even be in this class." Cosi had done poorly on another pop quiz.

"I didn't ask to be in this class, Sister." Cosi tried to hide her irritation. "I was put in here because of my test scores."

"Oh, balderdash." Sister Agatha wiped her finger across the board and examined the tip. "You're here on a needs-based scholarship, not a merit-based one. We always have problems with you needs-based people. Sister Valentine should know better."

Cosi looked at her. *What is she talking about now?*

"Don't pretend you don't know. I've got your number, Missy. Pretending to want to enter the convent so you can attend this school. Why, you're nothing but a little social climber, wanting to hobnob with your betters. You have no real interest in becoming a nun."

Cosi opened her mouth to argue, but knew it was pointless. Arguing with someone like Sister Agatha always made her tongue-tied and furious. She remembered how easily Marty handled his opponents at the party and decided to take Sister Valentine's advice. She would join the debate team at the next opportunity.

Cosi came home from school that afternoon to find her aunts sitting with her mother at the kitchen table, rubbing Aunt Mari's back. A tear fell from Aunt Mari's eye into her cold cup of espresso. "…and when I showed Tony the receipt for a gold bracelet, he admitted everything, including the fact this *puttana* works with him. What did I do to deserve this? I feed him, clean up after him—I even stir his damn coffee!"

"Men are bastards," Big Ange declared. "It's just a fact."

"It's their hormones," offered Aunt Rosa. "They got different ones than we do. They can't help themselves, Mari. It's not your fault. Not a thing you can do, if they wanna stray."

Big Ange's eyes flashed, but she said nothing.

"We should all go to the shrine to pray Tony comes to his senses." Aunt Franny looked heavenward. "My lips to God's ears he will find his way to become a decent husband again."

"Hah. There's no decency when it comes to men," countered Big Ange. "All we can do is try to outsmart 'em."

Cosi plucked up her courage. If she was ever going to stand up to Sister Agatha, she had better learn how to talk seriously with adults. Her father's confession had confused her, but after reading most of Little Ange's yellow book, she had a much better idea of what had been going on. She would never admit it, but she believed she was becoming quite an expert on sex.

Cosi cleared her throat. "Yes, Aunt Rosa, they have different hormones, but we have hormones too. So why is it OK for men to cheat on women, when it is not OK for women to cheat on men? Why are there different rules?"

The four women looked at her.

"Those are good questions," said Big Ange, finally. "And I got no good answers."

"You're right. Why do we always get the shaft?" Aunt Mari dabbed at her tears.

Aunt Rosa shook her head. "*Madonne!* You're starting to sound like a *feminiss*, Mari."

"What's a *feminiss*?"

"Don't you watch TV?" Aunt Rosa sighed. "Remember those women who went to Atlantic City to burn their bras at the Miss America contest? Claimed men treat us like sex objects? Men treat me that way, God knows," she said, eyeing her perfect red nails, "but I'm pretty sure there's nothing I can do about it."

"Maybe you can start by keeping your *nennès* out of everyone's face," muttered Big Ange, glancing at Rosa's exposed cleavage.

Cosi took a deep breath and tried again. "I saw a book at the library by a lady named Betty Friedan. Everybody at school is talking about it. She wants women to start sticking up for themselves. I can get the book, Aunt Mari, if it would help you."

"I gotta do something," Aunt Mari nodded, considering. "Maybe burning my bra and letting my boobs bounce around will get Tony to pay attention to me again."

"I'm not sure that's the idea," said Cosi, "but I'll get you the book."

"Well, aren't you all a bunch of Gloomy Gerties," declared Aunt Rosa. "There are times we really need a man." She grinned impishly. "I think I'm pregnant again!"

Aunt Mari started to cry. "Oh Rosa, I'm so happy for you. When are you due?"

"The doctor said I'm about three months along. He thinks I'll deliver in August if all goes well. Say a prayer for me."

Big Ange was scowling, swirling her coffee around and around her cup. Cosi had a momentary panic attack, counting the months since her father died, and realized it was well over a year ago. It could not be his baby. She let out her breath and smiled tentatively at Aunt Rosa, who had announced she was pregnant several times in the past. For reasons the aunts never discussed, Aunt Rosa's pregnancies always ended without a baby. Cosi wondered now if any of those lost babies had been her father's, and even worse, if any had ended up in the Erie Canal.

COACH Bannerman was studying Cosi from the back of the gym while she went through basketball drills with the rest of her class. When they finished practicing lay-ups, Coach barked, "McCarthy, get over here." Cosi ran over, wondering what she had done wrong. "You're in better shape than you were last semester," said Coach. "You shot up like a beanpole and you lost that baby fat. You still stink at dribbling the ball, but you're faster running around the court."

Cosi was surprised. Coach Bannerman never complimented anyone. Cosi had assumed Coach would not give her a second look after her failed attempt to make the basketball team.

"Well Coach, I've been trying something called the Metrecal diet and I…"

"Stop drinking that crap!" shouted Coach. "If you want to get in shape, you need exercise, not liquid food! Why don't you join our new cross-country team?"

"Our what?"

Coach folded her arms. "You're too slow to run track, but maybe not for cross country. We'll run long distances, on paths and open fields. You need stamina, and long legs help. Start running with the team and you'll be in shape in no time. Whaddya say?"

"I'll think about it," said Cosi.

"Well think fast. We start running as soon as the paths are free of ice."

All the way home, while the city bus pitched and rocked its way through early spring potholes, Cosi wondered why Coach was taking an interest in her. She ran up to the apartment and took another hard look at herself in the mirror, then at the photo of her eighth-grade graduation. She had grown six inches and lost at least 20 pounds since then. Her face had new hollows and her chin had lost its roundness. Her school uniform was too short, and in some places, too tight. She pulled the black dress up over her head and stared. Her breasts had swelled considerably and her old bra was much too small. For a fleeting moment, she wondered what Jack might think when he saw her in a bathing suit this summer.

She leaned out the bedroom door. "Mama, I need a new bra."

Her mother appeared instantly in the doorway. "Let me see."

Cosi bounced up and down on her heels, the tops of her breasts vibrating like jello.

"*Madre di Dio!*" Big Ange's eyes widened. "You can't let the nuns see you looking like that." She disappeared, and in a minute, returned. "Here. Wear one of my old bras."

"I can't wear that!" Cosi stared at the enormous Maidenform cotton brassiere with under wires and pointed cups. "I'll look ridiculous."

"What do you mean, ridiculous?" Her mother had an angry squint to her eye.

"I just mean it will be far too big on me," Cosi mumbled, not wanting to explain that pointy bras had gone out with the Fifties.

"Try it on."

She tried it on. She had to admit her mother was right. The cups covered her breasts completely, but with little room to spare. She looked at the tag and saw it was only a D cup, not the double D cup her mother usually wore.

She looked at her mother appraisingly. "Mama, you've been losing weight."

Her mother looked embarrassed. "Yeah, I lost some. I'm tryin' to slim down."

"Well, I'm not wearing your old bra. They have bras on sale at AM&A's for $3.99. I'll do some extra babysitting if we don't have the money."

"Since when do you talk so disrespectfully to your mother?

"Since when can't we afford $3.99?"

Big Ange's lips tightened. "Your Uncle Danny, the *scroccone,* hasn't paid the rent in three months. Why don't you ask him for the $3.99? And get the rest he owes while you're at it."

Rory and his gang were in the backyard playing "chicken" with a switchblade knife. "You lose, shit-for-brains," Rory was saying to a younger kid. "Pull it out of the mud with your teeth." Rory turned when Cosi came stomping down the back stairs. "Hey Cosi," he called. "Wanna see me stick my blade between your legs?" All the other boys guffawed.

"Wanna see me stick that blade between *your* legs?" Cosi retorted, staring Rory down. "I came to find out why your family hasn't paid the rent." The boys stopped laughing and looked away. There was nothing funny about your family being broke. They had all been there.

"Why you asking me? Go ask my dad. But get ready for a sob story about how they're threatening to lay him off at work."

She considered confronting Uncle Danny but thought better of it. There was worried talk all over the neighborhood about big layoffs at the steel plant. The newspapers said corporate headquarters was unhappy with the high taxes in New York, and some people were saying the company planned to move the whole plant to another state.

She hoped the rumors were not true. What would Uncle Danny do if he lost his job—move his whole family? Continue to live downstairs and not pay rent? If her mother threw them out, how soon could they get another tenant if most of other men in the neighborhood lost their jobs? Come to think of it, what would happen to the neighborhood? Most families were barely scraping by. Cosi sighed and headed back upstairs.

Dear Joey, I hope you are OK. I wish I could say things are good here. I'm not sure which is worse. War or poverty?

Chapter Sixteen: Invisible Wounds and Babysitting Nightmares

Joey Catalfano came home from Vietnam in early June. It was a Sunday, just after 3 p.m., Cosi remembered, because the McCarthys' were on their way back from dinner at Nonna's. She had nearly dropped the remains of her mother's lasagna on the front steps when she saw the station wagon pull up next door. Mr. Catalfano jumped out of the car and opened the back door.

Joey emerged from the car slowly, stiffly, his face blank as a sheet of paper. He was in jeans, no longer wearing the spic-and-span Army uniform he had on when his parents took him to the bus station. Cosi stared, searching for bandages, crutches, anything that might explain why he had come home early. His parents stood on either side of him holding his arms, talking quietly. Cosi saw pain etched in his face, though she saw no wounds.

She worried about him all night. "There's something wrong with Joey," Cosi told her mother the next morning. "Can we make him a rum cake? Remember how he always ate a huge piece at the church picnics?"

"Sure. That boy needs something to cheer him up. Bring it to him after church Sunday."

Still dressed in her church clothes, Cosi knocked on the Catalfanos' door. "Hello Mrs. Catalfano. My mother and I made Joey a welcome-home gift. We remember he liked this cake," she said shyly.

"Oh, hello Cosi. Well, how nice," Mrs. Catalfano said, then hesitated briefly. "Uh, why don't you come in for a moment?"

Cosi stepped inside and stood in the foyer, careful not to step on the spotless white shag carpet. Mrs. Catalfano took the cake and turned to walk toward the kitchen.

"Wait there just a second."

Cosi looked around the neat living room, where a huge framed picture of Joey in his Army uniform hung over the mantelpiece.

"Joey?" she could hear Mrs. Catalfano say in a low voice, "Honey, Cosi McCarthy is here, and she baked something nice for you. Would you like to come out and say hello?"

"No." Joey's voice sounded like he was talking into his pillow.

"Now, Joey…" his mother tried again.

"I said no! Tell her to go home!"

Mrs. Catalfano returned and handed the cake to Cosi. "He's feeling a little under the weather right now, but I know he would really appreciate it later. Maybe you can come back another time?"

Cosi hurried out the front door and burst into tears. What had she expected? She thought about all her unanswered letters and the awful things she was hearing on the evening news. None of her prayers to end the war seemed to be making any difference. And instead of trying to help all the poor people in Vietnam, she knew now, she should have focused on one soldier.

Dear Joey, what happened to you? I know you don't want to talk, but I'm praying for you. PS: The cake's in the freezer.

Just before school ended for the summer, Little Ange came running into the house waving a sheet of paper over her head.

"I got a summer job!" she screamed. "I'm gonna be working at the pool as a lifeguard, and it's full-time! Is that outta sight, or what?"

Her mother looked at her. "What kinda bathing suit you gonna wear?"

"Oh Mama, can't you ever be happy for me? The city gives us lifeguard outfits that we *have* to wear. I don't have a choice."

"Hmmph. You still gonna babysit for the Conways at night?"

"Of course not!" said Little Ange, "If I do, I won't have a life. Besides, I told them Cosi could babysit. That way she can make some money too."

"Could I, Mama?" Cosi pleaded, watching her mother's eyes narrow. "It would help the family if we're both paying room and board. How much do they pay, Angie?"

"Fifty cents an hour, and sometimes, when they go out and have a really good time, Mr. Conway gives me a big tip. It's a good job, Mama. Let Cosi do it."

A week later, Cosi was contemplative as she walked the several blocks to the Conways' house on 14th Street. It was beautiful summer evening, the sun slanting at a sharp angle, changing the shadows in a way that made Cosi sad for reasons she did not understand. She shook her head and told herself to be happy. She finally had a real job.

The Conways had agreed to drive Cosi home whenever they returned after dark. Tonight, they were leaving at 7:00 and Cosi wanted to be there at least fifteen minutes early to go over details. Although the evening was beginning to cool, her armpits were soaked with sweat and she sniffed them, checking for body odor. She knocked on the door twenty minutes early.

A boy of about eight ripped open the door and yelled, "Mom, the new babysitter's here!"

A harried-looking woman in a peasant dress came to the door, trying to wrestle her earrings into place. "Hi," she said, "Come in, come in. You must be Cosi. I'm Trudy. Let me introduce you to the children. Paul! Ringo! Come here please."

Mrs. Conway smiled at Cosi, "Did Little Ange mention we nicknamed them after our favorite Beatles? Their real names are Lester and Elmer but we love the Beatles and have all their albums. Your sister likes to listen to the 'White Album' while she smokes pot. I assume you like it as well? I've left it out for you."

Left it out? Does she mean the 'White Album'? Or the pot?

Both boys had wild mops of long curly hair that reminded Cosi of the poodle her neighbor never got around to grooming. They ran around the room screaming and randomly hopping onto the sofa, the coffee table, and the beanbag chair.

"Now boys, you need to calm down before bedtime. I want you to listen to some music and do some meditation." Mrs. Conway turned and whispered to Cosi. "They know what that means. Just make sure they don't eat anything with sugar before they go to bed. It makes them completely unmanageable."

Mr. Conway walked into the room, sporting a long brown ponytail and granny glasses. "Well now, if it isn't the new babysitter!" he said in a booming voice. He was a large man with a Southern accent and he grinned in a way that made her uncomfortable. Somewhere in the dim recesses of her memory, she recalled her father acting like this when a new babysitter arrived at the McCarthy home.

"We'll be home between 11:00 and 11:30," said Mrs. Conway, who seemed not to notice her husband's leering. "Help yourself to anything you like, including the carob brownies. And there's carrot juice in the refrigerator if you want something other than water or wine."

"Take good care of our boys, you hear?" Mr. Conway winked.

The Conways drove off, leaving Cosi looking out the window, wondering what to do next. Ringo solved that problem when he ran into the room crying.

"What's the matter, sweetheart?" Cosi knelt down to face the little boy.

"Paulie hurt my brain," said Ringo, pointing to his head.

She looked where he was pointing and saw a large lump. "Paulie, come here please," she demanded, using her sternest voice. "Tell me why you hit your brother in the head."

"He was trying to steal my candy," said Paul.

"What candy? You know you're not supposed to have candy before bedtime. Your mama is going to be very angry with you. Please bring it here and let's put it away."

"No," shouted Paul. "And you can't make me, you scuzz bucket!"

Cosi was shocked. She had never heard a child speak so rudely to someone older. "Ringo," she said, as calmly as she could, "show me the candy Paulie was trying to keep from you." Ringo took her hand and started walking toward the boys' bedroom.

"No!" screamed Paul running ahead of them. He tried to slam the door but Cosi was stronger.

"OK, where is it?"

Ringo pointed to the closet. "In the back."

Cosi got down on all fours to reach underneath the shelves full of clothes and toys. She felt around until she retrieved a large paper bag. Backing out, she felt Paul's hand on her rump.

"What are you doing?" she gasped.

"Copping a feel," said Paul, matter-of-factly.

"Get your grabby little hands off of me," she snarled. She opened the bag and saw dozens of small candy bars and lollipops, with just as many empty wrappers. "Where did all this come from?"

"Me and Dad got it last Halloween. Mom told him to take it to work, but he hid it in his closet. It's *my* candy too so I put it in *my* closet."

"Well, you can't have any more tonight." Cosi pushed past him and set the bag high atop a kitchen shelf. She took a deep breath. "Time for music. Do you have a favorite album?"

Paul scrunched his face. "Mom wants us to listen to some Maharishi crap, but I got something better. I'm gonna find my dad's album."

He ran into the living room, found the record, and set it on the turntable. Cosi looked at the cover. She had never heard of the band, Iron Butterfly, or the cover song, "Inna Gadda Davida." Paul turned up the volume on the Hi-Fi and sang along while he played air guitar, jumping around the room.

"This is not what your mother had in mind," Cosi yelled over the cacophony. Paul shot her the finger. She marched over and turned off the record player. "Go to bed *right* now."

Paul eyed her defiantly. "Little Ange lets us listen to whatever we want. And she's a stone-cold fox, not a dope like you."

"Well, I'm not Little Ange," said Cosi, "and I say it's time to go to bed."

"You forgot, we're supposed to meditate before we go to bed," Ringo piped up.

"Shoot," said Cosi wearily. "I forgot. Let's go meditate." She followed the two boys into a small dark room in the back of the house.

"Wait. I have to turn on the black light." Paul flicked a switch and the room suddenly had a strange glow to it.

Cosi could see several posters hanging on the walls in the dim light. One said "Power Plant" with marijuana leaves and mushrooms in the background. Another showed a silhouette of a naked man and woman embracing. "I don't think you're supposed to be in here," said Cosi. "This isn't a place for children."

"Yes, it is," Paul insisted. "This is where we meditate. We have our own mantra." He sat on the floor and looked at Cosi. "You're supposed to sit and close your eyes, stupid."

"OK," said Cosi, "But no more copping a feel while I'm not looking. Understood?"

The boys closed their eyes and made moaning sounds and chanted words Cosi had never heard before. She had no idea what this was all about, but had to admit it did seem to calm them. After 20 minutes or so, she finally managed to tuck them in. She went back to the living room and collapsed on the green velour couch.

With no TV in the room, she sat staring at the batik-covered walls, and eventually wandered into the kitchen looking for snacks. Little Ange told her that the only downer about babysitting for the Conways was the food. They were vegetarians.

"If she bakes brownies though," Little Ange had said with a smirk, "be sure to eat one."

Cosi found the brownies hidden in the back of the refrigerator. They tasted funny, nothing like the brownies her mother made. She found carrot sticks, nuts, and dates and decided to try them too. Still curious about the room with the black light, she wandered back to check it out. This time she noticed a small chest with a key underneath it. She opened it to find a baggie of what looked like dried oregano and papers like the ones Nonna used to roll her cigarettes.

While she contemplated the horrible possibility that the Conways smoked pot in front of their children, she started to feel funny, as if everything was slowing down. Her eyelids were suddenly heavy as silver dollars and her mouth was dry. She stumbled into the kitchen, gulped the carrot juice, and managed to find her way back to the living room.

She thought if she sat down, she might fall asleep. *Better put on some music so I can stay awake.* She rummaged through the milk crate and pulled out an album with the word "Cream" at the top, and below it, "Wheels of Fire." She tried to focus but the drawings on the cover began to move. Some expanded and contracted, some started to spin, and the whole cover appeared to be in motion. Her body felt all wrong. She had difficulty placing the needle on the album and it landed in the middle of a song that sounded like they were singing about black curtains.

Her head felt so heavy she thought her neck would snap. She staggered to the couch. The room slid sideways and she began hallucinating, scenes from her worst nightmares flashing rapidly before her. German Shepherds trying to tear her apart at an anti-war protest. Black men screaming at her in righteous anger. A pale baby pulling her down into the Erie Canal. Joey Catalfano lying in a pool of blood.

When the Conways came home, they found her curled in a ball, crying and babbling. "Uh oh," said Mrs. Conway. "Fred, check on the kids."

The next thing Cosi remembered was sitting in front of her house in Mr. Conway's car.

"Y'all OK now?" he asked, peering into her eyes.

"I don't know." She felt sick to her stomach. "What happened?"

"Too many hash brownies, I reckon. You gotta be careful with those things. If you're not used to them, they can blow your mind."

Mr. Conway grinned the same grin she'd seen earlier. "Hey, if you're feeling a little better, how about having a drink with me?" He held up a bottle. "I've got this stuff called Galliano. Sweet and sassy, just like you."

Cosi thought she might throw up in the car. She remembered Alessandro and his bulging eyes, and poor little Maria Goretti trying to fight him off. "I need to go up to my house now. I think I'm going to barf."

Mr. Conway laid his hand on her arm. "Don't rush off. Here's your money, $2.50 and a fifty-cent tip. I'll make it a fiver if you have a drink with me next time," he bounced his eyebrows up and down. Cosi mumbled her thanks, stumbled to the front door, and half-crawled up the stairs to her flat.

"You don't look so good." Her mother opened the door, hands on hips. Cosi's face was white as Elmer's glue. "Must be that vegetarian food."

Dear Joey, I know you're having a tough time, but whatever you do, don't do drugs. Especially hash brownies.

Chapter Seventeen: Moon Party

It was one of those rare, sultry days in July. Every fan was humming, every window was open, and every child on the West Side of Buffalo was on their way to one of the city's public swimming pools. The hot tar in the parking lot scorched Cosi's feet as she flip-flopped her way to the "Mass Avenue" pool entrance. She was hurrying toward the locker room when she saw Jack and Gabby already in the water, dunking each other, and waved. Running from the showers to the pool, she heard a whistle blow. Little Ange, seated like a queen on a high chair overlooking the pool, was leaning forward with a whistle in her mouth, while a boy Cosi had never seen before rubbed suntan lotion onto her legs and feet.

"Walk," said her sister, teeth clenched on the whistle.

Cosi made a face, but slowed to a fast walk and jumped in the pool.

"Hey," she said, swimming up to her friends. "Are you guys gonna watch the moon landing tonight?" They shook their heads.

She had been following the TV news coverage of the Apollo 11 mission for the past several days. Walter Cronkite was giving regular updates as the astronauts circled the moon, and sometime tonight, he said, after the lunar module had landed, two of the astronauts would step out onto the moon. Cosi could hardly believe it.

"Why aren't you guys more excited? Life on earth will never be the same after this. We all might be living on the moon in 10 years!"

"I know you're excited but I have to babysit," said Gabby. "You can come over and watch it with me. I'm sure the Zanghis wouldn't mind."

"Yeah, Cosi—I'll come over too. We'll make it a party." Jack smiled at her, openly admiring her new two-piece swimsuit. His smile looked too much like

Mr. Conway's right now and she tried to ignore it. What did all these new, strange looks mean? Surely Jack was not a creep like Mr. Conway.

"I'd like to Gabby, but Mama finally agreed to let me have a Moon Party for the family. She wants me to help her with the food." Cosi looked down at the water and made small circles on the surface with her hands. "Jack, you can come over to my house and watch with us, if you like." Jack hesitated for a moment, and her stomach clenched.

"Well sure, sounds like fun." he laughed. "What will you have to eat?"

Cosi sighed. One of the things that would show up at the party was Nonna's anchovy *bizza*. Unlike the pizza neighborhood kids could get at La Nova's, Nonna made her rectangular sheet of *bizza* from the same thick dough she used to make her bread, and slathered it with homemade tomato sauce, plenty of salty anchovies, and grated cheese. No one in the family liked it, but they dare not say anything to Nonna.

"I plan to make an antipasto." Cosi ticked off the items on her fingers. "Aunt Franny's making stuffed artichokes, and Uncle Carm said he would stop by the Anchor Bar to pick up some wings. Aunt Rosa's bringing fried *gardoons* and Aunt Mari will probably bring *cannoli*." She deliberately left out the *bizza*.

Jack's eyes lit up. "Far out. I'll be there."

Cosi ran all the way home. She was out of breath when she burst through the front door. "Mama, I have a friend coming over to watch the moon landing with us tonight, is that OK?"

"Who is it?" her mother shouted over the roar of the vacuum cleaner. "Gabby?"

"Uh, well actually, it's a boy."

Big Ange shut off the Hoover. "A boy?"

"Yes, Mama, a boy."

"Why do you need to bring a boy around here? You're gonna be a nun, God willing."

"He's just a friend, and for goodness sakes I'm almost 15! Little Ange brings boyfriends up here all the time. Why can't I invite someone over just once?" Cosi held her breath as her mother mulled it over.

"So, this is someone you hang around with? Maybe he should come to the party, so I can look him over." Her mother nodded, and added, "Your uncles will wanna get a look at him too."

Big Ange returned to her vacuuming. "Bring him. Why not? There's plenty of room for everyone." She looked pointedly at the couch and one chair that faced the small TV. "But he needs to be out by 10."

The party was set to begin at five, but Cosi turned the TV on early in the afternoon while she and her mother were making the *caponata* for the antipasto tray. She ran between the kitchen and the living room every few minutes to see if there were any new developments. Eventually, she dried her hands on the damp dishtowel, threw it over her shoulder, and sat down on the couch to watch as the *Eagle* maneuvered in for a landing.

Alarms began to sound aboard the lunar module. Walter Cronkite spoke in a hushed voice while Mission Control in Houston tried to figure out the problem. Cosi sat on the edge of the couch, holding her breath as she thought about what it would be like to crash into the moon. *Dear Lord, are the astronauts going to die? If not, how will they rescue them? How long can they last up there if they're injured or their spaceship's busted? Will they run out of food and starve to death?*

She had not considered all the dangers of space travel. Listening to the tense exchange, she found new respect for the three astronauts. She couldn't imagine she would ever be that brave. When she heard Neil Armstrong announce, "Houston, Tranquility Base here. The Eagle has landed," she cheered.

"Mama, they landed! They're on the moon!"

"*Merda,*" said Big Ange. "You believe everything you see on the boob tube? It's probably something they shot in Hollywood."

Uncle Carm and Aunt Franny were the first to arrive at the party, trailed by Nonna who came slowly up the stairs leaning on her cane, a long ash hanging precipitously from her cigarette. Uncle Carm juggled the chicken wings and Nonna's *bizza*.

Aunt Franny nervously set down the pan of warm artichokes. "I'm not sure I should even be here. A lotta people at church think it's blasphemous, men goin' up into heaven. Heaven is where God the Father, the Son and the Holy Ghost live. The saints too. It's not right, people going up there before they're dead."

"Franny, I told you, relax!" shouted Uncle Carm. "Father Mario thinks it's OK. He told me they set up a special TV for the Pope hisself to watch. Are we gonna question the Pope?"

Aunt Rosa arrived next with Uncle Benny. She stopped in the doorway to catch her breath and rubbed her swollen stomach. "I been feeling a little tired Ange," said Rosa, "but I made the *gardoons* anyways." She set the bowl of limp fried greens on the table, hugged Cosi, and gave Nino a small toy rocket to mark the occasion.

Big Ange eyed the *gardoons.* "They're cold," she muttered under her breath.

Aunt Mari arrived, for the first time in her married life, without Uncle Tony. Embarrassed, she set down the *cannoli,* hugged Big Ange, and whispered, "He wouldn't come. He's off somewhere with that *puttana.* He says my family is dead to him."

"That *testa di cazzo,*" Big Ange sneered. "Screw him. He's dead to us too. He'd better not show his ugly *faccia di bow-wow* around here."

Little Ange wandered in, darkly tanned and smelling of chlorine. "Mama, do we really have to watch this stupid thing all night?" She picked an olive off the antipasto tray. "They might have a good band on The Ed Sullivan Show."

"It's not even on tonight," said Cosi, offering glasses of red wine to the adults. "All the regular shows have been interrupted for this." She put her hands on her hips. "This is history, Angie." Little Ange gave her a look of disgust and went off to her room.

The doorbell rang. Everyone looked around the living room, counting heads, trying to figure out who was missing. Cosi took a deep breath and went to the door. Jack stepped in shyly, holding a newspaper cone full of roses he had snipped from the bush in front of his house.

"Good evening, Mrs. McCarthy." He smiled, handing her the flowers.

"So, who's this?" demanded Big Ange, dropping the roses on the table without looking at them. All eyes in the room were on Jack.

Cosi sensed her face turning scarlet. "This is my friend Jack. Remember, Mama?"

Uncle Carm and Uncle Benny came over and circled Jack like hyenas, looking him up and down. Then Uncle Carm slapped Jack hard between his broad shoulders.

"Hey Jack, how's your back?" He and Uncle Benny guffawed. Jack smiled broadly, as if this was his favorite joke.

"What's your last name, Jack? Jack is not a Sicilian name."

"I'm Sicilian. My last name is Tomaselli. My Christian name is Giacomo. Giacomo Tomaselli."

"Tomaselli? Where are your people from?"

"Catania."

There was a collective gasp around the living room. Uncle Carm scowled. "Catania? And you call yourself *Siciliano*? Real Sicilians are from Palermo!"

There was a heavy silence. Then Jack said, "Well, at least we're not from Napoli."

Uncle Carm slammed his fist down on the table. "You're right!" he shouted, then punched Jack in the shoulder. "At least you're not from that *bagnarole*! This guy is OK." Everyone laughed, including Jack.

Uncle Benny stuck his finger in Jack's face. "Just you remember, our Cosi's gonna be a nun. She's pure as the virgin snow. You ruin her and we'll stuff your mouth with your own meatballs. *Capisce*?"

"Don't mind them." Aunt Rosa put her arm around Jack. "They give everyone a hard time. Come on over and get some food." Jack helped himself to the buffet and, unfazed by the uncles' threats and needling, seemed to be enjoying himself immensely.

Several hours passed while everyone waited for the astronauts to emerge from the lunar vehicle. Cosi saw her mother look up at the clock. It was 9:50. The only food left on the table was half of Nonna's *bizza* sitting next to a pile of chicken bones.

"Almost time to call it a night." Big Ange looked at Jack.

Jack got up and helped himself to a cold slice. "Mmm. I can't stop eating this anchovy pizza," he told Big Ange. Balancing his plate with one hand, he sat down on the floor, scooted next to Cosi, and pretended to be interested in the TV.

Cosi was lost in thought. *When we start travelling all over the galaxy and living on other planets, we'll be too far away from each other to have family dinners and parties like this one.* She looked around the room, her early excitement now tempered by sadness. She could not bear the thought of ever leaving the home and family she loved. It occurred to her then that this was exactly what her Irish and Sicilian ancestors had done. Got on a ship to come to America, never to see home and family again. For them, the United States might as well have been the moon.

Aunt Franny was on Uncle Carm's lap in the overstuffed chair and both were snoring. Nonna had wandered off long ago to sleep on Big Ange's bed. Aunt Mari, Aunt Rosa and Uncle Benny were still in the living room sitting on the couch, but Aunt Rosa looked tired, ready to call it a night.

"Is that a foot coming out?" said Uncle Benny, sitting up.

"I can't tell," said Aunt Mari, leaning forward from her spot wedged in between Benny and Rosa.

"Come on Benny," said Aunt Rosa. "We gotta go. My back is killing me."

"You can't leave now!" said Cosi. "They're about to walk on the moon! It's historic."

"Yeah, yeah," said Uncle Benny grunting, as he pulled Aunt Rosa to her feet. "We'll watch it on the news tomorrow."

"Mama, please, can't Jack stay until they step on the moon? The party can't be over yet."

Big Ange looked at the clock. "Jack can stay until 11:00, but not a minute later."

Just before her mother's deadline, Neil Armstrong climbed down the ladder and stepped onto the surface of the moon. Cosi watched transfixed, stunned by the import of this moment. Jack took the opportunity to hug her tightly, brushing her breasts in the process. Cosi blushed, but pretended not to notice.

"That's it. Party's over." Big Ange glared at Jack.

"Mama, we have to watch them actually walk around on the moon. This has never happened in the history of mankind!"

Aunt Franny woke with a snort and shook Uncle Carm. "Get up, Carm. I'm gonna wake Nonna. We gotta go. They're already on the moon."

"What? You let me sleep through it?" Uncle Carm shook his head crossly. "That's just like you, letting me miss something important!"

Aunt Franny stumbled sleepily down the hall to find Nonna while Aunt Mari packed up her things to go. They all said their goodbyes, leaving only Jack and Cosi watching the TV. Cosi could see her mother lean her head toward the living room every few minutes as she washed the dishes. Each time Jack started to snuggle too close, she would walk in and stand next to them. "So, finish your walk already," she would say to the TV.

At midnight, Big Ange decided she had enough. "Time to go Jack. You'll have to watch it on the news tomorrow."

Cosi sighed, walked Jack out the door and down the front steps. Out of earshot, she hoped, of her mother. "Thanks for coming," she said softly.

"It was…different." Jack chuckled. He leaned over and kissed her softly on the lips.

"I saw that," came a voice from upstairs.

Cosi got into bed that night, her whole body taut and restless. She took a deep breath and said her prayers, thanking God for letting the astronauts land safely on the moon. Closing her eyes, she tried to focus on what life on the moon might be like, not because she intended to live there one day, but to push the lingering effects of Jack's kiss from her mind.

Dear Joey, what a day! I hope you watched. You're the one person I know brave enough to fly to the moon, but don't go. OK?

CHAPTER EIGHTEEN: BROKEN DREAMS AND REGRETTABLE CURSES

AT FIRST, COSI THOUGHT it was the alarm clock. It was still dark and when the ringing persisted, she realized it was the phone. She sat bolt upright in bed, listening as her mother's bedroom door opened and her footfalls moved toward the kitchen. Little Ange rolled over and Cosi could see in the dim light from the streetlamp that her sister was awake and listening too. A heavy silence hung in their room while their mother spoke to someone in a muffled voice. A moment later, Big Ange was at their door.

"Rosa's having her baby but something's wrong. Benny said we need to come quick. Angie, you stay here with Nino. Cosi, you come with me."

Cosi shivered as she climbed into the old car, her bare legs touching the cold vinyl seat. She looked at her mother out of the corner of her eye and saw the grim set of her jaw. The car screeched to a halt at each stop sign then lurched forward, often knocking the magnetized statue of Saint Christopher, patron saint of travelers, off the dashboard.

In the hospital waiting room, Aunt Mari and Aunt Franny rushed toward them. They all hugged while Cosi's stomach did somersaults. They walked together to where Uncle Benny was sitting and weeping into his hands. He looked up, his face red and swollen.

"I never shoulda punched her those other times," he blubbered, "but I swear to God, I didn't punch her this time. I never touched her. I knew this one was mine."

"Shut up, Benny," said Big Ange. "Pull yourself together, then tell us what's happening."

"Rosa and the baby...the doctor said they're in trouble. They could both die, Ange!"

"Die? How could she die? It's 1969 for God's sake! You'd think they know how to deliver a baby by now."

"The doctor said she's bleeding from the inside and they can't stop it. She lost a lotta blood. He called it a…a… I can't remember what it's called, but he said it's very dangerous."

"Where is this *stunad,* this doctor? He doesn't know what he's talking about," snapped Big Ange. "I had three babies. A little blood is normal. Nothing to worry about."

The doctor appeared without warning and walked up to Benny, ignoring the women. "Mr. Tedesco? It's over. We delivered the baby and he's still alive, but I'm afraid he won't be with us for long. Your wife is holding him. We've given her a transfusion and she's hanging in there, so far. We're not out of the woods yet. You might want to see her."

Big Ange stepped in front of the doctor. "You mean to tell me you couldn't deliver one little baby without screwing it up? What the hell kind of doctor are you, you *minchione!*"

"Mrs. Tedesco had a uterine rupture," said the doctor, looking Big Ange squarely in the eye. "It's a condition called vasa previa. She is lucky she's alive. She's lost a lot of blood."

"We're her family," Big Ange folded her arms, "and we demand to see her. I don't trust you stinking doctors, and if you did anything wrong you better believe there will be hell to pay."

The doctor sighed and looked at the ceiling. "Fine. She's in room 330. But don't stay in there long. She needs rest."

Big Ange marched down the hall with the rest of the family hurrying behind her. When they burst through the door, Rosa looked up with uncomprehending eyes from the small bundle in her arms. She looked back down again.

"There, little Benny, Mama's here, Mama loves you," she crooned, rocking the baby back and forth in her arms. "Nothing's gonna hurt you now. No, no one's gonna take you, you're gonna stay right here with me, sweet little Benny, right here with Mama."

Silently, her family surrounded the bed and looked down at the tiny infant. Benny stroked the baby's cheek gently with his finger then backed away.

"He...he's gone Rosa, he's gone." Benny dropped to his knees by the side of her bed and began to sob. "Somebody call the doctor."

"No!" said Rosa, pulling the baby to her breast. "No, he's not! He's sleeping, that's all. He's just sleeping. He's gonna be fine."

Franny and Mari sat on the side of the bed in tears. Big Ange looked at the motionless baby, her face frozen. Cosi could feel a lump forming in her throat.

"Rosa..." Big Ange reached for her sister's shoulder.

"No!" screamed Rosa. "Don't touch me, and don't touch Little Benny! You're nothing but bad luck!"

As if waking from a dream, Cosi remembered her mother's curse and felt a bitter taste in her mouth. Was this her mother's doing? Was the death of this innocent baby the result of the *malocchio*? She had never believed in those old Sicilian superstitions, but God forbid, maybe it was real. Maybe Aunt Rosa would be the next victim.

Cosi grabbed her mother's arm. "Mama, I need to talk to you." She could feel the bile rising in her throat. She mustered all of her courage and pulled her mother toward the ladies' room, locking the door. "Mama, I know what you did. I know you cursed Aunt Rosa. You gave her the evil eye and I know why...."

"You know?" Her mother slammed the flats of her hands onto the Ladies Room sink. "Don't say another word. We don't speak of such things."

Cosi looked at her mother, tears rimming her eyes. "Why not, Mama? Why can't we talk about such things, especially when Aunt Rosa might die?"

"Because." Her mother's eyes were cold and unfocused. "When secrets see the light of day, families are destroyed. Let the truth stay buried."

"But a baby is dead, Mama, a baby is dead! All because you're jealous of Aunt Rosa!"

Big Ange turned and slapped Cosi hard in the face. Cosi fell to the floor, sobbing. Big Ange stared at her daughter, then turned and steadied herself, gripping the edges of the sink. She set her jaw and studied the bowl, taking deep breaths. She stood for what seemed an eternity with her lips moving, the silence heavy with her anger, and perhaps, remorse. "Enough!" she shouted finally and stood straight up. She took one last deep breath and exhaled. "I will remove the curse. We will come back tomorrow with the implements."

Huddling together in a small group at Forest Lawn Cemetery, the Di Giacomo family buried Little Benny in a tiny grave. Uncle Benny, inconsolable, leaned on Aunt Mari's arm during the entire service. Aunt Franny fingered her rosary beads and Big Ange stood, arms folded and head down, between Little Ange and Cosi. No one mentioned what was on all their minds.

Cousin Vito had told them Aunt Rosa cut her wrists while in the hospital. She had snatched a pair of scissors from the nurses' tray but botched the job. Having already lost so much blood during the delivery, she would have died if her obstetrician had not discovered her shortly after. They transferred her to the psychiatric hospital, Vito said, and placed her on suicide watch.

Walking back from the gravesite, Cosi whispered to her mother, "Mama, you have to remove the *malocchio* now, before Aunt Rosa kills herself."

"What do you want me to do? She's in the nuthouse." Big Ange made the sign of the cross to ward off the demons and kept walking. "I'm not going *there*."

"Listen, I have a plan. Nonna has a *corno*—they say the golden horn wards off evil spirits, so that's a start. I'll go in first with the *corno*, then when you're ready, we'll go together and perform the other ritual." Cosi frowned. "The one you won't tell me about."

Big Ange ignored this last remark. All Sicilian families had their own secret method of removing the curse. "Nonna will never give you the *corno*, she said, changing the subject. "She thinks it protects her."

"I'll get Aunt Franny to help me."

Cosi caught Aunt Franny before the group reached the cemetery gate and slipped her arm inside her aunt's elbow. "I want to come over tomorrow to talk to Nonna. I want to borrow her *corno*."

"Why?" asked Aunt Franny. Cosi saw her mother's warning look.

"Um, because we think someone may have cursed Aunt Rosa. With the *malocchio.*"

"What? Who would do such a thing to Rosa?" Her aunt considered the possibilities. "OK. But let me talk to Nonna first. Come over tomorrow afternoon while she's watching her shows."

The next day, Cosi found them in front of the television absorbed in Nonna's favorite soap opera, *The Edge of Night.* Cosi knew better than to disturb her grandmother, who followed the action despite not understanding a word that was said. When a commercial came on, Aunt Franny leaned toward Nonna and began speaking softly in Sicilian. Cosi heard the word *corno.*

Nonna looked irritated. *"Eh? Ma che quest'?*

Cosi noticed that Aunt Franny already had the pendant in her hand. She must have taken it while Nonna was sleeping. Aunt Franny talked soothingly to her mother while she held the necklace out to Cosi. Nonna grabbed her arm.

"Mama, Mama è per Rosa," said Aunt Franny. Nonna slapped at her daughter's arms and chest and cursed at her bitterly. Eventually, Nonna gave in and threw her hands up at the two of them. *"A fanabla!"*

"What is she saying, Aunt Franny?"

"Never mind, *cara.* Take the necklace and don't lose it, or I'll never hear the end of it."

Cosi talked Big Ange into driving her to the psychiatric hospital that weekend but could not persuade her to leave the car. Her mother was perspiring and avoiding her eyes.

"You go in. See what it's like first. Give her the necklace and come right back. *Be* careful. The place is fulla whackos."

"OK, Mama," said Cosi, her mother's anxiety compounding her own fears. She had heard the horror stories about the hospital since she was a child—how it was filled with murderers, rapists, and fiends. The hospital's 19th century administration building, which looked like the forbidding Thornfield Hall on the cover of the book she was reading in English class, *Jane Eyre*, did nothing to assuage her fears. On each floor of the three-story structure, Cosi could see the outdoor balconies where patients sat or paced behind heavy steel mesh stretching to the ceiling. Inside, someone was screaming.

Cosi squeezed her mother's hand, took a deep breath, and got out of the car. From where she stood, she could see a small basketball court off to her right where men were shooting baskets. They stopped playing and watched Cosi walk toward the hospital entrance. One of the men walked up to the fence and curled his fingers through the chain link. He stared at her, unsmiling.

She walked through the front door, her footsteps echoing in the massive foyer, her heart rattling around her chest. A woman seated in an office behind a glass door had her sign in, gave her a visitors' badge, and pointed to an arrow with the words "Women's Ward." Barely breathing, she made her way down a long, dim hall.

In the Visitors' Lounge, a small woman sidled up to her. "Are you here to visit me?" she asked, grabbing Cosi's hand. The woman had a speech impediment and walked with a limp.

"Uh, no, I'm here to visit my Aunt Rosa." Cosi smiled tentatively at the woman.

The woman dropped her hand and walked away. A moment later, she was back. "My name is Harriet. Will you come visit me?"

Cosi felt sorry for the woman and was tempted to sit and talk, but she remembered her mother, fretting in the car. She searched until she found Aunt Rosa sitting on a sofa in the corner, her bandaged wrists crossed in her lap, her chin on her chest.

"Aunt Rosa?" whispered Cosi, not wanting to wake her if she was asleep. Rosa slowly turned her head toward Cosi.

"Hi Aunt Rosa, how are you?" She wondered what to say to a suicidal person. "Are you feeling any better?"

Large, fat tears rolled down Rosa's cheeks.

"Aunt Rosa, I'm sorry. I didn't mean to upset you. We think we know what's wrong. You've been cursed with the evil eye. Will you let us help you?"

Rosa seemed far away, unreachable. Cosi opened her hand and showed her the necklace.

"See what I've brought? It's Nonna's *corno*. It will protect you from witches and demons. Mama will bring the secret implements next time and remove the curse." Cosi knew her aunt was superstitious like her mother, and hoped she was buying all of this. She unclasped the necklace and reached behind her aunt's neck. She fastened it and let the twisted horn drape over Aunt Rosa's hospital gown. "There. See, nothing can hurt you now."

In slow motion, Rosa reached up and rolled the horn between her fingers. They sat in awkward silence while Cosi looked around the room. She saw only one other visitor, though there were several patients milling about and hoping, Cosi supposed, that someone would come. They did not look like murderers or fiends. They looked lost, and lonely.

Cosi said her goodbyes and walked quickly down the hallway toward the hospital entrance. She noticed a man standing in a long corridor on the opposite side of the entrance hall, leaning against a wall and looking in her direction. He was in the shadows, but she was sure it was the same man she had seen on the basketball court—the one who was clearly staring at her as he curled his fingers through the fence. Cosi shuddered and ran out to the car.

"Well?" said Big Ange, as Cosi climbed into the passenger's seat.

Cosi took a deep breath. "Aunt Rosa perked up a little when I gave her the *corno*. We should come back tomorrow. She's not looking too good."

When the McCarthys returned the next day, Rosa was sitting on the same sofa. Harriet limped toward them as soon as they entered. "Are you here to visit me?" she asked, grabbing Big Ange's hand.

Big Ange jerked her hand away. "Get away from me."

Cosi gave Harriet a weak smile and pulled her mother toward Aunt Rosa. Big Ange, looking nervously around the room, opened a large black bag and removed a bottle of olive oil, a flask of holy water, and a ceramic bowl. She set the bowl carefully on her lap and poured the water into it. She uncorked the olive oil and handed it to Cosi.

"Hold that carefully. The last thing we need is for you to spill the oil. That will bring *you* bad luck." Cosi held the bottle tightly while her mother stuck her baby finger into it.

"Are you ready?" Big Ange looked at Rosa, who sat mute.

Cosi watched as her mother let three drops of oil fall from her finger onto the water, muttering something under her breath. The drops moved to form one large blob of oil in the middle of the water and all three gasped.

"You see," said Big Ange, feigning surprise. "It's in the shape of an eye. You've been cursed, Rosa." Big Ange made the sign of the cross, stuck her finger into the holy water, and made the sign of the cross on each of Rosa's palms.

"Now we have to say one "Our Father," one "Hail Mary," and one "Glory Be." Big Ange held Rosa's hand with her left and Cosi's hand with her right and began to intone the prayers.

"Our Father, who art in heaven…" she murmured, eyes closed, head bent down. Cosi saw her mother open her left eye slightly to see if Rosa was praying. Rosa began to move her lips.

"…hallowed be thy name," Rosa whispered. Cosi gently squeezed her aunt's hand.

When they finished, Big Ange handed Cosi the bowl. "Go dump this in the toilet. It isn't holy water anymore—it has the evil eye in it. Make sure you flush twice."

Cosi did as she was told, and returning from the ladies' room, found her mother holding Rosa's hands. Cosi wanted to weep with joy. Maybe the feud between her mother and Aunt Rosa was finally over for good.

"The curse is gone, so get a grip, Rosa. You need to get the hell outta this loony bin," her mother was saying. "Besides, we're missing a fourth at our pinochle table."

When they arrived home, Big Ange set her black bag on the kitchen table and pulled out the empty holy water flask and olive oil. Distracted, she set the bottle of oil on the edge of a platter, and it tipped over, slowly rolling to the edge of the table and onto the floor with a crash. Cosi gasped, and as quickly as she could, dropped to her knees and began mopping the oil with a dishtowel. She looked up and saw her mother staring at the floor.

Big Ange's face was ashen. "It's too late. The bad luck will come. God is telling me I will pay for what I did to Rosa."

Dear Joey, why do adults believe in such nonsense? I wish I could cure you with a bottle of olive oil and a bowl of holy water!

Chapter Nineteen: A Guy's Got Needs

As the summer wound down and the school year approached, Cosi prayed for a way to get out of babysitting again for the Conways. She'd been asked several times and made excuses, but she could not do that forever. Her mother would ask why she was passing up a paying job, especially with new textbooks to buy in a few weeks, and Cosi was too embarrassed to tell her mother about the repulsive Mr. Conway. Finally, she had an idea.

"Hello Mrs. Conway," Cosi answered pleasantly, when the phone rang one Saturday morning. "Nice to hear from you. Sure, I can babysit tonight. Until 11? No problem. My friend Jack will stop by when you get back to walk me home. My mother thinks it's important for me to get more exercise. No, tell Mr. Conway I'll be fine. I won't need a ride. Thanks, Mrs. Conway, see you then."

This time, when she walked into the Conway house, she was prepared. "Hi boys, I've brought a game over for you to play. *Chutes and Ladders.* You like to play games, right?"

Paul looked suspicious but Ringo jumped up and down. "I wanna play, I wanna play!"

"We'll play as soon as your parents leave. I know you'll be really good at this, Paulie. You'll probably win every time. "

Mrs. Conway looked gratefully at Cosi and shouted to her husband, "Come on Fred, we're already late!"

Mr. Conway ambled by and smirked at Cosi. "You sure you won't need a ride home?"

"No, my friend Jack will come to get me. And no brownies tonight," she said.

"Suit yourself." He winked at her and followed his wife out the door.

Cosi easily manipulated the rules of the game, so Paul always won. "Hah! You numb nuts will never beat me," he boasted after winning the game for the fifth time. "Let's play again."

The evening passed quickly, and the kids were in their beds with the lights out at 9:00. Cosi was proud of herself. She sat on the sofa, opened her purse, and pulled out a box of Cracker Jack and a stack of 45s to put on the Hi Fi. She was struggling to wedge the small plastic adaptor into a new Three Dog Night record when she heard a knock at the door. Surprised, she looked out the front window.

"Jack?" she said, opening the front door. "What are you doing here? You're an hour and a half early." He kissed her on the cheek and handed her an album.

"I thought I'd come sooner so we could listen to the new Creedence Clearwater Revival album. It's got that song, "Bad Moon Rising" on it. It is *so* boss. I also brought a couple of Ted's Hot Dogs and some onion rings. I remembered what you said about the food here."

"But... I told the Conways you wouldn't be here until 11:00."

"Relax. They're cool and the kids are in bed, right? Besides," he said, setting down the food and album and putting his arms around her, nuzzling her neck. "Won't it be nice to have a little time to ourselves, without your mother watching my every move?"

"Well, OK, but no funny stuff." She ran her tongue over teeth and breathed into her hand to check her breath when Jack turned to put his album on the turntable. Thank goodness, her breath smelled sweet, like candied popcorn, and there were no kernels in her teeth. Jack sat on the couch and patted the cushion next to him. Cosi sat, and together they devoured the food and listened to the music.

After polishing off the last onion ring, Cosi sat back contentedly. She had started to wonder what it would be like to marry someone like Jack. He was such a nice guy and, unlike Joey, closer to her age. Surely after a few years of proving that she would make a lousy nun, the Virgin Mary would let her off the hook.

Jack put his arm around Cosi's shoulders. "Bitchin' song, right?" he said, rubbing a finger gently behind her ear and then down her neck. Cosi felt a trail of goosebumps where his finger had been. He leaned over and turned her chin toward him. He kissed her on the mouth while running his hand slowly from her neck down toward her breast. All she could think of at first was the sweet taste of ketchup on his lips. Then she pushed him away.

"What are you doing? You know I'm not like that!"

"Hey…calm down. I got carried away for a minute. Let's just kiss—OK? What could be the harm in that?" He put his hands up in the air and smiled. "I won't even touch you." He leaned over to kiss her again, and she let him.

She closed her eyes and enjoyed the sensations. She could feel the soft drift of hair above his lip. Occasionally she would feel his tongue flick against her teeth, and she wondered if this was sinful. She could hear Gabby's voice whispering in her ear: *Just because you're gonna be a nun someday, doesn't mean you have to live like one now.*

Jack had one hand on the back of the couch and another on the armrest. Slowly but steadily, he pressed against her as they kissed, until she was nearly prone. He moaned and kissed her neck as he took his hands off the couch and let the full weight of his body fall on hers. She opened her eyes, startled, while Jack, breathing heavily, kissed her neck and shoulders, moving his hands beneath her sweater. She felt something hard press against her thigh and began to panic. Didn't she read somewhere it was possible to get pregnant through your clothes?

She pushed herself up on her elbows, looked over Jack's shoulder and said loudly, "Good grief! Look at the clock!"

Jack turned to look, giving Cosi the opportunity to push against his shoulders and squirm out from under him onto the floor. She clambered to her feet and stepped away from the couch, trying to catch her breath.

"Aw, we still got plenty of time" said Jack, his face flushed.

"Yes, but I've got to go to the…." She ran to the bathroom and locked the door.

What must have been 10 minutes later, she heard a knock. "Cosi? Are you OK in there?"

"I'm not feeling well. Those hot dogs...my stomach...you know."

"Are you coming out? I need to get in there. "

"Well, OK, but what's the hurry?"

"A guy's got needs. That's what! Now let me in!"

Confused, Cosi flushed the empty toilet and washed her hands. When she opened the door, Jack rushed past her, pushed her out the door, and locked it. She stood there bewildered before remembering something she read in her sister's yellow book. Something about how if a man has an erection, all that's on his mind is how to deal with it.

Good Lord. Is Jack in there...?

Cosi heard a car door slam. She ran to the front window and watched the Conways get out of their car. She raced back to the bathroom and pounded frantically on the door.

"Jack, they're home early! Get out!"

"I can't right now...."

She thought she could hear voices outside. In a minute, they would be at the door. "Now, Jack! Get out *now*!"

The door flew open, and Jack looked around, zipping his fly. "What should I do?"

"Go out the back door and come around the front. Pretend you just got here." Jack tucked in his shirt and ran. Cosi locked the back door and hurried to the living room to greet the Conways.

"Hi," she panted, her hair disheveled. "Have a good time this evening?"

"Better than you," said Mr. Conway. "Looks like my boys gave you a rough time."

Cosi laughed nervously. "Oh, you know, boys will be boys."

"Yes, indeed I know that." Mr. Conway bit his lower lip and stroked his chin. A knock at the front door spared Cosi a longer interrogation. "That must be Jack," she said.

"Hi." Jack stepped in and avoided looking at the adults. "Ready to go, Cosi?"

"Yes! Let me get my purse and I'll be right with you." She walked into the small kitchen to get her denim shoulder bag and realized Mr. Conway was right behind her.

"Forgetting something?"

He stood blocking the doorway. She held her breath, prepared to hit him with her fists and cry out for Jack if he came near her. He reached into his pants and pulled out his wallet. "Here's your pay. I'm afraid there won't be a tip tonight."

Cosi exhaled and took the money. "Thanks." She tried to push past him.

"One more thing," he said, blocking her exit. "There's a red mark on your neck that wasn't there when you arrived. I sure hope Paulie didn't do that." He smirked and let her pass.

Jack and Cosi walked the several blocks to Cosi's house without saying a word. At the bottom of Cosi's steps, Jack gave her a peck on the cheek.

"Jack," she said, not looking at him. "Let's not do that again."

"Don't worry," Jack called over his shoulder as he walked away. "We won't."

CHAPTER TWENTY: AN AQUARIAN EXPOSITION

Late one sweltering August evening, when Cosi went out to sit on her upper porch, she was startled to look down and see Joey slumped on his front steps, smoking a cigarette. Gone were the short, neat haircut and military bearing. His now unruly hair was matted in the back, and she could see, even from this angle, that a thick, black beard framed his handsome face.

She leaned over the railing and called down to him, but he looked straight ahead, inhaling deeply, before flicking his cigarette toward the statue of Saint Francis sitting in the middle of his mother's irises. He stood up without a word and walked back into the house.

Something inside her died a little, but she shrugged it off. There was a time when she would have been devastated by Joey's coldness, but she had a boyfriend now. All the windows of her apartment were open, and she was listening intently as she had been doing nearly every evening, hoping the phone would ring and it would be Jack. She had not heard from him since that awkward night at the Conways.

She was watching the sky gather into the delicate pinks and robin's egg blues she once thought of as the colors of her future baby nursery, when she heard the first ring. She ripped open the screen door and ran into the kitchen. Her mother was holding the receiver.

"Guess who," Big Ange said, frowning.

Cosi's heart thudded. Her mother turned on the faucet to finish washing the dishes and Cosi whispered into the phone, "Are you mad at me?"

"Naw, forget it. It was no big deal." Jack sounded like his usual self. Maybe things were still OK between them. "Gabby and some other friends are talking about going to a music festival in White Lake next weekend. Did you see the poster at the record store?"

Cosi hadn't.

"They're calling it an 'Aquarian Exposition,' whatever that means. There's supposed to be an art show and crafts bazaar and food and everything...not only is CCR going to be there, the Grateful Dead and Hendrix are supposed to play. It should be far out. Think you can go?"

"Let me ask." Cosi knew what a big deal this music festival would be to Jack and her friends, and Jack's silence the past few weeks made her realize how much she cared for him. But she also knew her mother. She broached the idea with her carefully at first, then pleadingly, then petulantly.

"Please Mama," she begged again, a few days before her friends were leaving. "I'll do anything you want if you let me go. I'll babysit for Nino day and night, I'll clean the house, scrub the toilet, wash all the windows, I'll ..."

"*Basta!*" said her mother. "White Lake is at the other end of the state of New York and I don't like the sound of it. Where're you gonna sleep for two nights?"

"Gabby's cousin Marco has a van. We're going to bring sleeping bags and camp out under the stars. If it rains, we will sleep in the vehicle. Please Mama, they're supposed to have a big crafts bazaar. I can bring some of the Infant of Prague garments to sell."

"And where's Jack gonna sleep?" asked her mother, hands on hips.

Cosi was silent. She worried about that herself.

"Just what I thought," said her mother. "Out of the question. Kids traveling 300 miles to God knows where without parents? Sleeping near each other, temptation around every corner? You want to ruin your chances of becoming a nun for good?"

"Mama, please! I'm not like that...and Jack's not like that."

"Oh, really? I've seen him in action. Besides, with the bad luck we got coming, who knows what could happen. Best to avoid trouble." She turned away, ignoring her daughter's final protests. "You're not going and that's final. You'll thank me someday."

Cosi wiped away bitter tears while she walked to Gabby's house on the morning the group was leaving. Jack knew how hard she had tried to convince her unreasonable mother, and they all hoped Big Ange would relent. Now, on her way to deliver the bad news, she was more than a little worried. What if Jack met someone at the festival?

She spotted Marco's neon yellow Volkswagen van, its engine running. Cosi peered through the windows and saw piled up sleeping bags, Mexican blankets, and plastic milk crates full of food. Love beads hanging from the rear-view mirror jangled as Sly and the Family Stone belted out "Dance to the Music" on the radio.

She turned and saw Gabby, Jack, and several other kids coming out of Gabby's front door, talking excitedly. Gabby looked tanned and gorgeous in a midriff blouse and peasant skirt, her long black hair hanging down her back, a braided leather headband across her forehead. She was hanging on Jack's arm, laughing. A sudden image of Jack and Gabby sleeping next to each other on the floor of the van stopped Cosi in her tracks.

"Hey Cosi!" called Jack. He walked over and reached out to hug her but stopped when he saw the expression on her face. After an awkward silence, he said, "I wish you were coming."

"Yeah," said Gabby, smiling. "Want me to talk to your mother one last time?"

"Forget it," muttered Cosi. "If you really wanted me to come, you would've tried harder." She spun on her heels and headed toward home.

"What's got into her?" she heard Gabby say.

All weekend long, Cosi moped around her bedroom, unable to read, listen to music, or speak to her mother. It did not help that on all the radio stations the DJs talked about the big "happening" at what they were now calling "Woodstock." Whenever she thought of Jack and Gabby together, a white-hot ball of anger formed in her stomach and pushed up her throat.

"What's your problem?" Little Ange sneered. "You pissed because Mama wouldn't let you go to that stupid Woodstock thing? She wouldn't let me go either and I'm older than you."

Cosi pushed her face under her pillow and covered her ears. After hearing nothing for a while, she peeked out to see if her sister had left, only to find her standing at the mirror, curling her eyelashes with a metal contraption that squeezed them into a row of thick black exclamation points. She looked enviously at her sister; certain she would give her boyfriends what *they* needed without a second thought.

"What's it like, Angie?"

"What's what like?"

"You know…sex."

Her sister snorted. "Why are you asking? I didn't think the saintly Sister Cositina had any interest in that."

"I'm just wondering, since I'm never gonna know what it's like."

Little Ange sat down on the edge of her bed. "Well, I'm going to let you in on a little secret. I know how Mama worries, but I've never had sex. I'm saving myself for marriage. Yeah, sure, I've done some heavy petting. But that's it."

Cosi sat up. "You've never *done it?*"

Her sister laughed. "Just because every guy in town wants to have sex with me, doesn't mean I'm gonna let 'em. I'm waiting for the *right* guy, and I'm not gonna ruin my chances by getting knocked up. I'll be 17 next year and I got big plans to leave this effing dump."

Cosi searched Little Ange's face. "You're kidding, right? Who are you going to marry? That guy I saw you with at the pool?"

"Naw, stupid. I can't marry some low-class *guido* from around here. I gotta get out of Buffalo. I wanna marry a guy who lives in a big city, has a real job, and wears a white shirt to work. A guy who makes plenty of money and buys me the kinda clothes that suit my style."

"You mean you'd leave Buffalo, leave the West Side?" Cosi was incredulous. "Are you crazy? Our whole life is here, Angie. Our family, friends, church—everything. We're West Siders. That's what we are and always will be. I won't leave, even when I become a nun."

"Suit yourself. You'll find out soon enough, only losers stay here." Little

Ange put the finishing touches on her make-up and headed out the door with a little wave, leaving her sister with her mouth agape.

Marco was supposed to drive the group back on Sunday when the music festival was over. On Monday morning, when she called to talk with Gabby, Mrs. Mortadella answered the phone.

"I don't know where they are," Gabby's mother said in a worried voice. I haven't heard from them. I called the New York State troopers, and they said the traffic on the Thruway is still backed up because so many people went to that festival. They promised to let me know if there have been any serious accidents."

Cosi hung up the phone, her stomach turning. *What if they've been in a car wreck? What if they're dead?* She ran to her bedroom and knelt before the statue of the Virgin. "Mother of God, I'm so sorry for all my evil thoughts. Please don't let them die," she prayed.

Around nine Monday evening, there was a knock at the door and Cosi opened it to find Jack and Gabby, eyes sparkling with excitement, wearing identical strands of love beads. Marco had just dropped them off and they were barefoot, disheveled, and covered in mud. Her relief at knowing they were alive was quickly replaced by a mounting fury.

"Oh my God oh my God," said Gabby. "You won't believe it when we tell you..."

"There were like, millions of people," said Jack interrupting her, "at least half a million anyways."

"The Thruway was so packed we were on it for hours..."

"And on Saturday it rained and rained..."

"So here was this woman having a baby in the middle of the concert..."

"...everyone was stoned, rolling around in the mud..."

"...they decided to keep playing right through to Monday morning even though it was supposed to end Sunday..."

"... and Hendrix's version of the Star-Spangled Banner was so..."

"... all these naked people..."

"... lines were so long everybody just gave up and peed everywhere..."

Cosi stood up, arms folded across her chest in a perfect imitation of her mother. "Enough. Time for you two to go. There's something I gotta do. So, goodbye."

Jack and Gabby looked at each other.

"Did we say something wrong?" asked Jack.

"No, it's just…I'm not interested, that's all. Can you please go?"

They turned, confused, and started down the stairs. "I can't take this anymore," Jack said to Gabby, shaking his head. Gabby whispered to him to go on, and once Jack was out of sight, went back up the stairs and grabbed Cosi by the shoulders.

"What the hell is wrong with you? You've been acting weird since Friday. Are you mad at us because your mother wouldn't let you go? How is that *our* fault?"

"I'm not mad!" shouted Cosi, tears running down her cheeks.

"Then what is it? Tell me. I'm your best friend, aren't I?"

"You were," Cosi was choking now, her shoulders shaking with sobs.

Gabby put her arms around her. Cosi shook her off. "So, are you and Jack a couple now? Did you sleep with each other in the van? Don't lie to me, Gabby. Don't tell me it was all innocent. I won't believe you."

"What the hell? Cosi what has gotten into you? Jack and I are friends. That's all. We've known each other since we were babies. Trust me. Nothing happened, you silly goose."

"Nothing? Really…?" said Cosi, sniffling, wanting it to be true.

"Well, not with Jack anyway. I did meet someone fine as wine though. I hope someday I'll see him again…." She sighed. "And as far as I know, Jack didn't end up with anybody."

Cosi sucked in her breath, trying to calm down. Gabby studied her face.

"I get it now. You think you shouldn't be interested in guys, but you secretly really like Jack. Maybe you're even in love with him! Am I right?"

Cosi shrugged. "I don't know. Maybe."

"Well, stop being so damned uptight and possessive. That's the surest way to lose a guy. Besides, Jack seems really into you."

"Really? Do you think he loves me?"

Gabby smiled. "What do you think?"

Cosi laughed and hugged her. "Thank you, Gabby. You *are* my best friend. I'll never figure out why you're so good to me."

"You will someday," said Gabby softly, hugging her back.

Dear Joey, I'm in love. I hope you will be happy for me if I marry someone else. You're much too old for me anyway.

Chapter Twenty-One: The Cheater and the Protestor

With September came the cool rains. The leaves of the last few blighted elm trees on Fargo Avenue were turning bright yellow, and horse chestnuts would soon be falling to cover the wide green lawn in front of the Connecticut Street Armory. Cosi made a mental note to take Nino there when the rain stopped. They made an annual pilgrimage to the old stone building in the fall, armed with a brown paper bag to gather up the shiny nuts. Nino would take them home and play with them until they cracked and molded.

It was the first day of the new school year. Shortly after opening prayer, Sister Matthew announced that Sister Agatha would not be teaching math this semester. Cosi nearly jumped up and sang the Hallelujah chorus. Then the other shoe dropped.

"I am pleased to announce that Sister Agatha will be our new religion teacher, replacing Sister Margaret Mary who is taking a position at Our Lady of Perpetual Help. I'm sure you'll join me in congratulating Sister Agatha." There was a smattering of applause.

Cosi gripped the armrests and shook her head in disbelief. This was the worst possible news. Religion was a mandatory course, so there would be no way to avoid Sister Agatha. Worse, this year she was supposed to begin the discernment process in earnest. She had hoped she would have a religion teacher with an open mind, one who would encourage her to question whether God truly wanted her to become a nun. Sister Agatha still clung to the old ways of thinking, while Sister Valentine, her spiritual guide, pushed Cosi to embrace the new. Cosi had no idea how she was going to reconcile the two.

She was lost in thought as she juggled her books, umbrella, and lunch bag on the walk home from the bus stop. Up ahead, she saw a young couple huddling close together under an umbrella. She immediately felt a pang of longing. She had not heard from Jack in weeks. The idea of calling him—of calling any boy—was unthinkable. Only slutty girls did that.

The couple drew nearer and Cosi squinted. *Is that...Jack?* She stopped, confused, and stared at the other figure, a girl who quickly lifted her head for a kiss. Cosi looked frantically for a place to hide, but it was too late. Tina Mortadella came toward her, dragging Jack by the arm.

"Cosi McCarthy? Is that you? I thought I recognized that old raincoat."

Cosi ignored Tina and looked steadily at Jack, who looked embarrassed, but said nothing. She walked stiffly past them, not looking back, and made it to the corner of Fargo and Massachusetts before vomiting in some bushes.

Cosi tried to muffle her sobs as she walked into the house, but her mother followed her into her bedroom. "What is it?"

"Jack...Tina..." She could not go on. She dropped her wet schoolbooks on the bed and threw herself next to them.

"Listen to me." Big Ange squeezed herself onto the bed next to Cosi. "You're surprised? What have I told you about men? They cheat on women. They think it makes them big men. Shows they got big *coglioni*. So, they will break your heart every time unless *you* decide you can live without them."

"But I love him, Mama. How can I live without him?"

"You can live without him because *you* got a special calling. You don't have to waste your time on these worthless *stunads*." Big Ange lifted her daughter by the shoulders. "You're gonna turn 15 soon. You can meet with the head nun at the Mother House this year. Tell her you're ready to become a Bride of Christ."

Cosi pushed her mother away crossly. "I already know the head nun, Mama. I spent all last semester reading to the old nuns in the Mother House, and I'm not gonna do that again. I'm gonna work at the psychiatric hospital, visiting the patients there."

"What? Why waste your time there? How will that prepare you to be a

Bride of Christ?" Her mother stood up and shook her head. "You're talking stupid now. I'll chalk it up to being dumped by that little *testa di merda*."

Cosi was still moping on the bus the next day when the driver quickly braked and, as the vehicle rolled well past the stop and on into the intersection, resignedly opened the door for Gabby. Cosi looked fixedly out the rain-splattered window, pretending not to see her friend.

Gabby plopped down next to her. "I know what you're thinking, just hear me out."

"Why didn't you tell me?" Cosi hissed. "Your horrible sister, of all people."

"I swear I didn't know. I just found out from Jack. He feels terrible about the whole thing. He wants to call you, to explain. What should I tell him?"

Cosi hesitated. She was in love with Jack and could not believe he would willingly betray her. *Maybe it was just a friendly kiss.*

"Tell me one thing, Gabby—is it true? Are they an item?"

Gabby looked down at her books.

"Never mind," said Cosi, her voice breaking. "Just tell Jack I'm moving on."

Cosi stopped to wipe away tears before walking up the school steps. Her mother was right about Jack. She took a deep breath and told herself to do exactly as her mother said. Stop thinking about him and get on with your life. Instead of stopping for coffee in the cafeteria, she walked directly into the guidance counselor's office.

Cosi surprised Sister Claire with her brusqueness. "How do I join the debate team and how do I volunteer to work at the psychiatric hospital?"

Joining the debate team was easy enough. At the very first meeting, Cosi discovered she enjoyed discussing current events, history, and philosophy. She had absorbed more than she realized from the evening news and the books Sister Valentine had given her. She also surprised the debate team coach as well as herself, with her ability to analyze issues. Not only was she able to remember details, but she could also construct logical arguments based on what she remembered. The only thing she needed to work on, was confidence.

Getting a volunteer position at the psychiatric hospital proved tougher. "They only accept one volunteer per semester," said Sister Claire, "and we've already selected two candidates for this year. You'll have to wait to see if they make it through the interview process." Cosi thought about the man who had frightened her when she visited Aunt Rosa, and for a moment, felt relieved. Then she remembered Harriet, so desperate for visitors, and decided to leave the next step in God's hands.

At the end of September, while she struggled with her trigonometry homework, the phone rang. She answered, briefly hoping that Jack was calling to apologize. When it came to Jack, her logical, analytical brain seemed to fail her.

An unfamiliar male voice said, "Hello, Cosi?"

"Yes. Who's this?"

"It's Marty Paczinski. You might not remember me, but we met at Meatball's house."

"Oh…yes, sure," she stammered. She had given up on ever hearing from Marty.

"I'm sorry I didn't call before this. Things got a little crazy after the Buffalo Nine trial last winter, and I didn't think it was a good idea to get you mixed up in that. I am calling now because we're going to have a big symposium downtown tomorrow, with lots of great speakers. I would love to have you come and see what it's all about."

"I don't know. I'm sort of seeing someone…."

Marty chuckled. "I'm sure you are, but I'm not calling to ask you for a date. If I'm ever lucky enough to go on a date with you, it won't be to something like this." She remembered now, how charming he was. She had to smile despite herself.

"This is strictly for educational purposes," said Marty. "You can decline, no problem."

"Well, is anyone else I know going?"

"Dominic for sure. Gabby said maybe."

Cosi thought it over. After meeting Marty, she had eagerly read everything she could find about the war and particularly the Buffalo Nine, a group of local students arrested for protesting the draft. When the first trial was held, students and faculty from UB had picketed the courthouse, chanting "Free the Nine, the Trial's a Crime." This would be her chance to get involved in a real effort to stop the war.

"OK. I'll go if I can talk my mother into it."

"Would it help if your cousin Dominic talked to her?"

"I guess it's worth a try."

Dominic arrived the next morning and kissed Big Ange on each cheek. "How you doin', Aunt Angie? My Ma sends her love."

"How is poor Mari now that she's alone?" Big Ange pinched his cheek. "You get fatter every time I see you, just like your *boombatz* of a father." She stopped. "Of course, we don't speak of him anymore, the stinking piece of *bacalao.*"

"I know, I know." Dominic shook his head. "It's a terrible thing when a man cheats on his woman. A good man takes care of and respects women."

"Hah! You're the only guy around who thinks with his head instead of his you-know- what," said Big Ange. "Mari must be proud,"

Dominic hung his head, embarrassed by the compliment. "A man's gotta do what a man's gotta do. That's the reason I'm here. I hear Cosi's going on a field trip down to the courthouse with some other students. I'm offering to escort her, you know, to make sure there's no trouble."

"Trouble? What kind of trouble?"

"You know…could be any kind of trouble. Guys hitting on her, gawking at her, or saying some shit to her, excuse my language. Or maybe there might be some students—you know—carrying signs and stuff."

Big Ange squinted. "Students carrying signs? You mean Holy Martyrs is making her to go to a protest? *Madonna mia,* what will these hippie nuns think of next?"

"No, no," Dominic was getting flustered now. "It's not her school…it's a religious-type group that's going. I mean, it's like an interfaith thing."

Cosi watched her mother grow more suspicious and decided it was time to step in and help Dominic, who was shifting from foot to foot.

"Mama, you know how concerned I've been about our boys being sent to Vietnam, like poor Joey next door. The government even has this new program, the one they're calling 'Project 100,000.' They're drafting young guys who can't speak English, have low IQs, even ones who have physical problems—just so they can keep the troop numbers up. Can you imagine, Mama, if one day Nino was forced to go to war?"

Her mother fell silent. Cosi felt a little guilty, playing the Nino card, but she was learning new tactics during debate team practices. She looked her mother in the eye.

"I think I *can* do something to stop the war, something that will please the Virgin Mary. Our Lady told the children of Fatima to spread the gospel of peace, right? The Blessed Virgin told me I have a special calling, so like the children of Fatima, I need to go and spread that message. If I don't go to rallies like this, when will I have the chance? Please let me go. It's what the Blessed Virgin wants. Dominic will look after me."

Big Ange sighed and finally relented. She fixed Dominic with a hard stare. "You better make sure nothing happens to her, *capisce?*

"*Capisce*, Aunt Angie." Dominic winked at Cosi and hurried out the door.

Cosi grabbed her denim bag and flew down the front steps before her mother could change her mind. When she and Dominic reached the street, Cosi stopped short. Marty was in the front seat of a candy-apple red '69 Mustang convertible, top down, blond hair blowing in the autumn breeze.

"Whoa," said Cosi.

Marty hopped out as soon as he saw her and opened the passenger side door. "Domo, jump in the back, will you?"

Dominic grumbled but shoved his bulk into the small, uncomfortable back seat. Cosi stared as Marty expertly shifted gears and talked at the same time. He handed her and Dominic buttons that said, "Buffalo Nine—Right On!" that matched the one he was wearing. While she struggled with the pin, Marty talked excitedly.

"So, we were able to get Susan Sontag and a bunch of other famous activists from New York City to come to the symposium. Students, faculty, hippies, yippies, even Vietnam vets. I'm glad you could come, Cosi."

Cosi gave herself a little hug. She remembered feeling like an idiot the first time Marty had asked her opinion about the war. This time she was ready.

"I wish I could've been there when the Buffalo Nine took sanctuary in the Universalist Church. It had such a catalyzing effect on the anti-war movement here in Buffalo." She was proud she had remembered the word, "catalyzing" from the newspaper.

Marty smiled. "Someone's been doing their homework."

They drove down Niagara Street and circled Niagara Square, turning right on Court Street. When they arrived outside the massive limestone courthouse, they saw several hundred people already gathered in the streets, on the sidewalks, and around the building. A small makeshift stage had been set up and someone was speaking through a bullhorn. It seemed like a gigantic version of Meatball's party. Music thundered through the loudspeakers and the now-familiar smell of marijuana wafted through the air. People danced, hugged, and flashed each other the peace sign. The posters they carried around the courthouse read, "Big Firms Get Rich, GIs Die," and "Don't Tread on Me—Support the 9."

There was an energy to the gathering, a hum that sent adrenalin coursing through Cosi's body down to her fingers and toes. She pressed forward, straining to hear the speakers on stage, but could only make out a few words like "capitalist oppressors" and "that's how the pigs operate." As she scanned the crowd, she spotted a couple of priests and several nuns. She remembered Sister Valentine's words: *Some of us believe our calling is to get involved.*

When the symposium ended, there were chants of "Ho, Ho, Ho Chi Minh, the NLF is going to win." The crowd milled around, chanting louder and growing more agitated. Marty and Dominic each grabbed one of Cosi's arms.

"That's enough for today," said Marty. "Let's get out of here before the cops come. I've been tear-gassed before and it's no fun." Safely back in the car, Marty asked, "What do you think?

Cosi's face was flushed with excitement. "It was incredible. I want to come again. I want to be involved!"

"And so, you shall," Marty smiled. "Before I drop you off at home, I want to stop by my house to pick something up. Would you mind? It's not far out of the way."

"Sure," she said. "Where do you live? Near Broadway?" She assumed since his last name was Polish, he lived in the section of the city where Polish immigrants had settled.

Marty looked at her with an odd expression. "The East Side? No, I live near the zoo."

"Oh, that's right. You said you went to the Nichols School."

Cosi had vaguely heard of Nichols, a private high school for brainy boys somewhere near Delaware Park. They drove north up Delaware Avenue toward the zoo, past the enormous old mansions that lined the broad street, relics of a time when Buffalo was one of the most prosperous cities on the Great Lakes. Few of the stately old homes were privately owned now. Most housed schools, museums, or businesses.

"Wow," she said, as they passed the Wilcox Mansion. She vaguely remembered that President Theodore Roosevelt was inaugurated there, just after President McKinley was assassinated at the Pan American Exposition, right in the heart of Buffalo. "Can you imagine at one time people actually lived in places like that?"

Dominic and Marty exchanged looks. "Yeah," Marty said. "I can imagine it."

They drove by Delaware Park and Marty took a left onto Nottingham Terrace. They parked in front of an enormous grey stone building that looked like something out of Cosi's old "Knights of the Crusades" book. She was confused, afraid she had missed something. "Is this the Nichols School?"

"No." Marty looked sheepish. "I live here."

"You should go see the inside," Dominic whispered. Marty opened the car door for her.

Cosi shook her head and sunk lower into the bucket seat. "I'll just sit here while you get what you need." Marty shrugged and closed the door.

She tried to process what she was seeing, taking in all the turrets, gables, and leaded glass windows of the great stone house. There was a huge fountain on the wide front lawn and an iron fence that seemed to surround an entire city block. *What kind of person lives in a place like this? Those people do not hang out with the likes of Domo and me.*

From the time she was a small girl, Cosi had been lectured on the greed and malevolence of the rich. It was one of the few things upon which the McCarthys and Di Giacomos agreed. "Money's the root of all evil," her father would say. Despite her mother's recent worries about the family's finances, and her sister's desire to marry rich, Cosi agreed with her father. She would happily take a vow of poverty if she became a nun.

When Marty unlocked the front door and disappeared inside, Dominic leaned over the seat. "The place has 12 bedrooms and 11 bathrooms! Fireplaces in every room and a staircase like something you would see in a Hollywood movie. Its frickin' unbelievable."

"Good for him. So, what are *we* doing here, Domo?" Cosi demanded. "Does he think his big house is going to impress me? Why is he slumming with the likes of us?"

"Because he believes in his cause," said Dominic, as Marty locked his front door and walked back toward the car. "He wants to hang with people who believe in it too."

Marty jumped in the car and handed her a book. "A small gift for you. If you haven't read *Slaughterhouse Five*, Vonnegut's latest, you need to. It's a great satire on the absurdities of war." Cosi took the book and stuffed it in her bag without looking at it.

Driving back to the West Side, Cosi studied her fingernails. She would not look at Marty. She wanted to say something, to let him know she was not impressed with his money, big house, or fancy car. *You have no right to think you're better than us, mister,* she wanted to say.

When they pulled up in front of her house, Cosi waited until Marty parked and said coolly, "Thank you for bringing me to the symposium. It was…instructive." Marty's face fell, confused by her sudden lack of enthusiasm. Cosi got out and was about to slam the door, when Little Ange sidled up to the driver's side. She leaned over, letting her ample bosom fall close to Marty's ear.

"Well, who have we here," she purred, running her finger slowly around the steering wheel. "Cosi, aren't you going to introduce me to your new friend?"

Cosi sighed. "Angie this is Marty. Marty, this is my sister, Little Ange." She watched in disgust as Little Ange held out a limp hand for Marty to kiss. He dutifully lifted it to his lips.

"The feeling is mutual," Little Ange giggled, fluttering her hand in front of her heart.

Cosi ran around the front of the car and grabbed her sister's arm. "Let's go, Angie. I see Mama upstairs waiting for us." They looked up to see their mother standing on the top porch. Kids from the neighborhood began to gather around Marty's car.

"Bitchin!" Rory walked around the car, nodding his head up and down. "Has this thing got twice-pipes? Can I look under the hood?"

"Bye, Cosi," called Marty over his shoulder. "See you next time." Marty and Dominic peeled away with a screech, leaving half a dozen kids with disappointed faces.

When Cosi came upstairs, her mother was in the kitchen preparing dinner. "How'd you do at the protest?" asked Big Ange, without turning to look. "Is the war over?"

Dear Joey, yes I will do whatever it takes to stop the war. I'll never forgive the men in charge, after what this war's done to you.

Chapter Twenty-Two: Road Vultures and Niagara Falls

Cosi and Nino were in the living room watching *The Brady Bunch* one mild October evening, when she heard a dull roar through the open front windows. The noise grew thunderous, punctuated by popping sounds. Cosi ran onto the upstairs porch and looked down.

A frightening-looking, tattooed man in a dark leather jacket and heavy black boots was revving his motorcycle in Joey's driveway. She watched as another, then two more choppers, squeezed in alongside him, rattling and sputtering as they idled. Big Ange and Little Ange joined Cosi on the top porch to see what all the commotion was and all three peered over the side.

Little Ange mouthed, "Who the hell are they?"

Doors and windows opened, up and down the street, as neighbors peeked out of their houses. Rory and his gang talked excitedly on the porch below. Cosi walked to the other side of the porch, curious to see how Granny Archer might react. Granny was standing near her window, dropping bullets into the cylinder of a revolver.

Cosi ran back to the other side of the porch, just as Joey came out of his house and slapped the first man on the shoulder. The tattooed biker turned off his engine, the others followed suit and the neighborhood grew quiet. Joey went back in the house and came out with two six-packs of beer. The men sat together on the concrete steps, talking quietly at first, then more loudly as Joey went in and retrieved six-pack after six-pack, and the night wore on.

"Can you hear what they're saying?" whispered Little Ange. She and Cosi sat crouched in the dark, leaning against the porch railing.

"Not really," said Cosi. "Something about 'Nam' and 'brothers.' That's about it."

Little Ange shrugged and went back inside, but Cosi continued to watch Joey for a long time. In the soft glow of his porch light, she thought she saw a small spark of life in Joey, missing since he had come back home. *He seems to be at ease with these bikers,* she mused.

Long after Cosi went to bed, she heard the engines again. She wished she had been brave enough to go down and talk to some of Joey's new friends. "Who were they?" she asked Rory the next time she saw him.

"Road Vultures Motorcycle Club," Rory explained in a voice saturated with admiration. "They want Joey to join. Man, those bikes were truly righteous."

Cosi began to twist her hair, a habit she thought she had broken by now. She had read about the Road Vultures in the newspaper. The head of the Buffalo chapter was shot to death in a dispute a couple of years before, and other killings and arrests of the club's members popped up in the press from time to time. *Has Joey lost it completely?* She wondered why would a former soldier would even consider joining up with guys like that.

Dear Joey, I know the war must have done something to your mind. If you ever want to talk about it, I'm here for you.

INDIAN summer ended and by the third week in October, rust and pumpkin-colored maple leaves covered the sidewalks and temperatures were in the mid-30s. Cosi kept busy at school practicing with the debate team and studying for mid-terms, and when weather permitted, running with the cross-country team. While she ran, she looked up at the bare branches of the trees which reminded her of dark veins on a pale white wrist, and wondered how Aunt Rosa was doing.

She was still on the waitlist for the volunteer job at the psychiatric hospital, but now that Aunt Rosa was home, her guilty feelings about the patients were fading. She was helping her mother make a Halloween costume for Nino when Marty called.

"Another rally?" she asked sarcastically.

"Uh no, actually." Marty sounded nervous. "Gabby told me you're not dating anyone now, so I was wondering...do you think you might be interested in going out with me?"

It occurred to Cosi, that for once, she had the upper hand with a guy. If he wanted to see her, it would be on her terms. "I have to be honest. I am going through the discernment process right now to see if I'm going to become a nun. I don't mind going out with you, but our relationship has to be strictly platonic." She smiled. She was learning all kinds of fifty-cent words on the debate team.

"That's fine," he said, trying to hide his disappointment. "My birthday is this weekend, and I was hoping to go out to dinner, to celebrate. I have no one special in my life right now. So...," he hesitated, "could we just go as friends?"

"I'll have to get my mother's approval, of course. Can you call me back tomorrow?"

Big Ange shocked her by quickly agreeing. "I saw him from the porch. Seems like a nice boy, even if he does have the long hair. Nice car. Must have..." Big Ange rubbed her thumb and fingers together, Sicilian sign language for big money. "Does he know you're gonna be a nun?"

"Yes, Mama. I told him."

Her mother gave her a sly look. "Dominic said you two are just friends. Maybe this guy and Angie could...."

Cosi walked away, ignoring the mercenary gleam in her mother's eye. All that talk about money being the root of all evil! She deliberately waited until Friday to call Marty back.

"I can go, but I have to be back by 11."

"I'll have you back by 10:59, just to be on the safe side."

"Where are we going by the way?" She tried to sound indifferent. She did not want him to think this was her first date ever, although it was. She and Jack had never gone on a real "date." Her mother had seen to that.

"It'll be a surprise," said Marty. "It isn't far and I think you'll like it. Dress up a bit."

"I'll think about it." She hung up and smiled. She was in charge this time.

Despite her efforts at nonchalance, Cosi took a bath and started getting ready hours before Marty arrived. She looked at herself in the mirror a dozen times. She borrowed a soft pink angora sweater from Gabby and from Little Ange a black skirt that fell slightly above the knee. She thought about that disastrous evening with Jack and pulled her scapular out, placing it carefully atop her sweater, to remind Marty to keep his hands where they belonged.

"Wow," said Marty, when three smiling women opened the front door. "You look great, Cosi." He held three red roses in his hands, and gave one to each. "Flowers to the fairest." While her mother and sister gushed over the attention, Cosi hurried Marty out the door.

They drove in awkward silence north along the Niagara River, until Cosi began to see signs for Grand Island. "Are we leaving Buffalo?" she asked in surprise.

"Yes, but just outside of it. We should be there in another 20 minutes."

They drove through Grand Island and over the North Grand Island bridge to follow the river along the Niagara Scenic Parkway. Before long, Cosi spotted a magnificent arched structure up ahead. "What is that?" She was well acquainted with the Peace Bridge, which she could see whenever she walked down Niagara Street. This bridge was new to her.

"That's the Rainbow Bridge. We're on our way to Ontario." Marty hummed, "O Canada," as they began the climb over the bridge while Cosi peered nervously down at the thundering river below. "Look over to your left," said Marty.

Cosi could see the mist rising from the falls. "Gosh—what a great view!" She was ashamed to admit she had never been to the Canadian side of Niagara Falls.

"You haven't seen anything yet."

On the other side of the bridge, they made a brief stop at Canadian customs.

"Where were you born?" asked the bored Customs officer.

"Buffalo," they responded. He waved them on quickly, eyes moving to the next car.

Marty parked the car below an enormous tower Cosi had seen from the bridge. She threw her head back as far as it would go, trying to see the top. She was looking at the underside of a large circular structure that sat atop a grooved, concrete base. It looked like an alien spaceship had landed on top of a giant swizzle stick. "Are we going up there?"

Marty took her elbow and guided her to a small elevator that looked like a bright yellow bug climbing outside the concrete structure. Once inside, the tiny car rose and the ground fell quickly below them. Cosi grabbed the sides of the elevator and shut her eyes.

"Hey," laughed Marty. "You're missing the best part."

The doors opened and the elevator operator turned to them. "Welcome to the Skylon Tower Observation Deck. You're over 500 feet above the Great Gorge. From here, you will be able to see both the American and Canadian falls, the Niagara Wine District and the city skylines of Toronto and Buffalo. Enjoy your visit."

Cosi walked with Marty around the circular deck, mesmerized by the incredible views. She began to relax, bathed in the soft pearly light of the evening gloaming, listening to the muffled roar of the river far below. She stood gazing at the Horseshoe Falls when an unexpected burst of light and a half-dozen gorgeous neon colors shone upon the roiling waters.

"Oh!" Cosi clapped her hands, dazzled. "What a way to celebrate a birthday!"

"Come on." Marty took her by the hand. "This is just the beginning."

They went down one level and Marty guided her into the most glamorous restaurant Cosi had ever seen. "Welcome to the Revolving Dining Room," said the maître d'. They sat at a table overlooking the American Bridal Veil Falls, but within minutes the room had moved a half turn and they looked down at an amusement park in Canada.

"Would you mind if I order for you?" Marty asked. "I have something special in mind. Surf and turf, they call it." He leaned forward and cupped his handsome chin in the heel of his hand. The glow of the candle highlighted his strong cheekbones and softened his intense eyes.

"Tell me about yourself." Marty unfolded his napkin and dropped it in his lap. "I realized coming over here I really know very little about you."

"Well, I go to Holy Martyrs High School." Cosi followed Marty's lead and laid her napkin on her lap. *Do rich people often drop their food on their legs?*

"I know that school!" Marty's eyes brightened. "Sometimes we get posters for your dances. Mellow Brick Rode, my favorite band, played there not long ago. Maybe I'll go next time." He smiled. "Why do you go there? Isn't that a long way from home?"

"It is a long way." She touched her scapular. "I'm preparing to enter the convent."

"I guess you're serious about that, aren't you? Well, I envy you, already knowing the path you're on at your age" Marty dipped his fingers in a small bowl of water with lemon and dried them on his napkin. "I wish I thought Nichols would help me find my path. No one there seems interested in the things that interest me. I had to venture to the far west side of Buffalo to find a kindred spirit." He tilted his head in a charming way, his eyes locking onto hers. She blushed, and scrubbed her fingers with the lemon, hoping she was doing things correctly.

Their food arrived, and he showed her with quick and practiced moves how to remove the lobster tail from its shell. She dipped a piece in the bowl of melted butter and let out a moan—it was the most delicious thing she had ever tasted. She sliced the filet mignon and took a bite. The meat was unbelievably tender, better than her mother's *braciole*.

"Tell me about being a conscientious objector." She wanted him to talk so she could eat.

Marty told her about his cousin who was drafted despite his ambivalence about the war, and killed in the Que Son Valley. He talked about black men being drafted to fight in record numbers, about misguided US foreign policy, about body counts. "This war," Marty stabbed a piece of steak with his fork, "is being waged by the rich and fought by the poor. We need to either end the draft, or undermine it."

He spoke with a passion she had not seen since her father used to talk about his work at the steel plant, and the night passed quickly. On the ride home, Marty pushed an 8-track tape into a slot beneath the car radio. "I hope you like Crosby, Stills and Nash."

"I do. I like them a lot."

Cosi listened to the beautiful harmonies of the group as they sang "Suite: Judy Blue Eyes," and "Guinevere," and "Helplessly Hoping" and realized they were songs about love and longing. Every now and then Marty would glance over at her and she felt her chest tighten. *Is he trying to tell me something? Did I send the wrong signals again?*

She thought about how Jack hurt her heart and wounded her pride, and prepared herself to rebuff Marty's advances. In the end, it was not necessary. When he walked her to the door at 10:59, he said, "Thank you for a great birthday," gave her a peck on the cheek, and walked away.

"Spill your guts!" Little Ange pounced on Cosi when she came into the bedroom.

"There isn't a lot to tell." Cosi took off the black skirt and casually threw it on her sister's bed. "We had a nice dinner at a restaurant near Niagara Falls. We talked about the war. I told him I was going to be a nun. He drove me home. That's about it."

"You told him you're gonna be a nun?" Little Ange laughed. "Last time you'll ever see that guy. You're an *idiot* for letting *him* get away. Don't be surprised if he moves on."

"I didn't let him get away." Cosi angrily kicked off her shoes. She was getting sick and tired of her sister's bullying. "What makes you think he won't call me again? Just because I don't act like a two-bit floozy, like you?"

"Who are you calling a floozy, you little stick-up-your-ass, goody two-shoes?"

"You! You slutty sleazeball!"

Little Ange lunged at Cosi, pushing her onto the bed. "Why, you little bitch!"

Cosi jumped up and grabbed a hank of her sister's hair. Little Ange tried to pry Cosi's hand away while slapping Cosi's face with her free hand. "Let go of my hair or I'll pound you into the ground," screamed Little Ange.

Cosi fought with a fury that surprised her sister, channeling all her pent-up emotions into her blows. She kicked Little Ange as they fell onto the bed and punched her face. Little Ange managed to climb on top and pin her arms while Cosi bucked, trying to throw her sister off the bed. They were trading obscenities at the top of their lungs when they heard a scream at the door.

Nino stood in his pajamas, slapping his own face. He shrieked, his eyes wide and unfocused. Cosi pushed Little Ange off, ran to Nino and hugged him, holding his arms against his sides to keep him from hitting himself. He shrieked louder and stomped his feet. Out of the corner of her eye, Cosi could see her mother running down the hall with her father's belt.

Cosi let go of Nino, dove for the floor, and crawled under her bed. Little Ange, who had not seen her mother coming, caught the first whack of the belt across her legs. She grabbed the blanket off her bed to protect herself and shouted, "Cosi started it!"

Big Ange tried to drag Cosi out by the ankle, but Cosi grabbed the bed-frame and held tight. Little Ange tried to grab Cosi's other ankle, but Big Ange swatted her again with the belt. "I don't need your help."

Finally, Big Ange sat on the bed, winded. "What's the matter with you two, scaring Nino like that? Cosi what's got into you?" Silence from under the bed. "You two are grounded for a week."

Big Ange pushed herself up and turned to Nino. The little boy stood in a puddle, whining and biting the inside of his elbow. Big Ange dropped the belt on the floor, folded him gently in her arms, and guided him to the bathroom. Cosi heard the bathroom door close. Her mother's soothing tones. Nino's whimpering.

Little Ange glared at her. "You'll pay for this."

Dear Joey, tonight I learned not all guys are assholes (unlike sisters). I went to dinner with my friend Marty who hates war. You'd like him.

Chapter Twenty-three: Protests and the Battle for Purity

Nino was asleep when Cosi left for church the next morning. She found him in the bathroom playing when she returned. "Nino," she whispered, "I'm so sorry about last night."

Nino did not look at her. He had filled the sink and put all of his plastic animals in the water, and one-by-one he took them out and lined them up on the rim of the bathtub.

"Nino, can I please help you?"

Silence.

"Nino, please forgive me. I know that fight was scary and I won't do it again. I'll make it up to you, I promise. I'm gonna buy you some more animals. OK?"

Nino held a plastic dog in front of her face. "Woof," he said loudly. "Woof, woof."

On Monday, Marty called. Cosi stuck her tongue out at Little Ange, who flipped her the bird and stomped out of the kitchen.

"Hey," Marty's tone was serious. "Did you see the news? The verdict is in on the Buffalo Nine. Three acquitted, two convicted. We don't know about the rest. We're going down to picket the Federal building to protest the convictions. Want to come?"

"Yes," Cosi whispered into the phone, looking over her shoulder to see if her mother or sister were within earshot. "Pick me up in front of the Fargo Grill. I'll head there now."

She called to her mother as she rushed out the front door, "I'm going to the library to do homework, Mama. I'll be back in a couple of hours." She did not wait for an answer.

When Cosi and Marty arrived, there was a large crowd gathering in front of the courthouse. She sensed a mood distinctly different from the one at the summer symposium. These people were angry. She and Marty hurried to join the throng but stopped when Marty pointed at several police officers who were handcuffing one of the protestors.

"That's the guy who was freed by the hung jury. Hey!" yelled Marty, "why are you arresting him again?"

Cosi watched a teen-aged boy push his way toward the police car where the handcuffed young activist now sat. "You're nothing but pigs!" shouted the boy at the cops, shaking his fist. The crowd surged forward. The police cruiser began to pull away to the rhythmic chanting of "Off the Pigs! Off the Pigs!"

The shouting grew louder. Cosi heard a scream, then a loud bang. Suddenly, she could feel the tight press of bodies around her. The crowd was not only angry but panicked now, and it pushed and shoved her along toward the uniformed police officers and cars that lined the street. She smelled something and coughed—*Is that tear gas?* She looked for Marty. *Where is he?*

Dear God, she thought, terrified, *what if I'm arrested? What if I'm trampled or killed? Mama doesn't even know I'm here.*

Cosi spun around, looking in all directions for Marty while the surging crowd jostled her along. She tripped and fell, someone stepped on her hand, a knee hit her in the face. She tried to stand only to be knocked down again. Panicked, she shrieked, "Help me!" over and over until someone reached down and pulled her to her feet. Sobbing, nearly hysterical now, she pushed her way out of the mob and stumbled in between two parked cars. She climbed up on the hood of one as the crowd swept by. People began to throw rocks at the police. She screamed over the din, "Marty Paczinski! Where are you?"

Strong arms reached up and pulled her down. It was Uncle Tommy, in plainclothes, astonishment written across his face. "Cosi! What on earth are you doing here?"

"I'm sorry, Uncle Tommy," Cosi cried, shaking uncontrollably. "Take me home."

He took her in his arms and limping aggressively through the crowd, carried her down a side street where he had parked his car. She wiped her eyes with her now swollen hand and tried to compose herself. "A friend of mine is still out there," she managed to say.

"You're not going to find her now, not in the middle of that angry rabble."

"It's not a *she*." She looked away.

"I see. Let's get you home then. I'm sure *he* can fend for himself."

On the short drive back to Fargo Avenue, Cosi felt miserable, chagrined that she had been so terrified, and cowardly. Her uncle parked the car in front of her house, and Cosi looked at him with imploring eyes. "Mama doesn't know I was there."

He gave her a stony look. "I know how hot-headed your mother can be so I won't tell her this time. But you listen to me, girl. You have no business involved in something like this. I don't care how much you like this fella. If I ever see you at one of these damned protests again, I'm gonna throw the book at you. Understand?"

"Yes, Uncle Tommy," she said meekly. She glanced up at the top porch, saw it was empty, and said a quick prayer of thanks for the chilly weather.

MARTY'S red Mustang was sitting near her house when Cosi came home from school the next day, convertible top up and windows closed. She considered ignoring him but as she came nearer, Marty rolled down his window and smiled painfully. She noticed his black eye.

"I've been waiting for you. Can we talk?" Cosi hesitated, but got in the car.

"I wanted to apologize for losing you yesterday," said Marty. "When we got separated, I looked everywhere but couldn't find you. I figured you probably walked home. I was worried, but I guess I didn't need to be. You seem fine."

He ran his fingers through his hair, remembering. "Man, wasn't that something? It was all over the news last night. Now everybody wants to get together again at UB on the 29th. We're thinking we might...hey, what's the matter?"

Tears streamed down Cosi's face. "So, you thought that was *great?* Everything you wanted it to be? Did you know the crowd knocked me over and nearly trampled me to death? Thank God Uncle Tommy found me and brought me home, but he said if he ever caught me at another protest...." She started crying again before she could finish.

"Hey, it's OK." He smoothed the hair on the back of her head. "It's all my fault. You're too young for this. I just thought...because you were sympathetic to our cause...I'm sorry."

"You should be sorry!" she cried. "You said this was all about peace. That crowd was violent! How can you call yourselves a "peace movement?"

Marty handed her a Kleenex and she blew her nose. She looked up and saw Joey walk out his front door. He was wearing a new leather jacket and black boots. He sat on the front steps, lit a cigarette, and stared at Marty.

"Who's that guy?" Marty asked.

"That's Joey Catalfano, my next door neighbor. Something happened to him while he was in Vietnam. He hasn't been the same since."

"I wonder if he might want to join our cause. Some of the Buffalo Nine are vets."

Cosi eyed Joey's face, which looked none too friendly. "I know, but I don't..."

Marty swung open the door and was out of the car, heading toward Joey before Cosi could stop him. He extended his hand. "Hey man, what's happenin'?"

Joey kept one hand in his pocket, his lit cigarette cupped inside the other. He ignored Marty and called to Cosi who was hurrying to join them. "Who's this jerk? Is he bothering you?"

Marty withdrew his hand. "Hey man, no need to get hostile. I heard you had a rough time in 'Nam, just like a lot of guys. I imagine it was hell over there. There's a group of us here in Buffalo who are trying to stop the..."

"*You* can imagine what it was like? I can tell you don't know shit, Richie Rich. For you, the war is nothing but words you put on your stupid protest signs. A bumper sticker on the chrome of your fancy car. I went because I *wanted* to go. Get outta my sight before I puke."

Marty put up his hands. "Look man, I didn't come over to get into it with you. I just thought after what you'd been through…"

Joey stood, his full six-foot, three-inch frame towering above Marty. The tight black leather jacket accentuated Joey's broad shoulders and muscular arms, and the deep purple scar under his right eye added a touch of menace. He flicked his cigarette onto the sidewalk. Marty did not back away, but said no more.

Cosi stepped between them. "Joey please, Marty didn't mean anything. He just wants the war to end, that's all. Besides, he was just getting ready to say goodbye to me, weren't you Marty?" She grabbed Marty's arm and started pulling him back towards the Mustang.

Joey and Marty still faced each other, eyes locked. Cosi whispered in Marty's ear, "If you ever want to see me again, get in your car right now." Reluctantly, Marty backed up to the car, his eyes never leaving Joey. Once Marty was in the driver's seat, Cosi ran to the other side.

"Cosi!" Joey called. Their eyes met. For a moment, his face lost that hard edge.

She hesitated, then jumped into the passenger seat. "Drive," she ordered Marty.

At the corner of Fargo and Rhode Island, she told him to stop the car. "Look, Marty, I understand what you and the other protesters are trying to do, but you're not going to get anywhere making enemies with a guy like Joey. Believe it or not, he was a really good guy, and deep down, I think he still is."

"Really?" Marty turned on her, showing his first flash of anger. "I don't even like the idea of you living next door to that lunatic. Who knows when he might go off the deep end and kill everyone in the neighborhood?"

"How dare you say that!" She turned on Marty with a fierceness that surprised him. "You don't know Joey. He's been good to me all of my life and you're going to tell me what he's like?" Cosi got out of the car. "I'll walk back, thank you." She slammed the door.

A half-block from her house, Cosi could hear the steady rumble of the motorcycles as they sat idling in Joey's driveway. She was close enough to see him walk down the steps and get on behind one of the riders. The group roared past her and Joey stared straight ahead. She was dismayed, but not surprised, to see the "Road Vultures" insignia on the back of his jacket.

Dear Joey, what was that look you gave me? Don't worry, I'm still in your corner, even if you have gone off the deep end.

"Turn to Part Three, Chapter Two of your Catechism," announced Sister Agatha, striding into the classroom. "Today we will discuss the Ninth Commandment and the Battle for Purity." She underlined "Purity" on the chalkboard twice.

Cosi sat very still, head down, catechism opened. She had recently gotten a demerit for wearing her uniform an inch above the knee, the result of another growth spurt that added two more inches to her height. She began to worry she would soon be taller than the boys.

"Miss McCarthy, would you please read section 2522 aloud?" Cosi read a short section about modesty and decency, then stopped and waited.

"Thank you, Miss McCarthy. Can you give the class an example of how, in today's abhorrent culture, our young people have abandoned the concept of modesty in their dress and behavior? Wearing skirts well-above the knee, for example."

Cosi willed herself to take a deep breath and pause before answering, the way she learned on the debate team. "Well, Sister," she began as calmly as she could. "Isn't your question based on a false premise?"

"Excuse me?"

"You're stating the question in a way that assumes all young people today have abandoned the concept of modesty. At the very least you should qualify your statement by saying "some young people," since it assumes facts not in evidence."

Sister Agatha's face stiffened. "How dare you question my question."

Cosi had the attention of the entire class now. The sophomores leaned forward in their seats, looking at her, waiting to hear how she would respond.

"I'm not questioning the basic validity of your question, merely suggesting there's a clearer way to ask it." Cosi began to see smiles behind the hands of her classmates. Encouraged, she went on. "We should discuss the fact that 'modesty' is a relative term. It means different things in different cultures. A meaningful discussion about modesty in our culture requires a discussion of the holistic changes in our culture first, as well as the reasons for those changes."

"Are you questioning the teachings of the church, Miss McCarthy?"

"No. I'm simply saying before we jump into an important discussion like this, we should define our terms and not resort to hyperbole."

"Right on!" called a voice from the back of the room. Cosi turned to look. It was Amanda Burns, who no longer braided her long red hair or wore a bra. "Why can't we have a *real* conversation about modesty instead of just repeating what's in the books?"

"I've had just about enough," sputtered Sister Agatha. "We will spend the rest of the hour in silent study. Please reread the entire section on the Ninth Commandment, and begin your 500-word essays on what St. John meant by the three kinds of covetousness. Miss McCarthy, Miss Burns, see me after class."

The class fell silent, but Cosi caught the winks of several of her classmates. After class, she barely listened to Sister Agatha's reprimand, reveling in her first small victory.

Just before Thanksgiving, Cosi received a note telling her to report to the Guidance Counselor's office. She went immediately, concerned that Sister Agatha was complaining about her again. She sighed with relief when she found Sister Claire smiling.

"I've got good news for you, Cosi. Kathleen Malloy has decided to serve as a teacher's aide in one of our inner-city schools. That means the position at the psychiatric hospital is open. You can start next semester."

Cosi had forgotten her application to work at the hospital. How in the world was she going to fit it in with all of the other things she had going on?"

Sister Claire clucked her tongue. "I thought you'd be happier."

"I am happy, Sister. It's just catching me by surprise. How many hours will I need to put in each week? It's a long way from home and…"

"You'll go for three hours, three days a week, during the school day. You can substitute your volunteer work for one of your class electives. If you go at the beginning or end of the day, you can take the bus directly to or from home. You live on the West Side, don't you?"

Cosi was not listening. She thought again about Harriet and the lonely patients in the Visitors' Lounge. They surely needed her more than the elderly nuns upstairs. "OK. I'll do it."

"Good," said Sister Claire. "You'll benefit from the experience as much as the patients."

Dear Joey, they say that people in the psychiatric hospital were once just like you and me. That can't be true. Could it?

CHAPTER TWENTY-FOUR: BIRTHDAYS AND BETRAYALS

COSI AND HER MOTHER walked home from church one Sunday morning in early December, huddling close against the cold. "Do you wanna invite some friends over to celebrate your birthday tomorrow?" her mother asked.

"Who would I invite other than Gabby? My friends at school live too far away."

"Well, you could invite your cousin Dominic. And how about that nice boy with the red car, what's his name…Marty?"

"You know very well what his name is, Mama. Why do you keep encouraging me to see him? Why aren't I getting the usual lecture on becoming a Bride of Christ?"

"Why? He's such a nice boy. Very polite. Doesn't dress like a bum and has some moolah. I'll call him if you're too embarrassed."

"No! Don't you dare. I'll invite him, and some other friends, if it makes you happy."

Tina answered the phone when Cosi called to invite Gabby. "Well, if it isn't Jack's ex-girlfriend. Gabby isn't here."

"Can you tell her I called to invite her to my birthday party?"

"I'm not promising anything." Tina hung up the phone.

"Where's Gabby?" asked Dominic the day of the party. He was helping himself to another slice of cake.

Cosi poked at her piece and said nothing. She and Gabby had barely seen each other since Jack and Tina became an item. She was surprised, nonetheless, when Gabby neither returned her phone call nor showed up at the party. *I've had it with her,* Cosi told herself. *Just let her show her face around here again.*

Marty handed her a small wrapped box. "Happy Birthday, Cosi."

Little Ange smiled and rested her hand on Marty's forearm. Cosi winced when she saw her do it, but focused on unwrapping her gift. On a nest of cotton lay a small silver charm bracelet. Cosi held it up and looked at the tiny silver dove and a round, flat peace symbol attached to the bracelet.

"Don't you ever think about anything else?" Cosi snapped, irritated in general, with the way this party was going. She regretted her comment when she saw the hurt in Marty's eyes.

Little Ange diverted his attention. "Marty, tell me again about the SDS guys—Students for a Democratic Society—am I right? I'm *very* interested in the peace movement," she purred. Cosi gasped. She'd heard the SDS were violent. *I hope Marty's not involved with them.*

Little Ange pulled Marty gently over to the living room couch, and sat close, nodding her head as he spoke. Marty glanced at Cosi with a helpless smile. Little Ange firmly took his chin and moved his face back in her direction. Cosi shook her head, outraged by how easily her sister was able to manipulate him. She looked at her mother, who was smiling while she cleared the dishes. So, the two of them were in cahoots about this party. Why was she just figuring this out?

What do I care, she told herself. *Sure, Marty's been good to me but I'm never going to fall in love with a rich guy, especially one who hates Joey. Little Ange can have him.* But she went to her room and cried, just the same.

On the Saturday before Christmas, Cosi bundled up to shovel the front sidewalk. Usually, she loved to be out during the holiday season when it was snowing at night, the purity of the snow reflecting the soft glow of the colored Christmas lights, hiding all the shabby imperfections of her neighborhood. Tonight, though, as she searched the garage for a shovel, she could not shake the loneliness that weighed her down like a block of ice.

For one thing, Cosi could not seem to avoid running into Jack and Tina, who were together all the time now. She had even seen Tina showing off a new ring. Marty was calling the house regularly to talk to Little Ange, and Cosi still had not heard from Gabby. Her mother complained constantly about money and bad luck, and a dejected Aunt Mari left the two-timing Uncle Tony and moved in with Uncle Benny and Aunt Rosa. Aunt Rosa was still too sad to leave the house, and Cosi missed her.

It had been snowing for the past seven days and though the accumulation was light, it melted just enough during the day to refreeze at night, turning the sidewalks to ice. Walking around to the front of the house, Cosi was surprised to see Rory, shovel in hand, cursing as he stabbed the sharp edge of the shovel against the icy sidewalk.

"What are you doing out here?" Cosi walked to the opposite end of the sidewalk and began chipping ice, planning to meet Rory in the middle.

"What does it look like I'm doing, getting my rocks off?" snarled Rory. He jabbed at the sidewalk a few more times. "My old man's having a party tonight so he sent me out to shovel." He snickered. "Once they're in their cups, I plan to have my own party." He reached into his jacket and pulled out a bottle of Southern Comfort. "Want a swig?"

"No thanks." After her experience at the Conways, Cosi was careful about what she ate and drank. A car drove up and Uncle Tommy and his family piled out.

"Merry Christmas, Cosi!" Aunt Molly and several McCarthy cousins sang out as they climbed carefully over the snowbanks at the curb.

Uncle Tommy gave Cosi a kiss on the cheek. "No more adventures with the hippies?" She shook her head.

Uncle Jimmy and Aunt Tilly pulled up next. Aunt Tilly, proud to be a politician's wife, was wearing a real mink stole over her tailored black winter coat. They both gave Cosi a brisk hug. "Come see me if you want a job at a city pool next summer," said Uncle Jimmy. "You'd look pretty good in one of those red bathing suits."

Uncle Mack was behind them in his sporty new Grand Prix. He threw the keys to Rory and winked. "Move my car if the snowplows come through, OK?" Rory grinned.

More friends and relatives streamed in, many carrying bottles of whiskey or cases of beer while Cosi and Rory struggled to finish chipping away the sidewalk ice. When the music inside grew louder, Rory threw his shovel into the bushes.

"I'm cutting out," he said. "You sure you don't want to come back and party with us?"

"No, you go and have fun with your buddies."

"Suit yourself," Rory smirked. "See you in my dreams."

When Cosi's fingers became so frozen she could not bend them, she finally set her shovel on the porch and went inside. She was waiting in the lower hall for the stinging to stop when the door flew open and a man rushed past her. He stood unsteadily on the front porch, bent over the railing, and up-chucked into the snow. He came back into the foyer, wiping his mouth on his sleeve. "That's better."

While the door stood open, Uncle Danny spotted Cosi. "Cosi, get your arse in here! High time you joined us for a party. You're a feckin' McCarthy, you know."

Cosi began to demur when several McCarthy cousins pulled her inside. "We're having a hula hoop contest tonight," said one. "Come on in and try it."

Cosi sat on the edge of the couch and Aunt Joanie put a drink in her hand. "You need to be drinkin' something or this crowd'll have you drunk in no time," she whispered in Cosi's ear. "This is called a Virgin Mary. No alcohol."

Cosi smiled gratefully at her gentle aunt and sipped at the odd drink—tomato juice and ice cubes with a stalk of celery sticking out the top. Uncle Mack was in the center of the room, trying to rotate the hula-hoop around his middle.

"One, two, three, awwww…" said the crowd, as the plastic hoop dropped from Mack's waist onto the floor. Uncle Tommy and Uncle Jimmy were even less successful. Someone finally said, "Give up you stupid maggots. Only girls know how to make the feckin' thing work."

All eyes fell on Cosi. She put up her hands and shook her head. "No way."

"It's simple," shouted Uncle Danny. "Just rotate your hips like a warshing machine."

Several people dragged Cosi into the middle of the room and put the hoop over her head. She stood there, embarrassed.

"Just try it," called Aunt Joanie. "Make your hips do a big circle."

Everyone started clapping hands. "Go Cosi! Go Cosi!" they chanted. Cosi held the hoop in front of her and slowly started to move her hips. It circled a few times then dropped.

"Faster," the crowd yelled, and she swung her hips faster. To her surprise, the hoop stayed up. The faster she swung her hips, the louder the crowd cheered and clapped.

Everyone joined in. When the chanting ended, Cosi stopped, breathless, and let the hoop fall to the floor. They crowded around her, patting her shoulders, while she pushed her way back, sweaty and panting, to the couch. She could feel the adrenalin surge and, for a brief moment, she enjoyed being the center of attention.

Cosi wandered into the kitchen to douse her face with water and thought about sneaking out the back door when she heard Rory and his pals laughing and cursing in the backyard. Thinking better of it, she worked her way through the packed living room, where the men stood, arms wrapped around each other's shoulders, singing "My Bonnie Lies Over the Ocean," and swaying unsteadily to the music. She moved through the boozy crowd unnoticed.

She hurried upstairs and could hear the phone ringing just as she opened the apartment door. Her mother answered and motioned to Cosi. Big Ange peered at Cosi's flushed red face but said nothing, handing her the receiver.

"Hello?"

Silence on the other end. Then, "Cosi, it's me. Gabby."

Cosi nearly hung up, but something in Gabby's voice stopped her. "Why are you calling me, Gabby?"

"I can't talk over the phone. I need your help." Now Cosi was silent.

"Please, Cosi, you know I wouldn't ask if I thought I had any other choice. I can't tell you where I am right now, or what this is about." Gabby voice was muffled, barely audible. "We need to meet somewhere nobody knows us. Come to the North Park Theater on Hertel Avenue on New Year's Day. I'll be at the 5:20 showing of *Love Story,* sitting in the last row."

Cosi hung up. Part of her wanted to tell Gabby to go to hell, but she knew she would go. Maybe some people were feckless friends, but she wasn't one of them.

Dear Joey, Merry Almost Christmas. So, you're a bad boy now, a Road Vulture. Why then, do I still like you so much?

Part Three

Discernment
1970

Chapter Twenty-Five: Sisters, Sins, and Insanity

Cosi waited until her eyes adjusted to the darkened theater before she began her climb to the top of the stadium seats. Gabby was sitting in the middle of an empty row. Cosi sidled towards her and stopped short. Gabby was clearly pregnant.

Gabby shot her a look. "Sit down and listen, before people turn around and look at us."

Cosi sat, too stunned to say anything. *Why didn't this occur to me?*

Gabby whispered, clearly nervous. "Who the father is, doesn't matter. He won't be in the picture. I'm living in Clarence with my aunt and uncle who are helping me until it's time to have the baby."

"What will you do then? How will you take care of it?" Cosi had a hard time imagining Gabby's parents welcoming a new mouth to feed.

Gabby chewed on a knuckle. "I'm putting the baby up for adoption."

"What do you need from me?" Cosi could not take her eyes from Gabby's rounded belly. She wanted to touch, to feel the living thing inside. Instinctively, she touched her own stomach.

Gabby took a deep breath. "I need you to help me place the baby. I have someone in mind. I want the baby adopted by your Aunt Rosa and Uncle Benny. She always wanted a baby—now she can have one. But...you can't tell them it's mine."

Cosi shook her head. "How in the world do you expect me to do that? The first thing they'll want to know is something about the parents."

"I know, and I have a plan. You need to get Father Mario involved. He needs to be the go-between. They see him every Sunday at mass. They trust him."

"Father Mario? Why?"

Gabby sighed. "Don't you know anything? Catholic girls who get pregnant leave their babies at the church all the time. They know the church will take the babies, baptize them, and put them up for adoption. Haven't you ever heard of Father Baker?"

Cosi shuddered and thought of baby bones in the Erie Canal. "Why get me involved?"

"Look, I want my baby to go to Aunt Rosa and Uncle Benny. Nobody else. You're the only one I trust." She hesitated before adding, "I want my baby to stay in the family."

"Stay in the family? What are you talking about?"

Gabby's mouth twitched. She seemed to be struggling not to cry. She took Cosi's hand and squeezed tightly.

"There's something I haven't told you…been meaning to tell you…wanted to tell you so many times. I just couldn't find the right words. You and I… we're half-sisters."

"We're…*what?*" A smattering of people turned around in their seats to look. An older woman with a coil of gray hair put a finger to her lips.

"What are you talking about?" hissed Cosi. But suddenly she knew. Gabby's mother must have been one of the women who slept with her father. She felt her stomach lurch, certain she was going to be sick.

Gabby grabbed her hand and held it tight. "After your dad died, my mother told me he had gotten her pregnant. She said she always wanted to tell me, but was afraid I would confront your dad about it while he was still alive. He never knew I was his daughter. No one knew but my mom. She got pregnant with me a couple of weeks before she married Tommy Mortadella, so he thinks I'm his. Tina doesn't suspect anything either." Gabby hesitated. "I'm hoping you won't tell your mother or sister. It would be awkward."

Cosi couldn't think. This was too much. *My best friend, my half-sister, is pregnant with a child who is…what? My half niece or nephew?* She had to wonder how many other half-brothers and half-sisters she might have, and started to cry. *What kind of man was my dad? Why am I sacrificing my life for him? Maybe he should rot in Hell!*

Gabby put her arm around Cosi. "Let's get out of here." She guided Cosi, sobbing and shaking, out of the theater. They walked down Hertel Avenue, crunching snow underfoot as the frigid January night was descending.

"So, you get it, right?" Gabby asked, cupping her hands tenderly over the bump in her coat. "This is your father's grandchild. A member of your family, as well as mine. If you and Father Mario can convince Aunt Rosa, you and I will see this baby whenever we want. It will be our secret. We can even babysit together…assuming we can be friends again."

Gabby handed Cosi a handkerchief and Cosi blew her nose. Gabby put her mittened hands on Cosi's cold cheeks and looked into her eyes. "I know this is a big shock, and I know I have no right to ask you for such a huge favor. But I still think of you as my best friend, as well as my half-sister. I know I should have told you about this, and about Jack and Tina. Can you ever forgive me?"

Cosi pulled Gabby's hands away, unsmiling. "I'm sorry, but you're going have to give me some time. Right now, I don't know whether to hug you or smack you. I am *sick* of secrets! And as far as being sisters, well, having a sister hasn't exactly been the greatest joy in my life."

Gabby shrugged. "Mine either."

"Still, it would have been nice to know a long time ago that we were related. Now I understand why you befriended me. I feel like an idiot."

Gabby grabbed her by the shoulders. "Hey, I wanted to hang out with you because I really like you."

Cosi sniffed. "Yeah, sure. I don't know why I should believe you, but I guess I'll help you with the baby. We were good friends once. Maybe we still can be, even if we *are* sisters."

"BLESS me, Father, for I have sinned. My last confession was three weeks ago."

Cosi was perspiring in the small dark confessional, fully aware that Father Mario knew who she was. She could see him sitting on the other side of the mesh screen, his forehead resting on his hand as if he carried the weight of the world on his very shoulders. She sat on her hands, her new method of breaking the hair pulling, twisting, chewing habit.

"I don't really have any sins on my soul this time, Father, but I wanted to talk to you privately." She saw him take his hand briefly from his forehead, and quickly return it there.

"You see there's this girl I know from school…" Cosi hesitated, trying to figure out how much she should say. "She's gotten herself in a family way, if you know what I mean."

She heard a slight shifting in the seat on the other side of the screen. "Go on."

"She wants to give the baby up for adoption to a good Catholic family. I happen to know one. My Aunt Rosa and Uncle Benny have been trying for years, but all of their babies have died. My friend wants to give her baby to you, so you can give it to Aunt Rosa."

"I see. And why doesn't your friend simply give the child to Aunt Rosa herself?"

Cosi's cheeks burned. "She wants to stay anonymous. Her reputation would be ruined."

"I see. How far along is your friend? When is the baby due?" The priest tilted his head up slightly, and looked sideways through the screen.

"I don't really know. She's not huge or anything. Maybe about halfway there?"

"Uh-huh. Are you sure there isn't something else you want to tell me? I have heard just about everything in here, you know. Nothing is going to surprise me." Cosi began to panic. What was he hinting at? Should she tell him the truth?

"I know why you would want to keep a thing like this from your mother, and it's not my place to tell her," Father Mario whispered, conspiratorially. "Your secret is safe with me."

"My what?" Cosi paused, and laughed aloud. "No! You got it all wrong. I really do have a pregnant friend. It's not me! I'm just the go-between." She looked at him skeptically through the screen. "Will you help her or not?"

"I'm sorry, Cosi. You would not believe the number of people who come in here, talking about 'a friend.' I just assumed...."

Cosi stood up, indignant. "Well, you should know me better. I'm preparing to enter the convent. I'll tell my friend you'll help her out when the time comes. I hope I can count on you."

Father Mario was mumbling something when she slammed the door of the confessional. Walking home, vibrating with indignation, Cosi went over the conversation in her head and suddenly a particular comment struck her: *I've heard just about everything in here.* She knew her father confessed his sins to Father Mario, and now that her dad was dead, maybe the priest would tell her whatever her father owned up to. Next time she would ask him.

SEVERAL weeks later, when she arrived home from school, Cosi found the aunts sitting around the kitchen table. Aunt Rosa's face was alight, and Cosi was thrilled to see her favorite aunt so alive again.

"How did you find out about this so-called "opportunity," Rosa?" Big Ange was asking, wiping her hands on her apron. She squinted at her sister.

"Father Mario told me. He says he knows the girl and she's from a good family. Catholic *and* Sicilian, he thinks. She'll probably deliver in April or May."

"What about the father?"

"Who cares about the father?" Aunt Rosa retorted. "As long as he isn't black or Puerto Rican, what's the difference?"

Cosi was aghast. "Aunt Rosa—that's so racist!"

"Who cares what race he is?" interrupted Aunt Franny. "What if he's a *Protestant?*"

Aunt Mari laughed. "Who is gonna find a Protestant to fool around with in Buffalo?"

Aunt Rosa stood up, knocking her chair backwards. "You're all just trying to rain on my parade. Bad enough I gotta convince Benny. Says he's not sure he wants a kid in the house who isn't his. He better get used to the idea or I'll dump him, like Mari dumped Tony."

"Calm down." Aunt Mari poured a tablespoon of sugar into her espresso. "Why don't you pretend it's Benny's? So, he can save face, I mean. No one has to know,"

"What do you mean?"

"Buy three or four pillows of different sizes. Buy some maternity dresses and put the smallest pillow in there now. Every other month put in a bigger pillow. Make sure the neighbors see you walking around your yard, wave to them from the porch. When the baby comes, you and Benny go off with your suitcase, like you're going to the hospital, but instead you go to Father Mario and get your baby. You come back with the baby in your arms, no pillow on your stomach, and nobody knows the difference. Benny gets to act like the proud papa." Aunt Mari sipped her espresso, made a face, and poured in more sugar. Her sisters looked at her.

"You're a genius, Mari." Aunt Rosa grinned.

"Blessed by God with a big brain *and* big heart." Aunt Franny made the sign of the cross.

"Just make sure the father is white," added Big Ange.

Cosi started to object, but then shook her head. People over 30 were a lost cause. It was up to her generation to make things right.

At the end of January, Cosi left school shortly after lunch to begin her new volunteer job. She learned she would be working with the female patients on the chronically ill ward of the psychiatric hospital, and she looked forward to it. Her job was to keep them occupied for a few hours in the afternoons, three days a week. Maybe she would find her life's purpose there, helping those lost and lonely souls.

Sitting on the warm bus, watching the cars below navigate the snowy streets, her mind flashed back to the person she had once seen lurking outside the men's ward. She shivered, hoping there was a way to avoid that part of the building.

She got off the bus on Elmwood and ran through the wet snow to the facility's entrance, jumping over half-frozen puddles, sprinting toward the twin towers of the administration building, heart pounding. She needed to find Mrs. Claymore, the office manager and volunteer coordinator.

"Hello there!" boomed Mrs. Claymore in a hearty voice, throwing open her office door. She was a large woman with enormous hands, long earlobes, and a string of pearls around her neck. "You must be Cosi McCarthy. Happy to have you join us. I'll go over some ground rules, give you a tour of the facility, and then introduce you to Gigi, our Day Room supervisor."

Mrs. Claymore walked swiftly down the hall past a section she called Ward One. "You won't be allowed to go in there, that's the Men's Ward."

Cosi glanced through the meshed window in the large steel door. She caught a glimpse of a large, light-filled room where a dozen or so men milled about. Some were shuffling along, looking at their shoes, others sat and stared at the TV. Suddenly a face appeared in the window. The light behind him silhouetted his features but she was sure she recognized him as the man she had seen looking at her before. She hurried after Mrs. Claymore who walked and talked quickly, pointing out various rooms and offices.

"This is our library—you can see we have medical texts for the staff, as well as reading material for the patients. That room is where we keep all the patient files—you are not allowed in there. The files are strictly confidential." She shook the doorknob, demonstrating that the door was locked. They crossed the lobby again to reach the other side of the building.

"Here we are. Ward Two." Mrs. Claymore unlocked a heavy door. "This is the Day Room where patients come for recreational and occupational activities. This is where you'll work until the end of the semester. Now, let me introduce you to Gigi."

Cosi followed Mrs. Claymore into a small office with one large window that overlooked the Day Room. A pimply-faced young woman sat typing with two fingers.

"Gigi, this is Cosi McCarthy. Cosi, this is Gigi Blount, our file clerk and Day Room monitor here on Ward Two. Gigi also works with our volunteers. She'll show you where the cards and games are. Any questions?"

"No, ma'am." Cosi looked out at the listless patients. "I think I'll be fine."

"Any questions, Gigi?" asked Mrs. Claymore, in a tone not quite as friendly.

"No." Gigi went back to her typing.

"Good." Mrs. Claymore smiled. "I'll leave you to it. Cosi, let me know if you have any problems." She looked pointedly at Gigi, and left. Gigi said nothing until she heard the door to the ward shut and Mrs. Claymore lock it behind her.

"Bitch!" Gigi shouted with such vehemence that it startled Cosi. "I hate that two-faced snake in the grass!" Gigi stood up and stuck her finger in Cosi's face. "Don't trust that old witch is my advice."

"OK." Cosi took the measure of Gigi, wondering if she would be friend or foe. "I'll remember that."

Gigi began typing again, and stopped. "Well, don't just stand there—go on in. Some patients will glom onto you and get mad if you spend time with anyone else, so watch out for that. Otherwise, there isn't really anything to know."

Cosi hesitated, not wanting to sound fearful, but felt she needed to ask. "Hey, that guy in the Men's Ward? You know, the tall black guy who follows you with his eyes?"

"The guy who looks like a lean, mean Reggie Jackson? That's Rico Gonzalez." Gigi smirked. "Stay *faaaar* away from him."

"Why?" Cosi shifted nervously. "Is he violent?"

Gigi shrugged. "They say he killed somebody, but that's not why." She bit off a hangnail and spit it to the side. "He's smart, and he can charm the warts off a toad."

"Well, you don't have to worry," muttered Cosi. "I will definitely stay far away."

Cosi walked timidly into the Day Room and looked around. Immediately a woman with a badly scarred face came up to her.

"Who are you?" the woman demanded, looking at Cosi's shoes and rocking from side to side. Cosi introduced herself and asked the woman her name.

"Erma, but they call me Scarface. Like the gangster." Erma gnawed her thumb. "I don't like it."

"Well, I won't call you that." Erma was silent. "What games do you like, Erma?"

"Cards. I like to play cards."

"OK. How about if we…"

Erma walked away. Cosi was bewildered. Had she offended Erma? Another woman came over holding a record album.

"Have you seen my jewels?" asked the woman, pointing to a lavishly dressed opera singer on a worn record album cover. "These jewels are mine. They were stolen from me and I need to get them back." Her voice was tinged with desperation. "I am a member of the royal family. I've been kidnapped, and they are holding me here against my will." She lowered her voice. "I need to get out. Can you help me?"

Cosi's eyes widened. Could this woman be telling the truth? She knocked on Gigi's door.

"Oh, that's Eleanor." Gigi rolled her eyes. "She has what's called, 'Schizophrenia with Grandiose Delusions.' She's harmless, unless she thinks you're one of the people plotting to keep her here. Don't be surprised if she offers you millions of dollars to help her escape."

"How long has she been here?" Cosi asked.

"About 12 years, I think." Gigi turned back to her typing.

"What? Is that normal?"

Gigi shrugged, and nodded her head at Erma. "Scarface, the one you were talking to? She's been in institutions most of her life. When she was a kid, so the story goes, she was sitting between her parents in the front seat of the car. She had a tantrum, grabbed the steering wheel, and the car hit a tree. She went through the windshield. Her family, what was left of it, said they couldn't handle her. So here she is."

Cosi stiffened. "She doesn't like to be called Scarface. Her name is Erma."

"Whatever turns you on," Gigi retorted.

Cosi went back to the Day Room and searched for her new friend. She found her staring out the window. "Want to play cards, Erma?" she asked brightly.

"Naw," said Erma, walking away.

A small, cheerful woman came over to Cosi. "Oh, don't let Scarface upset you dear." The woman smiled broadly. "I'm Sarah. Pleased to meet you."

"Hello Sarah." Cosi sighed, relieved that someone would talk to her. "I'm supposed to help you pass the time, but I'm not sure what to do. What do you think the ladies would enjoy?"

"Oh, we all like to watch television," Sarah offered, "and some of us like to play cards or games. Anything that's not too, you know, distressing."

"Well, thank you. You're the first person who's helped me. Can you show me where I can find the cards and games?"

"Oh, I wouldn't know. I just got here. Suicide watch," Sarah whispered, and smiled. "I'll be leaving in a few days. I feel better already, now that I'm back on the lithium. But don't worry—I'll help you." She knocked loudly on Gigi's window. "Hello? The new young lady would like to know where the games are. Can you help us?"

Gigi, exasperated, got up and walked over to a closet in her office. She emerged with a stack of games and a deck of playing cards. "Stop screwing around, Sarah. You know damn well where they are." Gigi dumped the stack on a table. "Now quit hassling me." Sarah shrugged and smiled at Cosi again.

Cosi spent the rest of the afternoon trying to interest the patients in playing cards, but only Erma and Sarah agreed to play. The rest of the women sat with vacant stares in front of the television, including Harriet, who seemed not to recognize her. Cosi signed out and walked back toward the lobby, dejected. How was she supposed to help these patients? She considered going back to Sister Claire to request another assignment.

Dear Joey, good grief what have I gotten myself into? How do I help people who don't seem to want help? (Nothing personal intended.)

CHAPTER TWENTY-SIX: ROLL-YOUR-OWNS AND RIOTS

By HER THIRD VISIT, Cosi figured out how to entertain the patients on Ward Two. It was Sarah who whispered that they all smoked roll-your-own cigarettes and that Virginia Gold was their preferred brand. On Friday, Cosi brought a can of tobacco and a sheaf of rolling papers and told Gigi she was taking the patients out to the courtyard for a breath of fresh air.

Outside, the women crowded around her as she handed out the rolling papers. Sarah showed her how to take a good-sized pinch of tobacco, carefully drop it in a line on the paper, lick the adhesive, twist the ends, and lick them as well. They laughed at Cosi's first attempt, a fat, misshapen thing looking nothing like the ones the patients were making, and they nearly doubled over when Cosi tried to smoke it, coughing and choking for a good five minutes.

"Next time, we do this *after* we play cards or games," she told them. "Only those who play get to share my tobacco."

In the following days, she taught several of them how to play Gin Rummy and they taught her how to roll a tighter cigarette. She began to relax, settling into a predictable routine. One afternoon, Gigi suggested she walk over to the hospital library to get a stack of magazines for the patients. "They come in from the public library every two or three weeks. Don't bother reading them. They're old news by the time they get here."

Cosi pushed through the heavy wooden library door and inhaled the familiar, musty smell she loved so well. She spied the stack of magazines in a far corner and threaded her way through tables and chairs scattered throughout the cramped space.

"Hello." It was Rico Gonzalez, looking up from behind a stack of books at one of the tables. "I was wondering when we would get a chance to meet," he said, rising from his chair.

Cosi froze. She felt it would be rude, and possibly dangerous, to turn away. "I know who you are," she stammered. It was the first time Cosi was able to see him up close. He had a half smile which softened his face and he was obviously quite handsome. Gigi's comment about his charm now made sense.

Rico laughed. "So, my reputation precedes me. You've heard I'm a legal scholar no doubt." He nodded toward a large volume open on the table in front of him. He pulled the book toward him and folded half of it over his hand to show her the cover. "This is an annotated version of the U.S. Code. You know—The Law. I'm looking to see if there is a section on protections for people with mental illness. I'm researching my rights."

He pointed to another section of the library. "Over there are the most recent editions of the American Journal of Psychiatry. I am interested in this new movement to deinstitutionalize people like me who have been involuntarily hospitalized. I think I've read everything ever written by a cat named Thomas Szasz. Ever hear of him?"

What she heard was her heart pounding in her ears. This man, according to Gigi, was a murderer. Yet here he was, researching ways to get out. Should she report this to Mrs. Claymore? He stepped away from the table and reached to an upper shelf for a book. He stopped with his arm mid-air, and turned toward her, inhaling deeply. Cosi took a step back. He grinned.

"Sorry. It's been a long time since I've been near a woman who didn't smell medicinal."

He returned to the table and leaned back in the chair, his hands clasped behind his head, his face accentuated by a thick black mustache and a finely chiseled jaw. His features clearly reflected a blend of ethnicities. His skin was a rich caramel color, setting off dark almond-shaped eyes. Cosi realized she was staring, and blushed.

"What, may I ask, brings you here?" Rico asked in a friendly manner as he stretched, cat-like. Cosi was conflicted about whether to speak to him, but something held her there.

"I'm here as a volunteer, to help the patients." She began edging backward toward the library exit. "I plan to enter the convent and commit to a life of community service."

"I see. So, we patients are some sort of do-gooder school project of yours?"

His remark irritated her and she opened her mouth to give him a piece of her mind, then shut it. Rico Gonzalez was a patient in a psychiatric hospital. What did she expect? Perfect manners? She turned and walked out the door without a word.

Do not provoke the patients, she admonished herself, *or let them provoke you*. She looked back toward the library, but Rico was nowhere in sight.

ONE afternoon near the end of a bitterly cold February, Little Ange came home with Marty, reeking of something foul.

"They tear-gassed us, Mama," she reported, rubbing her red and runny eyes.

Marty had his hand on her shoulder. "Little Ange did real well—she hung in there." He glanced at Cosi, who quickly looked away.

"It was unbelievable, Mama." Little Ange beamed and warmed to her story. "We show up at UB and the riot cops are already there, dressed in scary-looking black outfits. I guess the trouble started last night at the basketball game, so today when we went, they start arresting people for *nothing*. The crowd gets mad, and someone throws a firebomb into the library. The police started clubbing everybody. It was crazy! People were screaming, running around. We aren't doing anything wrong but we get tear-gassed! Marty stands up to the cops, tells them to go to hell. He's got guts, my Marty." She looked admiringly at him. Marty smiled at the floor.

"Your uncle's a cop, remember?" Big Ange did not look the least bit proud of either of them. "I told you. You got no business being at UB. You're grounded."

Little Ange cursed, and mother and daughter spiraled into one of their pointless screaming matches, while Marty stood awkwardly to the side. Cosi would have wondered, once, why he put up with this. It finally dawned on her that while she was paying attention to other things, the relationship between Marty and Little Ange had gotten serious.

Cosi couldn't imagine why this bothered her so much. After all, she was the one who gave Marty the brush-off. Sure, she still held a grudge that her sister predicted Marty would lose interest in her, and was annoyed by the fact that he thought Little Ange was brave, thereby suggesting she was not. But there was something more.

Cosi thought about the dinner she and Marty shared in Niagara Falls and the love songs he played on his 8-track. He had obviously felt something for her, and she had to admit, she liked being liked by someone of his character. Her mother and sister seemed to see only dollar signs when they looked at Marty, and that was unfair. There was much more to him than that.

Cosi lay on her bed, staring at the ceiling, trying to push away the images kaleidoscoping through her brain. Jack's warm lips. Marty's soft eyes. Joey's broad back and shoulders. Rico's handsome face. This was to be her year of discernment, the year she must focus on whether she truly had the calling to enter the convent. Why then, did her mind constantly drift to men and the mysteries of their bodies? She sat up and tried to shake the thoughts from her head. She needed to focus on something else.

She opened one of the books Sister Valentine had given her a while ago, *The Seven Storey Mountain* by Thomas Merton. She began reading, then paused, surprised. So even Thomas Merton, the monk who became the conscience of the peace movement, wasn't sure he was doing what God wanted. How could she possibly know what God wanted? She quickly flipped through the pages and noticed Merton wrote a lot about love, too. Many religions permitted members of their religious communities to marry, so why was celibacy mandatory for Catholic nuns and priests?

She had once asked Sister Valentine if nuns had sexual desires. "Of course," said Sister Valentine. "We're human. We just figure out ways of dealing with our natural urges."

"Like, what ways?"

"We find other distractions."

Whatever those distractions are, Cosi thought, she'd better learn them, and soon.

Dear Joey, as far as I can tell, you don't have a girlfriend. How do you deal with your natural "urges?" Just curious.

ASIDE from an exasperating argument with Sister Agatha about the infallibility of the Pope, the second semester of Cosi's sophomore year was going smoothly. Her classes were more challenging and piqued her interests, especially her AP Biology course. One morning in April, Sister Francis, the biology teacher, wrote, "*Silent Spring* by Rachel Carson" on the blackboard.

"Anyone familiar with this book?" she asked. The class was silent.

"Can anyone tell me what the words, 'The Environment' mean?" Silence. "How about 'pollution'? Anyone familiar with that term?"

Amanda Burns, the redheaded classmate who now liked to entertain them with her wise-cracks, raised her hand. "It's the smelly stuff from the steel plant." The class laughed. Cosi played with her pencil and hoped her classmates were unaware her father had worked there.

"Thank you, Amanda. You are correct, but air pollution is not the only type. Thanks to Rachel Carson, we are now aware of the damage that industrialization has had on our environment—polluting the rivers, the air, the oceans—even the soil. We are beginning to realize the damage it is doing to our own health.

"As extra credit, I'm encouraging all of you to attend one of the activities being sponsored as part of the National Teach-in on the Environment. Senator Nelson of Wisconsin is the sponsor and they're having events all over the country on April 22nd. Find an event in your neighborhood and write a short report describing what you learned."

"Are you doing the extra-credit project?" Amanda caught up with Cosi after class.

"Sure, if I can find a place that's participating."

"My brother told me there's a bunch of stuff being planned at UB. People are calling it 'Earth Day.' They're organizing protests and marches to support this new cause."

Cosi rolled her eyes. "I'm sick of protests. Students are protesting everything! What's next on the protest list? Homework?" Cosi marched off, envisioning Marty and Little Ange at UB, carrying Earth Day signs and mooning at each other.

Cosi stopped to see Sister Valentine on her way home and was surprised to learn she was having her second-grade class participate in Earth Day. "You're never too young to be a good steward of the Earth," Sister Valentine explained.

"Can I help? I'll get extra credit at school if I do."

"Sure. The kids will be planting apple seeds in paper cups. Come after school on Tuesday to help me fill the cups with soil. We'll do the planting in class on Earth Day.

Wednesday, April 22nd, dawned bright but chilly and Cosi noticed the daffodils were finally in bloom as she got off the bus at school. She was in study hall, writing up the first part of her Earth Day report, describing how the kids in Sister Valentine's class had saved seeds from their apples, when she heard her name called over the PA system.

"Cosi McCarthy, please report to the Front Office. Cosi McCarthy."

She hurried to the office, filled with dread. This could not be good. *Is something wrong with Mama?* She stopped in her tracks, barely breathing.

"Phone call." The school secretary handed her the phone.

"Hello?" Cosi choked out the word.

"Now!" Gabby groaned. "Come now! I'm having the baby."

Cosi froze. She had not seen Gabby in months and they had made no real plans for when the baby came. "Come where? Where are you?"

"Millard Fillmore Hospital. My aunt brought me here. The contractions are only …ahhhhhh…. Shit, that hurts! Get here fast, Cosi!"

The secretary looked at her. "Family emergency." Cosi dropped the receiver onto the phone with a clatter. "Please let my teachers know."

She ran out of school to the bus stop and caught the first bus on Main Street. She got off at Lafayette and peered up the street to see if the connecting bus was coming, but there was nothing in sight. She decided to run the eight blocks or so to Gates Circle and finally arrived at the hospital information desk, barely able to catch her breath.

"I'm here… my sister," hoping that would get her in the door. "She's having…a baby."

"Her name?"

"Gabriella Mortadella."

"She's still in the labor room. You can go up."

Cosi ran up the four flights of stairs in terror, her only experience on the delivery ward was the time they lost Little Benny and almost lost Aunt Rosa. What if Gabby died before she got there? She was grateful she had continued her cross-country training. She flung open the door to find Gabby screaming and the doctor calmly timing the contractions.

"We've still got a bit of a wait." The doctor looked at his watch. "I'm going to give her a spinal to ease the pain." He rolled Gabby to her side and gave her a shot. After a while, she stopped screaming.

Cosi sat with her, holding her hand, patting her face with a wet cloth until well after dark. When the doctor and nurse arrived during the final contractions, they moved Gabby into the delivery room and shooed Cosi away. The next time she saw Gabby she was in a different room, holding a tiny infant in her arms.

"Isn't he adorable?"

Cosi looked down at the tiny face, the top of its head covered with thick dark hair. She stood up straight, and looked at Gabby.

"Gabby, I hate to ask…is the father…a different race? If he is, Aunt Rosa might not.…"

Gabby, annoyed at first, started to laugh. "Don't worry. The baby will look like all the other Sicilian kids in the neighborhood. He'll fit right in."

The baby started crying and Gabby soothed him. "It's gonna be hard to give him up," she admitted. The hospital scene with Aunt Rosa flashed before

Cosi's eyes. Would they have to pull the baby out of Gabby's arms like they did Little Benny from Aunt Rosa's? Cosi decided to call Father Mario immediately, before Gabby changed her mind.

Several hours later, Cosi sat next to Gabby's uncle who agreed to drive her to the rectory at Saint Michael's, the swaddled baby sleeping on her lap. Cosi kept looking at the infant's tiny mouth, as pink and delicate as a rose petal, suckling even in sleep.

"I would keep you myself if I could," she whispered to the child while they drove. "I would love to have a baby like you." The thought of never becoming a mother filled her with a grief she had not realized was there until she held this baby. One more sacrifice she was making to save the soul of a man, she began to think, who might deserve to be in Hell.

Holding the baby tight against her chest, Cosi walked slowly up to the rectory and rang the bell. Father Mario opened the door and she reluctantly handed him the baby. "Here he is, Father."

Father Mario nodded his head and quickly blessed the small bundle. "I called your Aunt Rosa and told her the baby was on its way here. You should leave now. I haven't told her about your…involvement."

"Thank you, Father." Cosi turned to leave.

"By the way, Sister Valentine was looking for you this afternoon. Something about an Earth Day class."

"Oh no!" Cosi had forgotten all about the Earth Day project. All the way home, she tried to think of an excuse for not showing up or remembering to call Sister Valentine.

"Where you been?" asked her mother when she walked into the apartment without books or school bag. It was nearly 11 pm. She would have to lie to her mother again.

"It's Earth Day, Mama, and I got caught up in the excitement. There were classes, tree plantings, music festivals. Didn't I tell you? I thought I did. I just lost track of the time."

"Yeah, yeah. I saw it on the news," said her mother. "More hippie dippy nonsense it looked like to me. What'll they think of next? Moon Day?"

Cosi was not listening. She would remember Earth Day forever, for reasons of her own.

Dear Joey, I have to admit, in my heart of hearts, I sometimes wonder what a baby of ours might look like. Like you, I hope.

Chapter Twenty-Seven: Four Dead

Big Ange and Cosi were at the kitchen sink, planting tomato seeds in eggshell cartons in early May, when Dominic came bursting through the front door and into the kitchen. "Have you heard what happened at Kent State? The National Guard shot a bunch of students—some are dead." Dominic was panting, trying to catch his breath.

Big Ange wiped the dirt on her apron, pulled him to the kitchen table and sat him down. "What are you talking about? Kent State? What's Kent State?" Little Ange came out of her bedroom and sat close to Dominic.

"Turn on the radio," wheezed Dominic. "It's on all the stations."

They turned on Little Ange's transistor, adjusting the antenna and turning the dial until they were able to find a news station. After a few minutes and despite the static, they could make out the voice of the announcer recapping the tragedy. "Four persons, including two women, were shot and killed at Kent State University's campus today, during renewed demonstrations involving hundreds of students...."

"OK, that's it." Big Ange snapped off the radio. "None of you are going to these stupid protests after this. It's too dangerous."

"But Mama..." Little Ange began to whine.

Her mother slammed her hand on the kitchen table. "You heard what I said. You are not going to UB again, and I don't care *who* wants you to go."

Dominic wiped his sweating face with a dishtowel. "Listen to your Ma, Little Ange. Things are getting pretty friggin' ugly and people are getting hurt. Marty went crazy when he heard. He's a friggin' lunatic right now. I never seen him so angry."

Cosi wanted desperately to call Marty, worried he might do something he would later regret. Little Ange pushed her chair back, grabbed the phone and dialed Marty's number. She stretched the extension cord all the way to the bathroom and shut the door. Cosi could hear her murmuring, raising her voice now and then. *He's her boyfriend now,* Cosi reminded herself.

Although Kent State was three and a half hours southwest of Buffalo, Cosi could feel the tension from the shootings rising and rippling through her neighborhood almost immediately. She sat in front of the television every evening, watching news reports of massive student strikes across the country. A week after the event, more than 800 colleges and universities had closed and more were closing every day. Angry protestors firebombed campus buildings. There were barricades across highways and city streets and reports that military guards armed with machine guns were protecting the White House. She prayed to her statue of the Virgin Mary, but the violence continued.

"I hope you listened to me and bought that gun." Granny Archer called out from her window, as Cosi and Big Ange carried the tiny tomato seedlings to the backyard.

"To do what?" Big Ange retorted. "Shoot kids barely older than mine?"

"Got what they deserve, if you ask me." Cosi looked at the hard-bitten old woman and hoped to God she never crossed her.

The phone rang late that night. Little Ange ran to it and started screaming for her mother. "Mama, they got Marty! Oh my God, they got Marty. He's been arrested. He got beat up and now he's in jail." Cosi tried to calm her hysterical sister while her mother grabbed the phone.

"Who's this?" demanded Big Ange.

Cosi could hear Dominic shouting into the phone as her mother held the receiver away from her ear. "I'm at UB. The place is going nuts."

"Well get your big fat *culoo* outta there. No good can come from you getting involved, and you'll get yourself arrested. Marty's rich daddy probably has a good lawyer. You don't."

Once again, her mother was right. Cosi heard Marty was out of jail the next day.

The war and the campus riots now dominated every Sunday dinner conversation in Buffalo, including those at Nonna's dinner table. In a stroke of terrible timing, Cosi's cousin Vito got a low number in the draft lottery and was awaiting his letter.

"Hundreds of GIs are deserting every day," Vito told them, shoveling a forkful of manicotti into his mouth. "Whole companies are refusing to go and some guys are even joining the enemy. What the hell? We still got a job to do over there."

Cosi saw Dominic glance at Vito, then quickly help himself to the chicken *cacciatore*. Vito caught the glance, and glared at Dominic.

"What's with the black armband, cuz?" Vito squared his considerable shoulders.

"Don't give me a bunch of shit." Dominic leaned on his elbows. "Even soldiers are wearing these now. Nobody supports this freakin' war. You're stupid to go and get yourself killed when nobody thinks we can win. Even Walter Cronkite."

Vito stood up, and so did Dominic. Hands reached up to stop them from going at each other's throats. Nonna stood up too, and leaning on her cane, walked over to Dominic. She reached up and slapped him in the face, then went to Vito and slapped him too. She shuffled back to her seat, mumbling under her breath. The table went silent.

"*Mangia!*" she commanded, and the family dug in, filling their plates.

Later, Cosi cornered Vito. "Please tear up your draft card. There's no shame in it."

"I know how to take care of myself." Vito rested his big hands on her shoulders. "Besides, a couple guys in the neighborhood have low numbers too. If we enlist together, we might be in the same company. My pal, Jimmy Fingers, said his older brother enlisted with his buddies, including your neighbor, Joey Catalfano."

"Your friend's brother knows Joey? They were in Vietnam together?"

"Yeah. They ended up in the same company. Got sent to the A Shau Valley. Jimmy's brother won't talk about it though. I guess they saw a lot of bad shit in that place."

Cosi sucked in her breath. "What happened there?"

Vito shrugged. "All I know is they were both door gunners. You know, the guys who shoot machine guns from helicopters? Any more than that, you have to ask Joey."

Cosi had not seen Joey in months. She had started sitting on her top porch again to watch the sunset on warmer evenings, but he never appeared. She decided to do some research in the school library on the place Vito mentioned and learned that not long before Joey came home, the A Shau Valley was the site of a battle the GIs called Hamburger Hill.

From old newspaper clippings Cosi learned that in 10 days of fighting there, more than 70 Americans were killed and nearly 400 wounded. The US Army finally took the hill but abandoned it to the enemy soon after. That alone would mess someone up, Cosi thought, but she learned something else. Something they were calling "friendly fire" killed or wounded some of the Americans there. Some soldiers even claimed to have seen their own door gunners shoot at them, mistaking them for the enemy in the thick jungle.

Cosi's aunts were sitting shoulder-to-shoulder on the living room couch, cooing over Rosa's new baby one sunny June afternoon. "We named him Luciano, but we're gonna call him 'Lucky,' even though we're the lucky ones." Aunt Rosa beamed at Lucky who was curling his tiny fingers around her thumb.

"He is one blessed child," agreed Aunt Franny. "He coulda ended up at Father Baker's."

"I got news." Aunt Mari had been unusually quiet. "I'm getting a divorce."

The sisters gasped, horrified. "Whattaya talkin' about, Mari? You'll be excommunicated!" cried Big Ange.

"I don't care." Aunt Mari set her jaw. "My so-called husband's no longer in the picture. He's living with the girlfriend. I shoulda divorced him long ago. Time to get on with my life."

"So, you're gonna do what?" demanded Big Ange. "Get a job? Go into business?" Cosi could see the wheels turning in her mother's head, pondering whether Mari had a new moneymaking scheme and might let her in on the action.

"Better than that. I'm going to New York City!"

Big Ange put down her coffee cup. No one in the family had been to New York City since the first wave of Di Giacomos arrived at Ellis Island. It was a big, intimidating, crime-filled place more than eight hours drive from Buffalo. All they knew was that it sucked away all of Buffalo's tax dollars.

"I'm gonna go work for NOW—the National Organization for Women," Aunt Mari explained. "After Cosi told me about it, I became a member of the Buffalo Chapter. Now they want me to go to New York City to help get ready for a big march in August. How about that?"

"You can't do this, Mari." Big Ange shook her head emphatically. "You can't leave the family and go off by yourself to a big city, where you don't know nobody."

Tears welled in Aunt Mari's eyes. "Don't make this hard on me, Ange. Everybody in the neighborhood looks at me like I'm some pitiful creature. The dumpy old, jilted wife. Don't you understand? The NOW people are giving me a chance to start over."

The sisters were silent. Cosi could hear the occasional click and hiss of the gas jet hidden deep inside the old oven in the kitchen. Finally, her mother sighed.

"Fine. If that's what you really wanna do. But don't call me if things don't work out."

"You'll see, everything is gonna work out great." Aunt Mari brightened, wiping her eyes.

Cosi smiled, secretly proud of her gentle aunt who had just stood up to her older sister for the first time. Maybe there *was* something to this women's rights movement.

"So," said Big Ange, unwilling to yield completely. "What's NOW gonna do for women like me? Find us jobs? Get full-time babysitters for our kids?"

"Well," Aunt Mari took a deep breath, "you're a smart businesswoman, Ange. Take charge of your life. For example, make and sell your Infant of

Prague garments at places like the Allentown Arts Festival in a couple weeks. It's supposed to be bigger than ever—600 vendors or something. I bet you'll sell a bunch."

Cosi held her tongue. The idea that her mother was going to sell religious garments in Allentown, a downtown Buffalo neighborhood known for its artists and bohemian lifestyles, was ridiculous.

"Not a bad idea," nodded Big Ange. "I'll look into it."

Cosi helped her mother set up a display of Infant of Prague outfits on two large folding tables at the festival. They had dressed a dozen or so statues in Big Ange's most elaborate garments, and arrayed a selection of additional garments in a large fan.

"I hope to God they got chairs for us somewhere." Her mother was already sweating profusely, unused to sitting out in the sun. Cosi found a chair and her mother sat and scanned the passers-by for potential customers.

Cosi's excitement grew with the swelling crowd. The festival was more street carnival than arts venue, so she left her mother sitting and walked down the narrow streets, taking in the live bands, face-painting booths, and the "Black is Beautiful" exhibit. There were clam bars, pizza stands, and vendors selling Buffalo's famous beef-on-weck sandwiches. All the bars were open for business at noon and Cosi could smell marijuana smoke wafting from the alleys.

She drifted toward the sound of drums and bells. A group of orange-clad Hare Krishna devotees invited people to dance with them. Drawing closer, Cosi could hear them chanting,

Hare Krishna, Hare Krishna, Krishna, Hare

Hare Rama, Hare Rama, Rama, Hare ...

She marveled at a religion that seemed so full of joy and attracted so many young people. Why couldn't Catholic nuns and priests dance in the streets like this, she mused. Big Ange was mopping her face when Cosi returned to the table. "*Merda*, what a waste of time. I should be home making sauce," said her mother. "I only sold three garments."

From down the street there was a shout and the sound of breaking glass. Minutes later there were people running through the street toward them, shouting.

"*Madonne.*" Big Ange looked around, bewildered. "Now what?"

"What's happening?" Cosi called to a young guy running by their table.

"Bar fight!" he yelled over his shoulder. "Mulligan's Brick Bar. Someone called the cops. Hope you brought a hankie."

"Brought a hankie...?" Big Ange looked to Cosi. Cosi knew exactly what he meant. With all the recent protests and riots, the police were on a hair-trigger. At the first sign of an unruly mob, they would call for reinforcements, K-9 dogs, and tear-gas canisters.

"Mama, we need to leave." Cosi still had nightmares about falling and being crushed by a rioting crowd after the Buffalo Nine trial. She and her mother were still shoving things into boxes when the first crack of a tear-gas canister sounded.

"Run Mama!"

They each grabbed a box and started threading their way through throngs of people, trying to get to the church parking lot where they had left their car. Big Ange waddled as fast as she could but Cosi could see the cloud moving closer until it enveloped them, the tear gas stinging her eyes and nose. Her mother stopped and bent over, coughing and gasping for air.

"I can't breathe!" Big Ange gasped. Parents carrying frightened children ran past them. Cosi willed herself to calm down. She pulled her mother's blouse up over her nose, exposing her belly. Her mother immediately pulled it back down.

"This is not the time for modesty, Mama. Cover your face," Cosi commanded. She pulled her own cotton top over her face and reached into one of the boxes. She held an Infant of Prague garment over her mother's face as the two of them struggled down Allen Street. "Stay close to me," Cosi instructed, as people ran by them in all directions, "and whatever you do, don't fall."

Her mother wheezed and stumbled behind her until they reached the parking lot. Cosi jerked open the door and helped her mother into the car, telling her to take deep breaths.

"The world has gone crazy," panted her mother. "You can't even sell the garments of Our Savior without getting tear-gassed." Cosi put the boxes in the back seat and her mother swung around. "Where are the statues?"

"We had to leave them, Mama. We couldn't carry it all."

Her mother's face was ashen. "Go back. Those statues have been blessed."

"Go back? Can't we wait until things settle down?"

"No! Go now. Who knows what those criminals will do to the holy statues?"

Cosi steeled herself, emptied a box of garments, and face covered, made her way back to their tables through clutches of riot police. When she reached the tables, she saw one completely knocked over and the other askew. Most of the statues lay broken on the asphalt. She put the remaining statues and all the broken pieces in the box, and brought them back to her mother in the car. Big Ange had her seat reclined, her eyes half closed, and her hand resting on her heart. Cosi got in the passenger side. Her mother looked into the box and gave a sharp cry.

"More bad luck for the McCarthy family!" Big Ange shook her head. "We have to find a decent place to bury them."

When they arrived home, Cosi got the garden spade and followed Big Ange as they marched solemnly to the back of the yard. Cosi was startled to find Joey, after months of not seeing him at all, in his driveway working on a banged-up old motorcycle. *Good Lord, he has his own bike now.* Joey stared at them as they carried the box of broken statues toward the chain link fence that separated their yards, and Big Ange eyed him, shaking her head before they started digging. Mother and daughter worked in silence, then gently laid the pieces in the hole and said a prayer when they were finished. Cosi started pushing the dirt back when Big Ange stopped her.

"Let me go get the rest of the tomato plants. Why waste the space? God won't mind, and a little holiness in the hole might help the tomatoes."

Cosi thought she heard a chuckle, but when she looked over the fence, Joey seemed to be studying some part underneath the seat of his rusty bike.

Dear Joey, I am glad you're back but please don't kill yourself riding that thing. Why do Vietnam vets keep looking for ways to die?

CHAPTER TWENTY-EIGHT: SUMMER IN THE CITY

SCHOOL ENDED THE THIRD week in June. Cosi managed to finish her sophomore year with an "A" in every subject but theology. She had gotten good grades on all of Sister Agatha's tests, but got a "B-minus" as a final grade, thanks to the "D" she got in conduct. She was mollified, though, by the glowing report from Mrs. Claymore on her service at the psychiatric hospital. "Miss McCarthy," the report said, "is a model of Catholic charity, piety, and comportment."

She had also scored well on a test called the pre-SAT. "These scores are fantastic, Cosi," Sister Claire, the guidance counselor, told her. "Do you know what this means?"

"No, Sister."

"It means you're in the top 5 percent of students who have taken the test. Your scores on the actual SATs should be good enough to get you into college. You can get a teaching degree at St. Bonaventure and be on a fast track to enter our Order." Cosi started to respond but thought better of it. Her mother would never agree to her attending college, even if they could afford it. She smiled at Sister Claire, who seemed to see a brighter future for her than Cosi saw for herself.

Cosi ran home from the bus stop, threw her book bag in a corner, lay back on her bed and smiled. School was over! Summer stretched out in front of her like a long, languid cat. She was thankful to be back in Sister Valentine's good graces after the Earth Day fiasco, had new babysitting jobs, and even considered resuming her daily trips to the Mass Avenue pool, then decided against it. Gabby wouldn't be there, so why subject herself to daily sightings of Marty and Little Ange, or Jack and Tina, rubbing suntan lotion all over each other? Instead, after watching the sunrise each morning, she would go for a long run through the neighborhood to get back in shape.

Cosi was surprised how flabby she had become after quitting the cross-country team to work at the hospital. She set a new goal for herself each day until she could run all the way to the foot of Porter Avenue where it met the Niagara River. She loved to run by the anglers standing on the break wall, casting their lines in the early morning light. By mid-July, she was turning left on Porter and running all the way to the end of La Salle Park, along the Black Rock Canal for a couple of miles, looping through the park, and back home without stopping. She would sprint up the back stairs, feeling strong, independent, and finally in charge of her life.

"How about some eggs in the hole?" Big Ange would sometimes ask, standing over her frying pan, hollowed-out slices of Italian bread with an egg in the middle already sizzling.

"Not hungry," Cosi would say, resisting the temptation. "Just coffee."

Early one morning, sitting on her back stoop and lacing up her running shoes, Cosi saw Joey walk into his backyard. He pushed his motorcycle out into the driveway without noticing her. He leaned it on the kickstand, and began to lay out rags and polish when he spotted her watching him. He lifted his chin at her, in greeting.

"Hi," called Cosi, with a little wave. They looked at each other for a few seconds and said nothing. Joey began polishing his bike in long, loving strokes. She got up to start her run, thought better of it, and walked over to the fence. He made circles of wax on his gas tank and took pains to avoid smearing any on the Harley Davidson logo. She took a deep breath.

"I haven't seen you in a long time. Guess you're hanging out with that motorcycle gang."

Silence. More waxing. Joey searched around and grabbed a different rag. He bent down to buff the black metal. She wanted to leave, go for her run, but curiosity got the better of her.

"My cousin Vito knows a friend of yours, who was with you in the A Shau Valley."

Joey stopped rubbing. He stood up and narrowed his eyes. "What about it?"

"I know it was bad…I read about it. If you ever want to talk…" Her heart thudded loudly in her ears.

He cut her off. "You wanna talk about your dead father?"

"What? No." She wondered what he knew about that.

He folded his arms across his chest. "There are things I don't bring up with you, and things you don't bring up with me. *Capisce?*"

Cosi, her face aflame, nodded. She turned to run but he called after her.

"Hey, Stretch. What, are you on the track team now?"

She stopped, startled, and faced him, jogging in place. She wasn't sure, but he seemed to be eyeing her long, muscled legs, barely covered by her running shorts.

"The running is doing you good. Keep it up."

He went back to work on his bike. She turned and shot out of the yard as if Coach was standing there, holding her stopwatch.

OK Joey, I'm dying to ask. What was that all about? Are you finally noticing I'm not a kid anymore?

JUNE was hotter than usual and it was stifling in the McCarthys' small apartment. Big Ange kept sticking her head under the kitchen faucet to let the cool water run through her hair. Nino sat in his underwear, playing with his toys on the linoleum floor, leaving little imprints of moisture wherever his thighs touched. Cosi kept a wet washcloth on her neck.

Little Ange sat in front of the apartment's only fan, whirring loudly in the living room window. "Mama, Marty's coming over tonight. Can you make my favorite cake? *Pleeease?*"

Her mother grunted. Cosi groaned. It was Little Ange's 17th birthday and she expected them to make a *Cassatta Siciliana* cake, with ricotta cream filling and a candied fruit topping. The cake was complicated to make and the oven would be on for at least half an hour.

"How about an ice cream cake this year?" her mother suggested, fanning her armpits.

"That's really dumb, Mama. It would melt in five minutes in this heat. Marty's taking me out for a fish fry tonight, and we want cake when we get back."

Little Ange graduated from high school in June and had been insufferable ever since. She was working full time at Tops Supermarket as a cashier and making decent money, enough to buy a new outfit every week, which she paraded in front of Cosi. Tonight, she was wearing a lime green, bell-bottom pantsuit, with a floral shell and a headband that matched.

"Got to look good for my man," she purred, inspecting her newly polished nails. "I wouldn't be surprised if he pops the question as a birthday present. Won't I look good with a diamond ring on my finger?"

Cosi watched out the front window while Little Ange and Marty walked arm-in-arm to his red Mustang. *Is he really ready to marry her?* Walking back into the hellish kitchen, Cosi felt a hollow place in her stomach, but she shook it off and went back to making her sister's cake.

Cosi was watching the news later that week when a story about a "Strike for Equality" in New York City came on. Cosi recognized a few of the women speaking into the microphone, including Gloria Steinem, Bella Abzug, and Betty Friedan herself. They talked about women having the right to jobs and education, to childcare, even the right to abortion.

As the news camera panned the crowd, Cosi tried to read the signs. She saw one that read: "Why Did I Wait to Dump the Bastard?" and shrieked. "Mama, come quick. Aunt Mari's on TV!"

Big Ange and Little Ange ran into the living room and peered at the small screen. "Where?" Little Ange's face was inches from the glass.

"Well, she's gone now," Cosi sighed, exasperated. "She was holding a sign."

"How could you tell it was her?" Her mother wanted to know.

"I could see that big mole of hers—geez, don't I know my own aunt?"

While the three argued, their eyes remained fixed on the small screen. They stopped arguing when the newscaster compared the feminist movement to a disease, and called the women who were protesting bubbleheads.

Big Ange was furious. "You got some nerve! Braless OK, but bubbleheads? That's my brainy sister you're talking about!" Cosi agreed with her mother. It was about time men stopped treating them all like dimwits, and take this movement seriously.

Little Ange rolled her eyes. "Mama, how many times do I have to tell you, people on TV can't hear you? Anyways, you saw most of them women. They couldn't get a man if they wanted to. That's really why they're pissed off." Having said her piece, Little Ange resumed the bad mood she had been in all week. Marty had given her a necklace for her birthday instead of a ring.

"It would be nice if those women were right." Cosi folded her arms. "If we could compete with men in the workplace, maybe we wouldn't be so broke, Mama. Little Ange wouldn't be moping around waiting for a ring, and I wouldn't have to become a nun."

"Whatta you talkin' about?" snapped her mother. "Who do you think runs most of the schools and hospitals in Buffalo? *Nuns.* Think about it. Who's more feminiss than a nun?"

Cosi had to admit, her mother had a point. She thought about the smart, college-educated sisters who taught at Holy Martyrs, or who were the school's administrators, and realized her impression of women who entered the convent had changed completely. Most of her high school teachers were savvy women who were "with it," dedicated to preparing their young charges for college, if not the convent.

Cosi was still angry about the results of the Kuder Occupational Test she had taken at school, which said a male with her scores should consider a career as a biologist, journalist, or psychiatrist. If these same scores belonged to a female, the results suggested, she should consider becoming a nurse, secretary, or drama teacher. How infuriating that she still couldn't be whatever she wanted! She could see the world was changing for women, thanks to people like Aunt Mari, but not fast enough.

ALL through the summer, Cosi looked to see if Joey was working on his motorcycle before she left for her morning run. She never saw him, only heard him late at night through her open window, the *bladda-bladda-bladda* of the engine coming and going while she tried to sleep in her stifling bedroom. She began to notice a pattern. He left at midnight and came back sometime around 4 a.m. When the bars closed, she supposed.

One torpid night, so still she could hear a dog peeing on a tree while she lay sweating in her bed, Cosi decided to creep downstairs with a glass of water to try to cool off. She loved to sit on the back stoop in the wee hours, catching just a hint of breeze, and listening to the night bugs sharing their endless gossip. She had checked her clock before she left the bedroom. It was just past 2 a.m. and Joey was not due back for a couple of hours. No one else should be out.

She kicked off her slippers, and sat with her bare feet and elbows resting on the cool concrete steps. She was looking at the stars when she heard a door open and saw Joey walk out the back door to his driveway. He had appeared too suddenly for her to run back upstairs, so she froze, hoping he would not notice her. He stared straight ahead for a while, smoking, then turned his head and looked straight at her. She flushed.

The next thing she knew he was in her backyard, sitting next to her, taking stock of the glass of water and her baby doll pajamas. "Too hot to sleep?"

"Um, yeah." Mortified, she slid her feet back into her slippers.

"Do you know what I do when it's too hot?" Joey stubbed out his cigarette on the concrete. "Go for a ride."

"Really?" she giggled in spite of herself. "That noisy motorcycle helps you sleep?"

"I'll show you." He took her firmly by the hand and pulled her up.

"What? No!" She whispered. "I can't go for a ride like this!"

"Why not? You can wear my helmet. No one will know it's you."

She protested all the way to his garage and continued arguing in hushed tones while he strapped the helmet on her head. She looked up at her apartment windows. No lights.

"Two things you got to remember," he said. "Don't let your bare legs touch the hot pipes, and hang on tight."

Why am I doing this? This is crazy, she told herself as Joey lifted her easily onto the seat. She remembered being in his arms like this when she had fallen as a child. He grabbed her hands and clasped them around his chest. He kicked the starter several times before the engine roared, and they shot down Fargo Avenue, past a barking dog expressing his extreme annoyance.

Now the night air felt cool and delicious. They headed west toward the river, and turned left on Niagara Street. A group of men standing around an outdoor clam bar turned to look when they blew past. Joey maneuvered the old Harley through Front Park, then La Salle Park, and on to the outer harbor, finally pulling into a deserted parking lot beneath the old Buffalo lighthouse.

He helped her off the bike and started walking. The entrance to the lighthouse had several boards nailed across it along with a large "Keep Out" sign. Joey squatted; his leather jacket stretched tight against his back. She noticed the Road Vultures insignia was gone.

"Crawl underneath," he instructed.

Cosi followed him up the stairs to the top. Joey walked quietly across the trash-strewn floor and stood by a glassless window, looking out over the Buffalo Harbor while Cosi picked her way carefully beside him in her thin slippers.

"How long has this lighthouse been here?" Cosi had never heard of it.

"It was built in 1833," said Joey as he lit another cigarette and inhaled, "when Buffalo was actually a happening place, thanks to the Erie Canal. I come here a lot. To be alone."

Cosi stared in surprise. Here she had been thinking he spent his nights in bars. "It's beautiful, isn't it?" She looked at the tiny boat lights winking far out on the lake. A gauzy moon, barely visible through the sultry night air, seemed to make this perfect night complete. She couldn't believe she was standing here, in this secret hideaway. With Joey.

He looked at her. They were standing so close she could feel the heat radiating from his body. There was something else, too, a tension, taut and feral, that made her shiver again. He put his arm tentatively around her shoulders.

"Getting cold?"

They looked at each other, and for a moment, she thought he might kiss her. She lifted her chin and looked in his eyes, smiling, while her heart beat out a military tattoo.

He froze suddenly and dropped his arm. He walked quickly to the other side of the lighthouse while she stood awkwardly in her skimpy pajamas, feeling confused and very exposed. Without a word, Joey headed down the stairs. Cosi followed mutely behind him. He handed her the helmet and stomped on the kick-starter while she searched her mind for something to say, desperate to make the evening magical again.

They eventually pulled up in front of Joey's house. Cosi followed him while he heaved the heavy machine up the driveway and into his garage. She held the helmet out to him, fighting back tears. "Go get some sleep," he murmured, turning off the garage light.

Dear Joey, I cried myself to sleep after our ride. Please tell me what I did wrong so I don't do it again.

CHAPTER TWENTY-NINE: SPITE SEX

W HEN SCHOOL STARTED AGAIN in September, Cosi was shocked to see Gabby standing in the locker room. She walked over to her as metal doors slammed and girls hurried past with armloads of books. "What are you doing down here Gabby, slumming with the Juniors?"

"I decided to come back and finish school." Gabby was shapely and beautiful again, showing no residual signs of her pregnancy. "Sister Matthew said I have to retake last semester's classes, but I might be able to graduate next June. Maybe we can take some classes together."

Cosi marveled at Gabby's insouciance. Surely, most of the school had noticed her absence and wondered about it. "Hasn't anyone asked you about... you know."

"Nah. Everybody knows the deal. When a Catholic girl disappears from high school for six months, it's no mystery."

"Why are girls in Catholic schools, who are supposed to become nuns or go off to college, ruining their chances by having sex?"

Gabby looked at her and grabbed some books from her locker. "Sometimes," Gabby said, carefully shutting her locker door, "the girl doesn't have a say, Cosi." Gabby waved to some friends and hurried off.

What did Gabby mean by that? Had she been forced to have sex and left to deal with the consequences? Cosi could feel the bile rising in her stomach. What gave men the right to pressure girls into having unwanted sex? Why did she have to work so hard to be virtuous, when men like her father and Gabby's mysterious "boyfriend" could do what they wanted without repercussions? It was time to demand some answers.

"Bless me Father, for I have sinned, in my mind, that is, many times." Cosi paused.

"Go on, child." She could see Father Mario's profile through the darkened screen.

Cosi took a deep breath. "Father? Did you ever hear my father's confession?"

"I hear everyone's confession. Why do you ask?"

"I'm worried my father died with sins on his soul—without having confessed them." She hesitated. "He had sex with women other than my mother."

Father Mario shifted in his seat. "Put your mind at rest, child. Your father confessed his transgressions many times. I'm sure he's in the hands of the Lord."

"Exactly how many women did he transgress with, Father Mario?"

The seat creaked as the priest leaned away from the small window. "You know I can't discuss what someone tells me in confession, Cosi."

She snorted. "You men all cover for each other, you mean."

Father Mario leaned forward and peered at her through the screen. "Don't be so quick to judge your father. He was a good man, but he had a man's appetites."

Cosi rose without a word. She wasn't supposed to judge her father? She was supposed to protect her virginity at all costs, but men could screw as many women as they wanted? The more she thought about it, the angrier she got. She decided she would find a guy and have sex with him, just for spite.

In October, Uncle Danny was one of thousands of local steelworkers who lost their jobs. There was talk of other layoffs too, along the waterfront, at the Ford Stamping plant, even at General Mills. What would Buffalonians do without the comforting smell of Cheerios in the air?

It was the only topic of conversation at Nonna's dinner table on Sunday. "This ain't good," Uncle Carm fretted, reaching over and helping himself to two more meatballs. "These layoffs are gonna ruin the city."

"Tell me about it," Big Ange fumed. "What am I supposed to do now? Throw Danny and Joanie and their five kids out on the street because they can't pay the rent?"

"I got a letter from Mari," Aunt Franny whispered, hoping her husband wouldn't hear. She says a lotta people from Buffalo are moving to New York City. She thinks we should too."

"That's the dumbest thing I ever heard!" yelled Uncle Carm. "We should all move to a big, dirty shit hole that's going bankrupt? Your sister's an idiot."

"She's not an idiot," said Aunt Franny defiantly, for the first time in her life.

Big Ange twirled her spaghetti. "If I ever win on Dialing for Dollars, I'm moving the family to Florida, not the Big Apple. New York ain't much warmer than Buffalo."

Cosi found the endless talk of job layoffs and money problems pointless and depressing. The psychiatric hospital, strangely enough, was the one place she could go and take her mind off all these problems by helping the patients with simple distractions. One afternoon, as the autumn sun sparkled through the meshed windows, Cosi sat next to Erma watching the Ward's favorite soap opera. Rico appeared in the doorway and leaned against the heavy metal frame, arms folded, smiling at the women in the Day Room.

"Get the hell out of here, creep!" shouted Erma. Several women began muttering under their breaths. "Pervert!" screamed Erma.

Cosi stood up and marched toward Rico. "Who let you in here? I thought you were confined to the Men's Ward."

"No ma'am." Rico flashed a friendly smile. "I have a job in the Laundry along with full grounds privileges. Gigi said I could come in for a minute." He waved at Gigi who looked away and resumed her typing. He reached into his pocket. "I know you and I got off on the wrong foot. So, I brought you a peace offering. I made it, of course. Not much opportunity to shop while you're in here."

"What is it?" asked Cosi, surprised.

In the palm of his hand lay a delicate, exquisitely carved wooden cross. He held it out to Cosi. "I thought you could wear it when you become a nun."

"It's beautiful." She was genuinely moved. "How did you learn to do this?"

He laughed. "I've spent so many hours in the wood shop I could have built a sailboat by now. You'll have to buy the chain for it. I hope you like it."

"Get the hell out," Erma shouted again. Rico winked at Cosi, and left.

THE phone rang one evening after dinner while Cosi was doing her homework. She ignored it until she remembered Little Ange was working the evening shift at Tops, and her mother and Nino were at Nonna's. Cosi grabbed the receiver on the sixth ring. It was Dominic.

"Marty's getting ready to leave for Canada," he blurted, without preamble.

"Why? He just turned 17. It can't be to avoid the draft."

"You haven't seen him lately, Cosi. He is out of control. He says he hates this country and can't stay here another day."

Cosi's mind was racing. *Is that really why he's leaving in such a hurry?* Maybe he'd gotten mixed up with violent people like the Weathermen, and was on the lam from the FBI.

Dominic paused. "He's leaving tonight and wants to say goodbye to you. Can you walk to the corner? We'll pick you up."

"Me? What about Little Ange? Can't he wait until she gets home from work?"

"No," said Dominic, and hung up.

She expected to see Marty's red Mustang but found Dominic's battered Corvair idling by the curb. Dominic pulled the front seat forward so she could climb into the back with Marty. They sat close together on the vinyl seat, and Cosi could see Marty was agitated and perspiring. They drove the short distance to a parking lot near the Peace Bridge entrance. Marty took a deep breath and let it out slowly. "Thanks for coming, Cosi."

The change in his appearance had startled her. Gone were his beard and long hair. He was dressed in a plain blue button-down shirt and jeans, and looked like a preppie on his way to college, not an angry young war protestor.

"Where have you been? What's with this new look?" Cosi wanted to know.

"The cops have lots of pictures of me," he explained apologetically. "Why make it easy on them?" He licked his dry lips. "I guess Domo told you I'm on my way to Toronto."

"Yeah, but not the real reason why. And what about Angie? She thought you were about to propose."

Marty grimaced and shook his head. "Your sister's a nice girl. She was fearless when things got ugly, and I admire that. But I don't want her involved in my new troubles. I got too close to some bad characters. And I don't know where she got the idea I wanted to marry her."

"Well, you sort of led her on," Cosi snapped.

"Look Cosi, I know things haven't been right with us, ever since that guy next door…" Marty paused when he saw a cloud pass over her face. He shifted in his seat. "I wanted to say goodbye to you because, well…" He reached for her hand. She pulled it away. He stared out the window. "Look, I know you're committed to becoming a nun, and I respect that. But…" he hesitated. "I thought there was chemistry between us, you know? Maybe it was just me hoping," he shrugged, "but I couldn't leave for Canada without telling you…" He took another deep breath. "I'm in love with you, Cosi."

She stared at him. Then, without a word, she turned to open the car door. He grabbed her arm. "Why do you think I came over to your house whenever I could? Sure, Angie encouraged me but I kept coming over just to be near *you*." He shook his head. "I hoped things might change, that I'd have another chance, and now I might never see you again. It's killing me."

She had struggled for so long to suppress her feelings for him that she could not give voice to them now. Her mind went blank and she sat mute.

Marty ran his hand through his short hair. "Would it be OK if I kissed you goodbye?"

She nodded reluctantly. The kiss was delicate and sad.

A car with a Canadian license pulled alongside them, engine idling. Dominic motioned for the driver to wait. "Well, this is goodbye then," said Marty. Dominic opened the door to let Marty climb out. Marty reached over and pulled the door shut. "Do you think I have any kind of chance with you? In the future, I mean."

"No," she said, turning away.

He brought her hand to his lips and kissed it. "Few people discover what their true calling is at such a young age. Take good care of yourself, Cosi McCarthy. If you ever change your mind and decide not to enter the convent, remember there's a man who loves you just north of the border."

Marty got out of the car and started walking. "Wait..." Cosi called, and scrambled out of the back seat. Marty turned back, hopeful.

"I want to give you something." She took off her scapula, put it over his head, and pressed it gently against his heart.

"Wear this and think of me. If you're ever in trouble, it will protect you."

Marty murmured his thanks and got into the waiting car. She watched the red taillights disappear over the bridge, and then collapsed, sobbing, against Dominic's car. Alarmed, Dominic jumped out and guided her to the passenger seat. "He shouldn't have gotten you all upset like that," he said, soothingly.

Months of Cosi's pent-up sexual tension and frustration exploded in a rage that frightened Dominic. "You have *no* idea why I'm upset Domo!" she cried, and the words flowed in a torrent. "I *want* to be in love. I *want* to be with a man. It's my *mother* who wants me to become a nun, because *she* hates men. *I* don't hate men. Why can't I fall in love, just once?"

Dominic stared at her. "Whoa. Where's this coming from?"

Cosi struggled to control her sobs. "All these "holy" men I've been reading about? Saint Augustine, Thomas Merton, Siddhartha? They got to fall in love, and *make* love, before committing themselves to God. Why can't I?"

Dominic handed her his handkerchief. "Calm down now. You're talking crazy."

Cosi looked out the window at the streetlights arcing over the Peace Bridge all the way to Canada, and took a deep breath. "No, Domo. It's all starting to finally make sense."

Dear Joey, something changed in me tonight. I've decided to find out what love (and sex) is all about.

Chapter Thirty: Girl on Fire

"THAT SHITHEAD!" SCREAMED LITTLE Ange. "What did I ever see in that jerk? I did everything he wanted and what did he do for me? *Nothing*. Now he leaves without so much as a goodbye!"

"Men," Big Ange tut-tutted. "What did you expect?"

Cosi kept a low profile at home, hoping her sister would never hear about Marty's farewell at the Peace Bridge. One dreary November afternoon, Little Ange ambushed Cosi as she walked in the door. She was grinning slyly for the first time in a month.

"Come here, I got something to tell you," Little Ange dragged Cosi into their room. "Are you ready for this?"

"Shoot," Cosi smiled. She was trying to be nicer to Little Ange.

"I'm moving to New York City with Aunt Mari. I'm gonna be a fashion model!" Little Ange hugged herself, dancing around in a circle. She thrust a business card at Cosi. "Read it."

Cosi read, "George Bingaman, Talent Scout, New York, NY, 212-338-9970. So what?"

Little Ange stopped dancing. "So what? He's a scout for all the big modeling agencies, you lamebrain." Little Ange sighed extravagantly and sat on her bed. "I'm at the Main Place Mall, on my way to buy new shoes, minding my own business. This guy stops me and says 'Hey pretty lady, you should be a fashion model,' and he gives me this card. And of course, I think, what a stupid pick-up line, so I say, 'I bet you get all the girls with a line like that.' He looks at me, real serious like, and says, 'I'm not kidding. I think you could be a model. Why don't you come to my studio and we'll take some pictures, see how it goes." Names some big agencies he works for, so I finally figure out, this guy is legit!"

"Angie, I hope to God you're not thinking of going!"

Little Ange laughed. "I already went, and got the pictures back. Wanna see?"

She reached into her suede purse and pulled out a manila envelope. On top of the stack was a photo of Little Ange, standing with her back to the camera, naked with the exception of a towel covering her rump. The next shot was of her lying naked on her stomach, her head tilted coyly to the side. The photos were not Penthouse pornographic, but left little to the imagination.

"Angie, I can't believe this!" Cosi shoved the stack back into the envelope. "These aren't the kind of pictures modeling agents take."

Little Ange grabbed the envelope. "What do you know about modeling agents? George is the real deal. He's gonna introduce me to people at the Ford Modeling Agency. They're *famous*, in case you don't know."

"Angie, listen to me," Cosi was frantic now. "Please don't do this. This does not make any sense. This guy could be a murderer or a rapist."

"You're just crapping all over my plans because you're jealous." Little Ange turned on her. "You think you're better than me. Well, screw you! You're not, and I'm gonna prove it."

"I'm just asking you to be careful. You can't trust anyone these days."

"Hah! You should talk about trust. You think I don't know how you were scheming to steal Marty from me? Oh yeah, Dominic spilled his big fat guts. I don't trust a word you say, backstabber!"

They went to bed that night without speaking and Cosi slept fitfully. When the alarm went off at 6 a.m. the next morning, Little Ange was already up, fully clothed, filling her brown Samsonite suitcase.

"What are you doing?" Cosi looked apprehensively from her sister to the suitcase.

"What do you think I'm doing?"

"Where are you going? You're not going to New York with that guy, are you?"

"Yep. Me and George are outta here in about…" she looked at the clock, "two minutes."

"You're sneaking out without telling Mama? She'll be furious."

Little Ange sneered. "Really? You think she gives a shit about me? Everything is 'Cosi this and Cosi that.' She'll be glad I'm gone." She snapped her suitcase shut and looked out the window. "George is here."

Cosi jumped up and grabbed her arm. "Please don't go, Angie. What if this guy kills you and throws you in the river? How would we know?"

Little Ange shrugged her off, her face hard and determined. "Look, I know you're gonna run and tell Mama, but give me a little head start. For once in your life, help me out. This is my chance to escape, Cosi. Give me a break." With a dramatic wave, she was out the front door.

Cosi immediately went to her mother's room, but by the time Big Ange was fully awake and understood what was happening, Little Ange was gone. Fat tears rolled down her mother's cheeks as Cosi told her what she knew. Big Ange walked into her daughters' bedroom in her nightgown and slippers, sat on Little Ange's bed, and shook her head, bewildered.

"How could she go to New York without telling me? What did I do to deserve this? All my life, I put my family first. I cook, make clothes, and since your father died, I try to scrape a few bucks together as best I can for you kids. I don't do anything for myself. And you know what? Nobody appreciates it. You remember that, Cosi. No matter what a mother does, or what sacrifices she makes, her children turn and walk away without a second thought."

Her mother's anguish surprised her, and Cosi tried to explain, "Angie thought you'd be glad she was leaving." The two had fought and argued for as long as Cosi could remember, so she had expected to encounter her mother's anger, not heartache.

"I love all my children," sobbed Big Ange. "Why would I be glad?"

Cosi tried to comfort her as best she could. "Don't worry Mama, I'm sure she'll be back."

"No." Big Ange wiped her tears. "She's gone. My heart has to lock the door behind her."

His lips brushed her eyelids and traveled down the side of her face. His tongue probed the inside of her mouth while his hands moved slowly over her breasts and down between her legs. He moved her legs apart as he began to…

Cosi awoke in a hot sweat. She was having the dream again, the one with the Faceless Man. She could see every detail of his body, but could never recognize who he was.

She kicked off the blankets and waited for her body to cool down. She rubbed the insides of her thighs, trying to make the sensations go away. *Damn it.* It was Saturday. This afternoon she was supposed to go to confession.

She decided, for once, to skip it and spend the afternoon with Gabby. Gabby was babysitting, bouncing little Lucky up and down on her knee. "Who's my handsome little man?"

"You shouldn't say things like that," Cosi warned. "You'll confuse him."

"Like he'll remember." Gabby set the baby on the floor. "Hey," she said, changing the subject. "Tomorrow's December 8th. How are you celebrating your 'Sweet 16' birthday?"

"Not sure. Meatball's having a Christmas party next weekend. Maybe I'll go."

Gabby looked thoughtful. "Remember the last party at Meatball's house? Sex, drugs, and rock n' roll? Be careful this time. Once you're 16, everyone knows you ain't jail bait no more."

Cosi remembered Meatball's party all right. Loud music, rooms thick with pot smoke, and couples in dark corners. She had been uncomfortable that first time. This time it would be different. "That's right," she said, coolly. "I won't be jail bait anymore."

On the night of the party, Cosi dressed in a new, snug-fitting outfit, bought with birthday money from Aunt Mari, who must be doing okay on her own in New York City, Cosi decided. Cosi was far taller than her mother now, and the hip-hugger jeans she wore emphasized her long legs and newly slim waist. She dabbed patchouli oil behind her ears and in the hollow of her throat, hoping the musky smell resembled the pheromones she'd read about in the yellow sex book.

She leaned over and brushed her long hair vigorously forward, then stood up quickly and pulled it back into a ponytail. She put on mascara and lipstick and did a serious appraisal of the final look. Her black hair, now well past her shoulders, shone from the brushing. Her blue-green eyes sparkled behind the dark mascara, and the red lipstick emphasized the fullness of her lips.

The party was well underway when she arrived with Dominic, who insisted on escorting her. They walked into the backyard and smelled roasting pork. Smoke appeared to be coming from a pit covered with corrugated tin from an old roof. Some fifty people were squeezed into the small yard with an even larger crowd inside the house. Meatball walked around like a Master of Ceremonies, handing out beers, slapping people on the back, shaking hands with new arrivals.

"Meatball!" yelled Dominic. "You remember my cousin Cosi, right?"

Meatball came over and laid a beefy paw on Dominic's shoulder. "Domo, my man. Good to see you. Your cousin, you say? How are you, pretty lady?

Meatball's eyes traveled slowly over her sweater and jeans and lingered at her exposed navel. "Say," his voice was low and oleaginous. "We've met before, haven't we? I wouldn't forget those curves. Like the racetrack at Watkins Glen, am I right Domo?"

"Careful." Dominic was not smiling. "She's planning to be a nun someday."

Cosi smiled at Meatball and ignored her cousin. "I turned 16 last Tuesday. I've got plenty of time before I become a nun. I was sort of hoping to celebrate tonight."

"Well, walk into my parlor, said the spider to the fly," Meatball laughed, put his arm around her shoulder, and ushered her into the house.

"Hey," called Dominic, alarmed.

Cosi looked over her shoulder. "It's OK, Domo, don't worry."

They walked to Meatball's room. Once inside, he shut the door, locked it, and turned on the lava lamp, casting a soft glow. He patted the colorful Indian batik blanket that lay across his bed, motioning her to sit near him.

She froze. She thought Meatball would bring out his water pipe like last time so she could shed some of her inhibitions. She had not planned to jump into bed with him.

"I was hoping we could smoke some pot?"

"Huh? Oh, sure. Hold on just a minute."

He went to his closet and pulled out a rainbow-colored ceramic bong and a large plastic bag. She watched carefully while he filled a metal bowl attached to the side of the pipe.

"Hold this." He handed her the pipe. "We need some mood music." He put on an album by The Doors, and Cosi recognized the eerie, sitar-like strains of "The End." Meatball lit the pot and inhaled deeply. He held the smoke in his lungs for what seemed an eternity. "Here you go," he said in a tight voice, still not exhaling.

Cosi took the pipe and looked at it, trying to figure out how it worked. Her only experience with smoking was the one puff she had taken from a roll-your-own cigarette at the psychiatric hospital. She put the pipe up to her mouth and looked at him expectantly when he finally exhaled with a long whoosh. He brushed a strand of hair back from her face.

"Go ahead." He held the match to the small bowl again. "Take a deep breath."

She inhaled deeply, following his example, but was unprepared for the harshness of the smoke. She choked and coughed violently, pressing her hands against her chest, gasping for air. Meatball thumped her back and she dropped the bong on the bed, neither one of them noticing the smoldering pot that spilled out across the beautiful cotton bedspread. It caught fire and Cosi shrieked. Meatball tried to douse the flames with the remaining water left in the bong.

"Get more water!" yelled Meatball.

Cosi ran and tried to open the locked door. "I can't get out!" she screamed, while the room filled with smoke. Meatball moved surprisingly fast for a large individual. He unlocked and yanked the door open in one motion, and ran out, smoke wafting from the door behind him.

"Fire!" screamed someone at the party. Everyone rushed for the doors of the old wooden house. Meatball ran into the kitchen, grabbed a cooler full of beer and ice, and dumped the contents on his bed. The small fire went out quickly. Meatball was still trying to fan the remaining smoke toward the open windows when the first fire truck pulled up.

"Everything is under control gentlemen," Meatball told the firefighters. They looked irritated and insisted on finding the source of the fire. One spied the large burn hole on the bed.

"Did anyone ever tell you not to smoke in bed?" quipped one of the firemen. They checked out the smoking pit in the back and politely turned down Meatball's offer of beer.

When they left, Meatball stood on his back porch and whistled. All eyes turned toward him. He cupped his hands around his mouth and yelled, "Hey, everybody. We had a little excitement, but it's all over. Who's ready to eat some pig?"

Everyone cheered. Meatball, Dominic, and several other guys refilled the beer cooler and brought out bottles of "Mad Dog" 20/20 and cheap whiskey from the smoky kitchen, setting up a makeshift bar in the blackened slush next to the roasting pit.

Cosi tried to make herself invisible. Her plans to get stoned, have a good time, and maybe even lose her virginity had gone up in smoke, literally. She was too embarrassed to face Meatball again. She waited until he went inside, told Domo she was walking home, grabbed a nearly full bottle of Mad Dog, and left the party.

The fortified wine felt good going down, like the whiskey her father used to give her at the Saint Patrick's Day parade. It was not long before it had its desired effect. She dropped the empty bottle in the snow and walked unsteadily up Fargo Avenue.

When Cosi reached her front steps, she sat down heavily, the lower half of her face numb. She shut her eyes, trying to stop the spinning, and heard the clink of metal coming from the yard next door. She stood up and stumbled down Joey's driveway, bumping between the side of her house and Mr. Catalfano's car. When she reached the garage, she saw Joey inside, working on his motorcycle. She leaned precariously against the wall. Maybe the day wouldn't be a total loss.

"Hi, hassome," Cosi slurred.

Joey stood up, dropped his wrench, and caught her as she stumbled forward. She tried to look longingly into his eyes, but the look he was giving her was not encouraging. *Who cares?* She decided. *I'm doing this.* Cosi reached up and put her hand behind his head and pulled his face toward hers, pressed her chest into him, and kissed him. She tried to slide a hand down the front of his jeans.

He grabbed her arms. "Stop it."

She blinked, took a step back and swayed. "Please, Joey. I want to."

He took a deep breath. "You're drunk."

She started to cry and crumpled to her knees as if she were about to pray. She leaned against the wheel of his motorcycle and clung to it; her face pressed against the gleaming spokes.

"C'mon." He pulled her to her feet. "Let me help you home."

Cosi avoided her mother's face when she opened the front door. She heard Joey mumbling "…a touch of the flu" and her mother grunting. Joey helped Big Ange lay Cosi on her bed and the room began to spin again. Cosi reached for the wastebasket and threw up over and over again. Joey held her ponytail away from her face and handed her a tissue when she finished.

He left the room without another word. Cosi could smell the sour vomit while the sound of hushed voices lingered outside her bedroom door. She wondered if a person could die of humiliation. If so, she would never see the morning light.

Dear Joey, I was too sick to write last night and today. Sick at heart, that is. Believe me that won't happen again.

CHAPTER THIRTY-ONE: THE SNOWPLOW

O<small>N THE</small> S<small>ATURDAY</small> <small>BEFORE</small> Christmas, Cosi headed out after dinner to shovel the front sidewalk. She could not shake the sadness that now always seemed to weigh her down every holiday. She had gotten Christmas cards from Aunt Mari ("Come visit New York, you would love it here"), and Marty ("There are thousands of Americans here in Toronto…we held a huge demonstration on Yonge Street this week"), even one from Little Ange ("Enclosed is my new Z card. It's like a business card for models"). Cosi noticed her sister looked different in the photos on the card. Older and more world-weary, somehow.

When Cosi finished with the sidewalk, she walked into the back hallway to return the shovel and was startled to find her 8-year-old cousin Moira sitting next to Lady, Rory's one-eared mongrel. Two young puppies clambered over their mother.

"When did this happen?" asked Cosi, bending down to play with them.

"They're about eight weeks old," Moira told her. "Mom's been trying to give them away before Aunt Angie finds out. We've only got these two left."

Cosi picked one up and nuzzled it against her neck. "You're so cute! Nino would love you—you look just like Dustmop!" Moira looked at her, uncomprehending. "You know, the little dog puppet on the Commander Tom show? He's black and white, just like this one." Cosi smelled its milky, warm, puppy scent and let it lick her nose. "I've got an idea," she said, suddenly. "Don't give this one away."

On Christmas morning, the McCarthys' gathered in front of the Christmas tree to open presents. Cosi unwrapped hers, a new Daily Roman Catholic Missal and a slim book with the title, *Confidentially Girls!* She looked at the back cover and read that this little book would explain how the church would help a girl stay on "the high road" of life. Cosi sighed. "Thank you, Mama."

Cosi could barely hide her excitement when she went to retrieve Nino's present from the back hall. She had carefully wrapped the cover of the box so she could go downstairs and easily put the puppy in it just before handing it to Nino. "This is for you," she told him. Nino reached out his arms and the box shifted. Cosi saw the alarm on her mother's face.

"*Madre de Dio*, what on earth is that?"

Cosi helped Nino open the gift and watched her brother's expression when he saw the puppy. He picked it up, ran in circles around the room, and wet his pajama pants. The puppy squealed, and peed on Nino as well.

"It's OK, Nino." Cosi peeled the wet pajamas off her little brother. "Just don't squeeze Dustmop so tight."

"What in the name of God are we going to do with another dog around here," Big Ange cried. She refused to hold or even touch the puppy. "It's bad enough the yard is full of dog crap from that mongrel downstairs. Who's gonna feed and clean up after this one?"

"I will Mama, don't worry. Did you see the look on Nino's face? He is *so* happy. Can't you make this one little sacrifice, for Nino?" Her mother grumbled, but the argument was over.

The snow fell steadily all afternoon and most of the neighborhood kids were outside, playing with gifts they received that morning. Boys with new hockey sticks pushed a puck up and down the slick street, calling "car!" when they needed to let someone pass, flipping the bird at any driver who was not from the neighborhood. Cosi went out to shovel again, determined to enjoy *this* Christmas day. She inhaled the crisp air and smiled. She had made Nino happy.

She began to shovel at the far end of their sidewalk, near the Catalfanos' driveway. She looked up to see Dustmop scamper out onto the porch, with Nino close behind him. Nino bent to grab the puppy. He was careful not to squeeze too tight and Dustmop wriggled out of his hands. The dog ran down the steps toward the street.

What happened next would replay in Cosi's head for the rest of her life. Nino running down their driveway after Dustmop into the street. Nino between the parked cars, bending down to grab the puppy. The snowplow barreling down the street. Too slowly, she understood what was about to happen.

Cosi screamed at Nino, waving her arms, shouting for the snowplow to stop. A voice shrieked in her brain. *Run!* But her feet moved too slowly. She managed three steps before she saw Nino's small body tumble through the air, land on the hood of a car and roll off to the side.

She was still screaming, they told her later, an eerie, incessant scream, as neighbors came to their doors and Big Ange came running down the stairs. Screaming when the city worker jumped down from the snowplow, his hands clawing the sides of his face, moaning "No, oh God, no." Screaming when mothers ran panicked into the street, terrified it was one of their children.

When the neighborhood mothers saw it was Nino lying motionless, they stood in respectful silence as Big Ange pushed through them. Someone ran to Cosi while she screamed and screamed, though she remembered none of it.

It was not until Big Ange was cradling Nino that Cosi stopped screaming. She ran to her mother and clung to her, unable to speak, or breathe. Big Ange held Nino's small, crumpled body, legs twisted at impossible angles, the puppy panting with its leg broken, lying nearby. She moaned as she rocked her youngest child, and all sounds ceased except the rhythmic keening of mother and daughter.

Long after the ambulance drove away, Cosi stood on the sidewalk looking blankly at the street. She saw Nino's shoes lying in the snow and gathered them to her chest. It grew dark and the snow turned to hard, wet sleet, but Cosi stood motionless.

Mrs. Catalfano came and put an arm around her. "Come on, honey, let me take you inside and get you warm." Cosi shrugged her off, and walked back into the yard, back to the alley behind the Infant of Prague shop. She crouched in the darkening, snow-covered alley where she once prayed to the Blessed Virgin for guidance.

She looked up at the black sky, icy pellets stinging her face, and shrieked at the heavens, her throat raw now. "God, why Nino? Why didn't you let me run out and stop the snowplow? I would have gladly sacrificed my life for him. Nothing I ever do works out. I'll never save anyone. Why don't you kill me now and put me out of my misery?"

There was no response, only the tap-tap of the sleet as it hit the back of the garage. Cosi slumped down, hugging Nino's shoes. She was unaware of the rapidly dropping temperature, and after hours of not moving, she could no longer feel her fingers or toes. Her jeans and mittens were soaked and stiff, her hair matted with sleet now turning to snow. She began to shiver violently. She tried to put Nino's shoes in her coat pockets but found her hands were not working. She felt very tired, her head heavy, as if the hand of God was pressing her down. She could not stand when she tried to get to her feet, and sank back into the snow that piled ever higher in the narrow alley.

Then the shivering stopped and she tore blindly at her coat. Her skin felt like it was on fire. She began hallucinating, and a dark shadow loomed above her.

"Daddy?" she mumbled, as strong arms picked her up and carried her through the snow. She tried to focus, but she was so very tired. All she wanted now was to sleep. "Daddy is that you?" Her tongue was thick and her words slurred. "Daddy, am I dead?"

Cosi became conscious of being placed on a bed, rolled gently on her side, and covered with several blankets. She began to shiver again. She heard a woman's voice, floating far away. "It's hypothermia, poor thing. Keep her warm, Joey. I'll get the hot water bottles."

She felt someone slide in behind her, an arm cover her protectively, a chest press tight against her back. Struggling to stay conscious, she heard a deep voice murmuring against the back of her head, felt warm breath in her hair.

"It's OK, Cosi. I'm here. I'll *always* be here when you need me."

She closed her eyes, and let the darkness wash over her.

Part Four

Free Will
1971

CHAPTER THIRTY-TWO: ACTS OF CONTRITION

"OH MY GOD, I AM heartily sorry, for having offended thee. And I detest all my sins, because of thy just punishments. But most of all…"

Cosi rolled and faced the wall, pulling the blanket and pillow over her head. Several times a day in the months following Nino's death, she would hear her mother through the thin plaster wall, the floor creaking as she knelt in front of the Last Rites crucifix, repeating the Act of Contrition. Sometimes in the early morning, Big Ange knocked lightly on the door.

"Cosi, are you getting up today?"

Cosi would hold her breath and wait, not moving, until she heard her mother shuffle away. Only when she heard the front door click and the heavy footsteps going down the hall stairs, would she get out of bed. Watching from the window, she could see her mother join Aunt Franny on the sidewalk below, the two mothers walking arm and arm to church, the frigid February wind whipping the mantillas bobby-pinned to the tops of their heads. They were on their way to Mass to pray for their sons—one in Vietnam, the other already in Heaven.

Alone in the house, Cosi crawled back into bed and counted the ticks of her alarm clock. Why it was still ticking? She had not wound the key in… how long was it? She could not remember the first week after the accident at all. There must have been a funeral but she could not remember it. She had vague recollections of struggling to open her eyes, to breathe.

She was aware of a persistent ache in her fingers and toes, and someone told her she had suffered frostbite. Her hands and feet were still in bandages, but she was glad for the constant, dull ache that distracted her from a deeper pain.

Cosi had been back from the psychiatric hospital for a couple of weeks. Her stay at Millard Fillmore Hospital, her mother said, was supposed to be brief, just long enough to recover from frostbite and hypothermia. But when the aides had come with trays of food, Cosi would not touch it. They told her she had to eat and would watch until she did.

"When you started throwing your food at the nurses, they said they were gonna insert a feeding tube," Big Ange explained, wiping away tears. "And when the doctor came in, you bit him and called him...a bad word. If you don't eat for a while, they put you on suicide watch."

Cosi did remember the stay at the psychiatric hospital, the irony of it, especially. Although she was in the Children's Acute Care ward, she stayed for a month, enduring an endless cycle of insomnia, sedatives, fitful sleep, and nightmares. Every morning at six, the nurses got her out of bed and marched her with the rest of the young "suicides" and anorexics down to get their medications and on to the dining hall for breakfast. Confined to her room unless she ate, she would put small bits of food in her mouth and chew for as long as possible. She would then go to the bathroom, stick her finger down her throat, and get rid of what she ate.

When Aunt Rosa came to visit her at the psychiatric hospital and sat on the same couch where the two had sat the year before, Cosi wept. "I don't want to live anymore, Aunt Rosa."

Aunt Rosa put her arm around her. "I know, sweetheart, but you gotta pull yourself together. Your mother needs you now more than ever. You're all she's got left." She lifted Cosi's chin. "Look at you. Skin and bones. I brought you a *cannolo* from Balistreri's. Eat, or they'll never let you outta here."

They sent Cosi home once she started eating again. Joey dropped by every day at first—Cosi could hear him talking quietly with her mother—but she refused to see him or anyone else. Her diary lay under her mattress, untouched since Christmas Eve. *Dear Joey,* she had written. *I have a big surprise for Nino. It will be the best Christmas we've had in a long time!* Now, on this bitterly cold February morning, Cosi lay in bed, fingering the wooden cross Rico had given her, trying to make sense of it all. Something Sister Valentine asked her long ago haunted her now.

Why do you believe in God, Cosi?

Why indeed?

She thought she saw things more clearly now. She had been a gullible little girl who believed whatever adults told her. She trusted her father, who turned out to be a liar and philanderer. Her faith in God, the Virgin Mary, her belief in the Catholic Church and its teachings, seemed like fairytales now, told to *naïfs* desperate to believe there was some greater meaning to life. She had been lonely, willing to cling to a fevered hallucination that she had a special purpose, that her sacrifices she would *mean* something. Now that Nino was dead, she knew there was no hand of God ensuring good triumphed over evil. Life was pointless after all.

Monday afternoon the doorbell rang. She recognized Sister Valentine's voice, talking softly with her mother. When she heard the knock at her bedroom door she hesitated, but finally sat up and smoothed her hair. "Come in," she said, her voice hoarse from disuse.

"Hello Cosi."

Cosi stared at the person dressed in an ordinary skirt and blouse, a woman who vaguely resembled Sister Valentine. Sister Valentine misread Cosi's look, and smiled. "What do you think?" She turned around slowly. "Our Order finally got the word. We no longer have to wear our habits. It's the first time I've worn clothes like this in a long time."

Cosi knew she was supposed to say something, and was taking too long to say it. Sister Valentine was not a blonde. On the contrary, her veil had hidden rather plain, short brown hair. She did not have a figure like Marilyn Monroe; in fact, she had a thick waist. The first thing that came to Cosi's mind was that while Sister Valentine, in her imposing black and white habit, was a topic of frequent speculation at Saint Michael's, with the mystery gone, she was boring.

"I have another surprise," said Sister Valentine. "I've decided to use my given name, now that Saint Valentine is no longer liturgically venerated. Please call me Sister Barbara Mullen, my name before I took my vows."

Cosi gave her a look of disgust. "What other Vatican II surprises are you going to spring on me?" She folded her arms. "Next you'll be telling me God is a woman."

The former Sister Valentine looked hurt. "I thought you'd be happy for me and happy for yourself. You'll be free of all those tired old rules when you become a nun."

"Happy?" Cosi could feel her voice tightening. "I'm disgusted with the Catholic Church. What is the point of it, now that we know all the rules we were following were bullshit? Everything about it is fake, made up. Are you even a real nun anymore?"

"Of course, I'm a real nun." Sister Barbara bristled. "But I accept that the world is changing, and I have to change with it." She stood and smoothed her skirt. "I'm sorry I didn't come over sooner to tell you about all this, but your mother said—well, you needed time to recover. She asked me to come over today to see if there is anything I could do to help you."

"You can go away." Cosi burrowed back under the covers and turned toward the wall. "There's nothing you, God, or the Virgin Mary can do to help me now.

Cosi went back to school at the end of February, but only after a number of visits and a great deal of patience on the part of Sister Barbara. They would meet for coffee Sunday mornings at the Your Host restaurant, away from the stares of fellow parishioners.

"When you lose a person you love, no one can help you through it," Sister Barbara would say while her coffee grew cold. "Let the grief wash over you. Don't resist it. Grieving is part of the healing process. So is being angry. You're not the first person to be mad at God. I'm sure he's use to it by now."

Cosi scowled. What would she know, anyway?

Sister Barbara reached over and squeezed Cosi's hand. "I know you don't want to face your classmates, but it would be foolish to drop out of school now. Getting back into a regular routine will be a welcome distraction. You'll see."

Cosi stared at her coffee cup. "What if I don't want to be a nun anymore?"

"There's no shame in that. That's what discernment is all about." Sister Barbara signaled for the check. "Just don't make any hasty decisions."

SISTER Barbara was wrong. Going back to school was not a welcome distraction; it was a misery. Cosi avoided her classmates and ate alone in the cafeteria. Sister Claire called her into her office after she had returned, and Cosi sat sullenly, picking at the dead skin on her fingers, while Sister Claire looked through her file.

"You've missed quite a bit of schoolwork over the past two months," the guidance counselor gently explained. "You'll need to spend more time in study hall to catch up with your class." Sister Claire leaned her head forward, trying to make eye contact. "Cosi, you're a good student, and with all of the advanced placement courses you've taken, you could have enough credits to graduate as a junior, in June. You can still do it, if you put your mind to it."

Cosi lifted her head. The idea of leaving school as soon as possible now appealed to her. "What do I have to do to graduate in June?"

"Pass all of your AP courses. Take the SAT. Finish your service project." Sister Claire paused. "Do you still have your heart set on taking your vows?"

Cosi paused, wanting to be honest with Sister Claire, who had always looked out for her. She looked down at her fingers and noticed that when she pulled the blackened skin away, there was smooth, pink skin underneath. Perhaps there was a whole, new Cosi under there.

"I ask," Sister Claire was saying, "…because Sister Agatha thinks taking your vows might not be the right thing for you now…."

Cosi bristled. *So, the old witch is blackballing me. I should have known.* She did not like being pre-empted by Sister Agatha. "I haven't made up my mind yet, Sister Claire. I want to talk it over with my spiritual guide, Sister Barbara."

"Well, you'll need to decide soon, especially if you're going to graduate at the end of the semester. If you're not going to begin your novitiate, you should think about going to college. You'll be throwing away the chance of a lifetime if you don't go."

Sister Barbara stopped by to check on Cosi at the end of her first week back at school. She had trudged through an early March snowstorm and stood in Cosi's living room wearing a black wool coat and a fluffy hat that resembled a grey snowball. Cosi thought she looked ridiculous. She waited until Sister Barbara had taken off her coat and was sitting on the couch.

"I've decided I'm not going to become a nun."

Sister Barbara sighed. "I understand you've struggled with this decision. And if you're sure you don't want to enter the convent, there's nothing more I can do for you. You won't need a spiritual guide and mentor anymore." She leaned forward. "Are you certain?"

"Yes." Cosi squared her shoulders.

"OK then." Sister Barbara put on her coat and hat, gave Cosi a brief hug, and left. Cosi was stunned. She had prepared a long, involved defense of her decision, but Sister Barbara seemed completely uninterested. In fact, she seemed relieved.

Cosi's mother was in her room a minute later, a bottle of oil soap and a rag in her hands. "I hope to God I didn't hear what I thought I heard."

"Mama!" Cosi turned on her mother. "Were you listening to our conversation?"

"I was washing the baseboards in the hallway. I can't help what I overhear."

"Fine! It's better you know anyway."

"Is it true what you said?" Big Ange looked shaken. "You don't wanna be a nun anymore?" She made the sign of the cross and kissed her thumb.

"No, I don't," Cosi muttered under her breath, "and I doubt the Virgin Mary cares."

Big Ange hurried into her own bedroom. Cosi found her kneeling on the floor in front of the crucifix, eyes closed, head bent.

"Dear Lord, she doesn't know what she's talking about. Help her come to her senses."

Cosi sat on her mother's bed. "Mama, listen to me. I just need some time. I'm so confused right now. I don't know what to do or what to believe anymore."

Big Ange, still on her knees, moved awkwardly over and took her daughter's hands.

"Listen to your mother. Somewhere in the back of everybody's mind, there is always a little doubt about God. Not many people have actually seen God, at least not while they're alive to talk about it. So how could you know for sure? But the way I figure is this. If there is a God, and I been praying to him all these years, then I got points in my favor and might get into Heaven. If there is no God, and I been praying all these years, then what's the harm? There's a fifty-fifty chance there *might* be a God and I learned from my Uncle Salvatore, go with the odds. Uncle Sal, he was a good bookie you know."

"This isn't helping me, Mama."

Cosi's mother got painfully to her feet. "Well, I'm not sure Sister 'whatever-her-name-is-today' is helping you either. Maybe you should talk to Father Mario."

"Father Mario? Oh please, Mama. What does he know? All he does is spout the usual religious claptrap. He's the last person I want to talk to. He even defends my scumbag father."

Big Ange's face reddened and she raised her hand to strike her. "Don't you dare speak of Father Mario, or your own father, that way!"

Cosi raised her own arm, hand opened, ready to grab her mother's wrist. "Don't you touch me, Mama. Don't you dare hit me."

They faced each other, breathing hard and vibrating with anger, until Big Ange grunted suddenly and put her hands over her heart. She took two staggering steps and fell heavily to her knees. She leaned against the bed then rolled slowly to the floor.

"Mama!" screamed Cosi. "Mama what's wrong? What's happening?"

"I think I'm having a heart attack. Call an ambulance."

Her mother lay sprawled on the floor, her long black dress askew, exposing her support hose and girdle. Cosi ran to the phone, but not before pulling her mother's skirt down, so she would look decent when the ambulance arrived.

In the back of the ambulance, Cosi sobbed and held her mother's hand. "I'm so sorry, Mama. Please don't die on me. I can't bear to lose you too." Big Ange lay with her eyes closed, not moving, as the ambulance men moved around her.

"Hey Vinny," the pudgy one called, looking around the ambulance. "Have we got one of them new whatchamacallits, a defibrillator?" Cosi was incredulous. Whose palms did these goofballs have to grease to get this job?

"Naw. Mr. Bonnano says they're just a gimmick."

"He would. He's a funeral director. Why they let funeral directors own the ambulance services, I'll never know. You know how to do CPR?"

"Is that the thing where you push on their chest until they start breathing?"

"Yeah, and you have to blow in their mouths too." They looked dubiously at Big Ange.

"We're almost to the hospital," said Vinny. "I think she'll make it."

Cosi jumped up and punched Vinny's arm. "Jerk! Do something! My mother could die!"

"Relax, chickie. We are doing something. I took her pulse, listened to her breathing, it all seems normal. She's ain't gonna die."

Cosi laid her cheek on Big Ange's chest, and her mother's eyes opened a bit. She stroked Cosi's hair. "In case I die today, there's something I gotta tell you."

Cosi looked at her mother. *Dear God. Not another deathbed confession.*

"You need to understand, I made a promise to God. When your father was dying, I did something that was wrong in the eyes of Our Lord. So, I told God I would sacrifice one of my children, like Abraham in the Bible, to get back on His good side. It didn't seem right to offer Nino, God rest his innocent soul, and your sister, that *puttana*, was not in a state of grace, so I promised God you could be His. When the Virgin Mary visited, I knew He heard my prayers."

"What do you mean, I could be His?"

"I promised Him you would become a Bride of Christ." Cosi's mother gripped her arm with surprising strength. "I promised Him! If you break that promise, God will go on punishing this family forever, and He'll send me to Hell for my sins."

Big Ange began to cry and Cosi felt helpless. She remembered her father, begging for forgiveness on his deathbed, and the torment in his face when he did not receive it. She could not deny her mother's final request. Cosi held her mother's hands. "I'll keep your promise," she said. "Now stay calm."

The ambulance brought her mother to the emergency entrance at Millard Fillmore Hospital and the admissions staff hurried the gurney into a large room. A doctor and nurse came immediately and pulled a curtain around them. Cosi stepped inside the small space.

"I'm her daughter," Cosi declared, daring them to tell her to leave.

The doctor ignored her. "Check her vitals," he said. The nurse scurried around, pulling out a blood pressure cuff while the doctor put his stethoscope to her mother's chest.

"Mrs. McCarthy, how are you feeling?" the doctor asked loudly, as if talking to a child. Big Ange opened her eyes.

"Not good, doctor. My chest hurts."

"We're going to hook you up to get something called an electrocardiogram. It will tell us what's going on with your heart."

"Is that really necessary?" Big Ange leaned up on her elbows.

"Don't worry. It isn't going to hurt. We'll get the machine and be right back."

The doctor and nurse returned wheeling a frightening-looking metal contraption adorned with multiple dials and wires, and began to lubricate the electrodes. "These are going to be a tiny bit cold," said the doctor while placing the lubricated pads on Big Ange's chest. They all turned to watch as the machine recorded Big Ange's heartbeats.

"What's it saying?" asked Cosi, watching the lines bounce up and down on the monitor.

"Just as I thought." The doctor shook his head. "There's nothing wrong with her heart."

"What? Are you sure?"

"All of her vital signs are normal—her pulse, her breathing, her blood pressure. Everything checks out. She seems quite agitated though."

The doctor turned to Big Ange. "I'm going to give you something that should help you, Mrs. McCarthy." He handed her a couple of pills and a glass of water. "If these work, I'll write you a prescription." The doctor watched while she choked down the medication.

"Well?" Cosi looked anxiously at her mother.

"I feel a little better," said Big Ange, looking sheepish. "What did you give me?"

"An antacid and a new medication called Valium, to relax you. Is your chest still hurting?"

"A little bit. Maybe it wasn't a heart attack after all. Maybe it was just the *agita*."

"The what?" asked the doctor.

"Heartburn," Cosi translated irritably.

On the ride home, Cosi and her mother sat in silence in the back of Uncle Mack's Grand Prix while he tried to fill the vacuum with one of his monologues. "Hey, have you heard the Knox Family is putting up money to buy Buffalo a new hockey team? They held a name-the-team contest, and guess what won? The *Sabres*." What does a sword have to do with Buffalo?

Cosi ignored him and turned viciously on her mother. "How dare you do that to me."

Big Ange shrugged and gave Cosi her practiced I-have-no-idea-what-you're-talking-about look.

"Don't give me that!" shouted Cosi. "You know exactly what you did. You deliberately scared the wits out of me to get me to make a promise."

"My chest did hurt," said Big Ange, defensively.

"I agreed under false pretenses to keep your promise. Well, the deal is off! I am not gonna be a nun, I'm not gonna go to church, and I might never believe in God again!"

Big Ange looked out the window at the passing cars, pulled her rosary out of her purse, kissed the worn cross, and began fingering the beads. "You're blaming God right now," she said to the window, "and I hope you get over it. But if you decide you won't be a Bride of Christ after I made a promise, the next time something bad happens to this family, it will be all *your* fault."

Chapter Thirty-Three: Rico Revealed

THE WEEK AFTER BIG Ange's fake heart attack, Cosi stood hesitating outside the guidance counselor's door. She had promised Sister Claire she would come back this week with a decision on taking her vows, when a last-minute thought occurred to her. If she withdrew from the discernment process, her volunteer project at the psychiatric hospital might end as well.

Cosi thought about the women in Ward Two who hadn't seen her for months. They were probably sitting in the Day Room now, wondering what had happened to her. Her work at the hospital with the patients was the one thing left in her life that gave her a sense of purpose, especially now that she knew personally what it was like to live behind those locked doors. She knocked on Sister Claire's door and mumbled something about needing more time.

Cosi arrived early on her first day back volunteering at the hospital, looking around as she bounded up the steps. She ran into Rico in the library, not entirely by accident, and he motioned her over.

"Where've you been?"

She was sure he knew about her stay there as a patient. "Busy writing my memoirs," she said, sarcastically.

"So, you're a writer now?" he asked, playing along. "Did I tell you I write poetry?"

"No, you didn't."

"You ever hear of the Last Poets?"

Cosi admitted she had not.

"Why am I not surprised? They're world-famous." He smiled. "But black."

Rico opened the composition notebook in front of him. "I've written this poem about the future, when they change the law and people like me won't have to sit and rot for the rest of our lives in places like this. I call it, '*The Crazies Will Not Be Hospitalized*.'"

Rico began to drum a steady beat on the library table.

> *You will not be safe, my brother*
> *You will not be able to drop your guard and mow the yard*
> *You will not be able to sleep well, raise hell*
> *let your kids play farmer in the dell.*
> *Because the crazies will not be hospitalized.*
>
> *The crazies will not be hospitalized*
> *supervised, sanitized, or lobotomized*
> *You will find them in a theater near you*
> *You will find them buying grapes in your supermarket*
> *You will find them sitting on a park bench*
> *Watching your pig-tailed little daughter*
> *Talking to her stuffed animals*
> *The crazies will not be hospitalized.*
>
> *Oh Lord, what should we do?*
> *The crazies will not be hospitalized*
> *When we can't tell them, from me and you*
> *What will we do?*
> *When the crazies will not be hospitalized*

Rico laughed at the look on her face. "It's supposed to be funny. Ironic, you know?"

Cosi was not sure which unsettled her more, the poem or the poet. "It's certainly…different," she stammered.

"When I get out, this is what I want to do. Write poetry. Put it to music," Rico said, keeping a steady rhythm on the library table. "First thing I'm gonna buy is a pair of congas."

Cosi felt a pang of sympathy for him, listening to his dreams. If he was a murderer, as Gigi said, the hospital would never release him. She wondered, now that she was getting to know him better, if Gigi was telling the truth. How many poets murder people?

Cosi thought about asking Rico outright, but came up with a better plan— she would look at his file. She remembered the locked room Mrs. Claymore noted on the tour of the building and knew Gigi kept a ring of keys hanging on a hook in her office. *I'll bet Gigi has a key to the file room. Why else would she have stacks of folders next to her typewriter?* The old Cosi would never dream of doing such a thing but this one looked down at the bright pink skin on her now healed fingers. The fingers of the new Cosi.

Cosi found it easy enough to slip the key ring into her pocket while Gigi was on a smoke break. Making her way to the file room, Cosi matched a key to its lock on the third try. Looking up and down the hallway before slipping inside, palms sweating, she felt for the light switch on the wall. A single overhead bulb blinked on. There were rows of grey metal file cabinets crammed into the tiny space, and she saw immediately that the filing system for the patient's records was not by year of entry but by alphabetical order. Rico's last name was Gonzalez, according to Gigi, and there were several Gonzalez files, but no Rico. *Maybe Rico is a nickname.* She pulled out a fat file labelled "Ricardo Gonzalez" and opened it up. This was definitely his.

The first sheet was a summary of all Rico's particulars. His illness, it said, was "paranoid schizophrenia," and his admission date was June 3, 1961, with the words "court-ordered" in parentheses. *He's been here nearly 10 years*, thought Cosi. His race was listed as "Black/Puerto Rican," and both his mother, Isabel Gonzalez, and his father, Richard Martin, were listed as "deceased."

Cosi was puzzled. *That's odd. He goes by his mother's last name, not his father's.*

Rifling through the rest of the file, she noted it included the things one might expect to find there—a status report updated by a doctor every three months or so, dietary guidelines, a compilation of grounds privileges given and revoked, a list of medications that seemed to grow shorter over time. She almost missed the small newspaper article stuck between the forms when something about it caught her eye. A headline about a murder. *Where have I seen that article before?* Reading quickly, she remembered. Uncle Tommy's scrapbook.

Why would an article about the stabbing of Slick Martin, the man who shot Uncle Tommy, be in Rico Gonzalez's file? Cosi read the article carefully and sucked in her breath. "Slick" Martin must be "Richard Martin, deceased," and Ricardo Gonzalez—Rico—must be his son, the "kid" who stabbed him 14 times. With a shudder, she realized what Gigi told her was true. Rico *was* a murderer. Shaking, she was trying to reassemble the file in the order she found it when she saw him out of the corner of her eye, standing in the doorway.

"Interesting reading?"

The voice in her head screamed, *Run*! She turned and Rico caught her arm. "You were reading about me, weren't you? Wouldn't you like to hear my side of the story?"

Cry for help, the voice said. But who would hear her? Mrs. Claymore might, but she would wonder what Cosi was doing in that room. *Better to stay calm and quiet. Placate him.*

"Of course, I would," she told Rico, trying to keep her voice steady.

"Let's walk back to the library," he said. "We don't want to be caught in this dark hall together." He took the key from her and locked the door.

They sat at a table and when Rico began to tell his story, his face changed. Gone was the sarcasm and cockiness. In its place was something else. Pain? Grief? She wasn't sure.

He told her about his mother. Isabel Gonzalez was a maid at the Lafayette Hotel downtown. They lived on Peach Street in the Fruit Belt section of Buffalo's lower East Side, where his mother had met Slick Martin. Slick was *"ostentoso"* in those days, his mother told him. He would come into the hotel bar flashing a wad of cash, dressed to the nines. Their relationship was short and Rico was born several months after it ended.

Rico first met his father when he was 10. Slick showed up one day and Rico remembered his mother acting strangely. She was afraid of him, he figured out later. Slick left after a few days. "I was glad he was gone," said Rico. "I didn't like him, and we were fine on our own."

Slick showed up from time to time after that, drunk or high, looking for money, Rico continued. If his mother did not give Slick what he wanted, he would beat her while Rico watched, furious but helpless. There were times his mother whispered to him that Slick was hiding out from the cops. "Why don't we just turn him in, Mommi?" Rico would ask. "He'd kill us for sure," his mother would say. "I'll kill him first," Rico would promise, though he knew he'd never win a fight against the much older Slick.

When he was 17, Rico said, he walked in on the two of them going at it again. This time Slick was choking his mother. She was on the bed, arms flailing, Slick on top of her, his hands at her throat. "Bitch," he was saying, "you're gonna pay."

Rico said he remembered little of what happened next, only the white-hot anger that consumed him. He ran to his room and grabbed his switchblade. "I did go a little crazy," he admitted. He remembered sitting on the bed, covered in Slick's blood, when the police came.

"The neighbors all say you threatened to kill Slick more than once. Your only hope is an insanity plea," the public defender later told him. "Otherwise, it's the electric chair."

"I had no choice," said Rico, "so here I am. My mother came to visit every week until she passed two years ago from breast cancer. My only regret is that I wasn't with her when…" he paused, trying to control the quaver in his voice.

To Cosi's surprise, she began to feel sorry for him, hearing his story. What would she have done if someone was strangling her mother? Killing a person was wrong, of course. What kind of society would it be if murderers were not punished? But maybe society had punished Rico enough. He was a hot-headed teenager when he walked in on Slick strangling his mother. He acted on instinct, to protect her. Cosi thought she might have done the same. If so, would *she* be given the same choices—the insane asylum or the electric chair?

Maybe it was time to cut Rico some slack.

Chapter Thirty-Four: Surprise, Surprise

The following Friday Cosi went directly to the library, looking for him.

"Do you know where Rico is?" she asked a patient methodically turning the pages of a dog-eared magazine. The man pointed at the window. Cosi looked out and saw Rico on the basketball court, sprinting from one end to the other, the basketball lying in the corner. She hurried out one of the side doors and when he saw her, he stopped and bent over, hands on his knees, trying to catch his breath.

"Got...to get... in shape...before...I get out," he wheezed.

"I read the book you were talking about," she said, trying not to look at Rico's muscled chest, outlined by his damp white t-shirt. *Focus on what you came to tell him,* she admonished herself. "Szasz' new book, *The Manufacture of Madness.* Szasz doesn't think people should be kept in psychiatric hospitals involuntarily. He's pushing for something he calls deinstitutionalization."

"I know all about it." Rico came to the fence. "He wants us out of hospitals, working our way back into society. He thinks we should get help from shrinks on the outside."

"I think he's right," Cosi said, warming now to her argument. "At some point, you've learned from your experience and paid your debt to society. You need to find a lawyer who will help you get out."

"Whoa...slow down. Maybe that won't be necessary." Rico pulled off his wet shirt to cool down and stood bare-chested. "There's a big push to let patients out on a trial basis, and they're looking for candidates. I've volunteered."

"Who decides who's a good candidate?" Cosi looked steadily at the ground.

"Dr. Mooney, the head of the hospital. He's looking for patients no longer a danger to themselves or others, who can get along in a group home. I think I've won him over."

"What will you do if you get out? A poet doesn't make enough money to live on, no matter how good you are."

"My aunt—my mother's sister—and I keep in touch. She works at the Concord Baptist Church of Christ in Brooklyn. The Reverend Taylor, a good friend of the late Dr. King, runs it. My aunt's offered to let me live with her for a while when I get out of here."

Rico picked up the basketball and started to bounce it. "I want to work with someone like Reverend Taylor. Shit, I'd work for him for free. Like Dr. King, he's all about non-violence. And violence..." he paused, sending the basketball up and through the hoop, "...is what got me into this place. Besides, maybe I can hang with the Last Poets. They're jammin' in Harlem."

"You'd leave Buffalo?" The thought strangely upset her.

"Of course."

"Why? You can stay here and do the same kind of work. We need advocates for the poor here in Buffalo. There's this group of black men in Lackawanna...."

"Are you serious, Cosi? You told me your whole family remembers that article from back in '61. You think people in this town are gonna forget what I did? I'll always be thought of as a crazy-ass negro that nobody trusts."

"They would if they knew your story," she said. "I trust you."

"Took you long enough." He laughed. "Listen, no offense, but you don't know what it's like being black in America. When it comes to black men, white people believe, 'Mercy but murders, pardoning those that kill'."

"I don't understand."

You know, that line from Shakespeare? *Romeo and Juliet?*"

She looked blank.

"Shit, you didn't see that movie? We all saw it in the dining hall. It means if you show mercy to killers, they will kill again. That's what white people believe about black men."

"Not all white people are like that," she said, defensively.

"Oh, really?"

"Yes, really. The world has changed while you were in here."

He looked at her curiously for a long moment. "Did anyone ever tell you; you look like her? That chick in the movie, Olivia Hussey?"

Cosi blushed. "I need to go."

On the bus ride home, she thought about Rico. What happened to him seemed so unfair, the way he told it. He killed a man trying to kill his mother, and he paid with 10 years of his life, even though he was a juvenile at the time. And she knew he was right. If released, he would always be an outcast in Buffalo. He had no choice but to leave, and it made her sad.

When Cosi walked through the front door, her mother was waiting. "Something came in the mail for you, from Sister Barbara."

That's odd, Cosi thought. Sister Barbara had never sent her anything in the mail, not even a birthday card. She tore the envelope open and found a letter inside, dated three days earlier.

April 2, 1971

Dearest Cosi,

I am writing to let you know I have made an important decision, probably the most difficult decision in my life. I have decided to leave the convent. I am heading to Cleveland tomorrow where I plan to start a new life.

I have recently been in touch with a man who has been a friend since childhood. He is an important leader in the United Freedom Movement, working to end segregation in Cleveland's schools. You know how I feel about racial inequality. I have tried, unsuccessfully, to make progress here in Buffalo. I am moving on, hoping I can make a difference in Cleveland.

I also want to get married. I realize now that having a partner in life, a husband, is something I have yearned for subconsciously, for many years. You made me realize that, Cosi, with your many questions, and I can deny it no longer. I would like a family, children. If I delay any longer, I may never have the opportunity.

I also realized, after our last meeting, that I have failed you, as your spiritual guide. It was hubris on my part to think I could tear down your earnest religious beliefs and build them up again, stronger and more resilient than before. While I succeeded in tearing them down, I obviously did not have the wisdom necessary to help you build them anew. As a result, I have left you bereft, with no spiritual anchor in your life. For this, I ask your forgiveness.

I will offer you a few last thoughts, now that I am finally at peace with myself. I know you will never measure your worth using other people's metrics. You will base yours on how faithfully you fulfill your destiny, your special purpose, as you call it. Leave your options open, and one day you will know in your heart what that special purpose is.

In the meantime, be the most decent, kind, and forgiving person you can be. Cultivate your soul, rather than your dreams and ambitions, so that when you are confronted with difficult challenges, your soul will lead you in the right direction without any thinking on your part. That is how you will know your life's purpose. Follow the voice of your soul.

I want you to know it has been a privilege to work with you these past few years. I consider you a dear friend. Cleveland is not that far from Buffalo, and I hope we will keep in touch.

Yours in Christ, Barbara

Cosi sat down on the couch and crushed the letter into a ball. Sister Barbara was the one adult she thought she could trust to be open and honest with her. But in fact, she too had been hiding things, keeping secrets from her, all these years. She turned to see her mother reading the letter over her shoulder.

"Forget about her," said her mother, wiping at Cosi's wet cheeks with the corner of her apron. "A phony nun like that tells you not to become a nun? She knows better than your own mother? Like I told you before, the only ones you can trust are your family. Family knows best."

ERMA shuffled beside Cosi, walking ahead of the rest of the women from Ward Two. It was a sunny, breezy morning in the middle of April, and Cosi knew this walk was important to Erma, her way of establishing her place in the pecking order among the patients. They had gone out to admire the yellow forsythia bushes, now in full bloom, and Erma walked with a lift to her chin. She picked three daffodils and shyly handed them to Cosi. Rico looked up as the group walked past the basketball court, waved, and trotted up to the fence.

"Hey Cosi, when you're through for the day, there's something I'd like to show you."

"Sure." Cosi wondered if he had made her something in the wood shop, and she instinctively touched the crucifix he had given her earlier. Curious, she signed out early and went to look for him. After checking the library, she walked outside, toward the basketball court.

"Cosi," he called, "over here." He was leaning against the fence.

"What did you want to show me?"

"Follow me," he said.

She had told him that she trusted him, but she was not sure this was wise. Yet if she refused to go, wouldn't that signal that she *didn't* trust him? Against her better judgment, she followed him along the path behind the building, back toward the wide expanse of field that lay behind the hospital. Alarm bells went off in her head as they walked farther away from the building.

"Rico, where are we going?" She tried to sound firm.

"Almost there," he said, not turning around.

She was on the verge of running back to the hospital when he stopped walking.

"There," he said. "Isn't it beautiful?"

Rico was pointing to an enormous weeping willow tree. It was at least 40 feet tall and its graceful fronds swept the ground in the soft breeze. It stood beside a small brook, and Cosi could see a bench positioned beside it, making a lovely tableau.

She walked over and touched one of the long branches. "Wow," she said appreciatively. "It's the most beautiful tree I've ever seen." She glanced at him. He did have the soul of a poet.

Rico reached over, put his hand gently over hers, and slid it slowly down over the small fuzzy catkins and tiny feather-veined leaves. An electric charge ran up her arm. "Soft, aren't they?" He kept his hand on hers and pulled her gently toward the bench. "You can see the tree better from here," he said, patting the spot next to where he sat.

Cosi hesitated, unsure of Rico's motives. It was not too late to run.

He took a deep breath, and sighed. "Do you know the poem, 'The Willow Tree' by William Makepeace Thackery? They have it in the library. I remember a few lines."

Know ye the willow-tree
Whose gray leaves quiver,
Whispering gloomily
To yon pale river;
Lady, at even-tide
Wander not near it,
They say its branches hide. A sad, lost spirit.

He was silent then, contemplating something, and Cosi listened to the swish of the willow in the April breeze. Rico turned abruptly and said, "Sometimes I look at you, and I see a sad, lost spirit and wonder, why would a smart, pretty girl be sad?" He looked up at the tree. "I know you stayed here as a patient, on suicide watch." He turned slowly back to Cosi. "I told you why I was here. Now you tell me your story."

The question caught Cosi by surprise. Over the past year, the sadness would creep up and overtake her at times, like a kudzu vine, choking her. Rico could see this, obviously, but the last thing she wanted was to talk about her own troubles. She hesitated; if she did not explain, it would destroy the fragile trust they were trying to establish. She sat down on the bench beside him.

Cosi could smell the strong, sharp scent of the soap all the hospital patients used. She had never been this close to Rico before, and glancing at him, she could see fine lines forming at the corners of his eyes, a few stray gray hairs threaded among the black. He was only 27, but looked old enough to be her father.

Slowly, bits and pieces of her story came tumbling out. She talked mostly about Nino and her stay in the hospital, since he seemed to know about that anyway. While she talked, Rico never took his eyes off her face. When she stopped, he put his hand over hers and said, "I know how bad it hurts to lose someone you love. We got some things in common, you and me."

There was an awkward silence, and then he said, looking at the ground, "I feel like you need a hug right now. Would that be OK?"

She had worried that he might assault her. She did not expect a request for a hug.

"No, that wouldn't be a good idea."

He looked crestfallen. He put his hands on his knees, took a deep breath, and stood up. "I'm sorry. I thought it might make you feel better." He looked up at the sky. "I misread the signals. I thought maybe you liked me as much as I like you. I should have known. Why would you want to be friends with someone like me?" He started to walk away.

"Wait." She wondered, was she treating him unfairly? Was she guilty of her own prejudice, of being racist, like others she condemned? She touched his arm and something stirred in her. Every nerve ending was tingling, her heart hammering in her chest. "I do like you. "It's just that...."

Rico stepped closer and folded his arms around her, and she began to cry. She let him hug her for a while; it felt so good to be held. Then he took her face in both of his hands and kissed her. The hunger in that kiss frightened Cosi, but she did not stop him.

When he pulled away, he inhaled and exhaled deeply. "You have no idea how long...." Rico was leaning forward to kiss her again, when they heard the angry voice of Mrs. Claymore.

"Cosi McCarthy, is that you? What are you doing out here with one of the patients? Gigi said you were getting a little too friendly. I just hope I didn't see what I think I saw."

"What you saw was my fault." Rico calmly stepped in front of Cosi. "Miss McCarthy had no idea I was going to kiss her. I talked her into coming out here to see this tree in all its spring glory. She wasn't expecting me to do what I did."

"This is an outrage!" sputtered Mrs. Claymore. "I will speak to Dr. Mooney about your behavior, Mr. Gonzalez, and I expect you won't be enjoying grounds privileges after this. As for you, Miss McCarthy, I intend to speak to your principal. I doubt this is the kind of behavior they encourage at Holy Martyrs."

Cosi tried to speak but no words would come. Mrs. Claymore turned her back on Cosi and said to Rico, "Let's go, Mr. Gonzalez." Cosi watched helplessly as Rico walked away, two steps ahead of Mrs. Claymore, who watched him like a hawk.

Cosi ran to the bus stop and got on the first bus that would take her home. All she wanted to do was flee and nurse her mortification in the privacy of her own room. She was relieved to find the flat empty. Her mother must be in the back, still working in the shop. She locked the bedroom door and sat on her bed, wondering what the principal would do when she found out. Would she be expelled just before graduation?

She got up and paced the room. Despite her worries, Rico's kiss kept intruding upon her thoughts, especially the urgency of it. *He must have feelings for me,* she concluded. She knew such feelings were dangerous for both of them, but Rico was right. There was a strong physical attraction between them that was hard to ignore.

Cosi's mind was wandering into perilous places when she noticed Mr. Schiavonni striding down her driveway, obviously intent on seeing her mother. Was he finally here to collect the "seed money" he'd given her? She watched him disappear into the backyard.

She had not seen him in a long time, had not even heard her mother mention his name. After a while, her curiosity got the better of her, and she headed down the back steps. She walked toward the door of the little shop and could see Mr. Schiavonni through the garage window. She peered inside and saw his face, his eyes closed, hands resting on something, blocked somewhat from Cosi's view by the table full of statues in front of the window. Cosi leaned closer and could see his hands were resting on something broad and fleshy—something that looked like a woman's rump.

Cosi shrieked. Mr. Schiavonni was raping her mother! She tried to open the door and found it locked. She pounded on it, screaming, "Let me in this instant, you bastard!"

A minute later, the door opened and out rushed a flustered Mr. Schiavonni. Big Ange calmly smoothed her dress. Cosi stood with her mouth open, speechless.

"What?" asked her mother. "I was hemming his pants."

"You liar! What were you doing? How long has this been going on?"

Big Ange folded her arms. "By 'this' you mean what? Pete's visits?"

"Oh, it's 'Pete' now, is it? Have you been doing this since you opened the shop? Cosi sucked in her breath, furious now. "Is this how you repay the so-called loans he gives you?"

Big Ange shrugged her shoulders.

"Mama! If you're being paid for sex, it is not only immoral. It's illegal!"

Big Ange narrowed her eyes. "You watch your mouth. Before you go getting all high and mighty, let me tell you a few things about the real world. What Pete and I got going is none of your business. I scratch his back. He scratches mine. He's not getting what he needs at home, and neither am I. He wanted my girls to grow up good Catholic girls, so he contributed to their education. What's illegal about that?"

"Can't you even see what a *hypocrite* you are? All these years you've been telling me that sex outside of marriage is a sin. Now I find you doing—that!" Her face twisted in disgust.

"What am I supposed to do? No matter what I tried, the money wasn't coming in. I did what I had to do for my family. So, what's the problem? It's not like I'm cheating on a husband."

Cosi could feel the blood rushing to her head, her temples pounding. "You are the worst kind of mother," she screamed. "You ruined every relationship I ever had, scaring me with stories about pregnancy and sinning in the eyes of God. Now I catch you in the act, and you don't even apologize!"

She walked out of the shop, slamming the door in her mother's face.

Chapter Thirty-Five: Truth and Consequences

"Can I stay with you for a while?"

Silence on the other end of the phone.

"I don't think it's a good idea," said Gabby, finally. "I was lucky my mother let *me* come back home. You staying here is out of the question."

"Please Gabby, it won't be for long. It'll only be a few weeks until I graduate and get my own place." She hesitated. "I thought we were family."

Gabby sighed. "We *are* family Cosi, but…it's complicated. My mother thinks your mother knows about her affair with your father, although not that I'm your dad's love child. Big Ange hates my mom, regardless. How do you think your mother would react if you ran away and came to live with us? Should I tell her it's because you're 'family'?"

"So, what do I do? Something's happened and I can't live here anymore."

"Meet me at the School 18 playground after dinner, OK? I'll try to think of something."

The two girls had not seen each other since Christmas. As soon as Cosi sat on the wooden swing, Gabby pounced. "I'm dying to know. What's happened?"

It all came out in one great gush. Cosi told Gabby about her stay in the psychiatric hospital, her loss of faith, her decision not to become a nun, Sister Barbara's abrupt departure, and her mother's shenanigans in the Infant of Prague Shop. She also told her about her complicated relationship with Rico, along with the trouble they had gotten into.

"Wow," said Gabby. "That's a whole lotta living in a short amount of time." She made circles in the gravel beneath the swing with the toe of her sneaker. "I can see why you want to get out of that apartment, and I've been wracking my brains, trying to think where you could live. Realistically, you have to wait until we graduate. Then we can get jobs and rent a room together. In the meantime, just avoid your mom. And Cosi..." Gabby paused, "maybe cut your mom some slack. She deserves to have a life too."

Cosi twisted the swing slowly around the way she did when she was a child. She lifted her feet, and as the swing dizzily unwound she closed her eyes, pretending she was unwinding her life, going back to a time when things were so much simpler. When the swing stopped, she opened her eyes. Nothing had changed. She told Gabby she was going back home.

Cosi expected the principal to expel her when she arrived at school the next day, or at the very least, have her volunteer job terminated. She waited nervously, watching the clock, but the call from the front office never came. On Wednesday, she decided to go directly to Mrs. Claymore's office. The woman beckoned her in and shut the door.

"Sit down, Cosi. Do you know how dangerous it is to be out on the grounds alone with someone like Rico?" She hesitated. "Do you know he murdered someone?"

Cosi looked at the floor. "Yes, Mrs. Claymore. I know."

"Why on earth would you risk your life with him? I am surprised, Cosi. I thought you had more sense. Rico admitted he lured you out there. Being naïve and trusting, you fell for it."

Cosi screwed up her courage. She was just as much to blame as Rico, and she could not understand why he was covering for her. Why would he ruin his chances of getting out? The worst that could happen to her was they would fire her from a non-paying job that was nearly over anyway. He risked losing his privileges, even his chance for release.

"It wasn't his fault," Cosi blurted out. "It was my choice to walk the grounds with him. He didn't hurt or threaten me in any way. He shouldn't be punished. I should. I'll leave today."

"It's noble of you to try to take the blame, but I happen to believe Rico's version of the story. I've decided you can finish out your assignment here, but as part of your final report, I want you to include something about the lessons you've learned in dealing with the mentally ill."

"What will happen to Rico?"

"That's up to Doctor Mooney." Mrs. Claymore stood up. "Go on now. The ladies are waiting."

Cosi hurried to the Ladies' Day Room, glancing at the library in hopes of seeing Rico. He was not there. She ran to Erma and hugged her, and Erma grunted in surprise. Gigi looked up from her desk and then down again, her index fingers searching for the typewriter keys.

"Hey Miss," said Erma, rocking back and forth. "Someone left something for you on the table." Cosi looked over at a roll of old magazines held together by a rubber band. A slip of white paper with the single word, "Cosi" was wedged beneath the band.

Cosi picked up the roll. She slipped off the rubber band and a small, unmarked white envelope hidden between the magazines dropped to the floor. She picked it up, tore through the flap and pulled out a single sheet of paper:

O! She doth teach the torches to burn bright
It seems she hangs upon the cheek of night
Like a rich jewel in an Ethiop's ear
Beauty too rich for use, for earth too dear....
Did my heart love till now? Forswear it, sight!
For I ne'er saw true beauty till this night.
Romeo and Juliet, Act I, Scene V

Cosi shoved the piece of paper into her pocket, hoping that Gigi had not seen her reading it. She walked down the hall to the restroom, and read it again. *Did my heart love till now?* What was he trying to tell her? Was he in love with her? The thought made her palms sweat. She was confused by her feelings for him, some mix of sympathy and loyalty and yes, sexual attraction. But love?

Cosi didn't see him all that week, but on the following Friday she saw him on the basketball court. She kept walking when he stopped dribbling the ball and stared after her. He said nothing, and she did not turn back to look, though she knew he followed her with his eyes.

At night, she lay in bed, thinking about the lines from Shakespeare, wondering if Rico was thinking about her. The memory of his kiss confused and tormented her. She wondered what it would be like to kiss him again, but that first one had cost him dearly. He might be stuck in the hospital for a long time now because of her lapse in judgement.

Cosi ran to the bathroom and splashed cold water on her face. What was she thinking? That she could have a relationship with Rico? She realized how ludicrous this was. Instead, she should focus on helping him get out. Rico had paid his debt to society. Enough was enough.

She dried her face and smiled. Yes, she would put all of her energy into helping Rico get into Doctor Mooney's program. She would help him ease back into society and move to Brooklyn, if that's what he wanted. She took a deep breath. Her life had purpose again.

Cosi ran down the stairs Saturday morning and grabbed Rory's bike. She pedaled as fast as she could until she could see the spires of the hospital's administration building. Instead of entering the way she usually did, she rode her bike around to a side entrance, then behind the hospital to the back of the basketball court. She found him there, practicing foul shots.

"Rico," she hissed, pushing the bike behind a bush. He looked quickly around and came to where she stood outside the fence, her hands gripping the chain link as she once saw him do.

"What are you doing?" He shook his head. "Do you know how much trouble we could get into?

"I...I need to talk to you," she stammered, suddenly losing her nerve. "What did Doctor Mooney say?"

"He gave me a lecture and told me to take my pick: lose my library privileges or my basketball privileges. I chose to keep basketball. What about you? I can't believe they didn't end your school project."

"I wouldn't care if they did," she said. "I graduate in two weeks. Then I'll be able to come and visit you whenever I want." She added defiantly, "And I won't care who knows it."

"Cosi, listen to me. I have to be very careful. They might release me soon, maybe this month. The hospital is under pressure to select people for the new program. I might be able to start a new life."

Her heart sank. It was good news for him, of course, but it meant he would get out without her help. Soon he would leave for Brooklyn and she would never see him again. He put his fingers through the fence, covering her fingers with his own.

"I thought you'd be happy for me."

"I am," she said, miserably. She searched his eyes, and thought she saw a hint of sadness there. "Please don't leave Buffalo."

He reached up and grabbed the fence high above his head, and pressed his forehead against the chain link. She could feel the heat from his body and thought about Romeo and Juliet, the star-crossed lovers who would rather die than live apart.

"We talked about this, Cosi. I can't make a life here." He looked down at her, touched her nose tenderly through the fence, then brushed her lips with his finger. They stood in silence, not knowing how to break the tension that lay between them. Finally, his face relaxed in a smile.

"You could always come to Brooklyn. What's keeping you in Buffalo?" He stepped away from the fence, picked up the basketball and began to bounce it. "From what I hear, this town is dying. You said you have an aunt and sister in New York City. Would you consider it?"

She looked at his face. *Is he teasing me?* "Leave Buffalo? My whole life is here."

"Your life until now. You told me you decided not to become a nun, so you're trying to find a new purpose in life. You think you'll find it here? Come with me and we'll work for Reverend Taylor, together. It's a way to put our pasts behind us and work on a righteous cause."

"I've got to go," she said, grabbing Rory's bike. "But I'll think about it."

Cosi lay sleepless the entire night. She got out of bed sometime around

4 a.m. and sat on the back porch in her bathrobe, shivering in the chilly pre-dawn. She looked for Joey, hoping to find him in the garage working on his motorcycle. She needed someone to talk to about the crazy thoughts going through her head, but the garage was dark and silent.

Cosi didn't give a second thought to the junior prom—she had no one to go with anyway—and instead threw herself into her schoolwork, determined to finish up high school and graduate with Gabby. Two weeks before school ended, Sister Claire called her into the guidance office. "Congratulations, Cosi! We've just learned you won a New York State Regents Scholarship. You'll be getting a letter from Governor Rockefeller soon. We're all thrilled for you!" Sister Claire beamed as if it were her own accomplishment.

Cosi was confused. "I won a scholarship? What does that mean, exactly?"

"It means you can go to any state college or university in New York, tuition-free." She looked at Cosi. "You don't seem very excited. I hope you'll knuckle down now and start filling out your applications."

Cosi shook her head. "I don't know what to say. I never gave college any serious thought. I'm not sure what subjects I'd take if I did go."

"There's no need to decide on a major right away. Go to a good, liberal arts school and take a variety of courses. In time, you'll figure out what comes next for you."

Cosi left the guidance counselor's office decidedly out of sorts. What a thing to find out just before graduating. A few weeks ago, she had given no thought to what she would do next. Now a bewildering array of choices confronted her. Find a job and apartment with Gabby, go off to college, or follow her heart and go to Brooklyn with Rico. There wasn't much time to decide.

CHAPTER THIRTY-SIX: DOOR 1, 2, OR 3

THE HOLY MARTYRS GRADUATION ceremony was scheduled for June 18th, a Friday evening, at Kleinhan's Music Hall. Cosi stopped by the psychiatric hospital on Wednesday to hand in her final report and say goodbye to the patients on Ward Two. She decided to say goodbye to Rico too, though she dreaded it. She had managed to avoid him for weeks.

She wrestled with the idea of going to Brooklyn, but the longer she kept her distance from Rico, cold logic prevailed. Cosi could just imagine her mother's face when she informed her that her only remaining child was about to abandon her to live in Brooklyn with a murderer. She decided she would thank Rico, tell him she truly cared for him, wish him well, and if she had the chance, give him one last kiss. She owed him a meaningful goodbye.

"Cosi, this is excellent," said Mrs. Claymore, thumbing through the 40-page report. "Obviously my faith in you was not misplaced, and that little mishap with Rico taught you a valuable lesson. I'll be pleased to tell Sister Matthew your volunteer work here was an unqualified success."

Cosi shook Mrs. Claymore's hand, thanked her, and said goodbye, happy to get out of her office without further discussion. She hurried down the hall to Ward Two.

"I made something for you," said Erma, standing shyly in front of Cosi. She handed Cosi a crayon portrait. "It's you," she said, pointing to the tiny brown cross hanging from the stick-like neck.

"Erma, it's beautiful. Thank you," said Cosi. Erma stood awkwardly while Cosi hugged her. A few other patients came over to say goodbye as the tears rolled down Cosi's cheeks. Even Gigi stepped outside her office to join the chorus of farewells.

"Well, I can't say I'll miss you," said Gigi, arms folded, gum popping. "But it was nice to have someone around who didn't have a screw loose."

Cosi grinned. "Yeah, I won't miss you too," she said, heading for the door.

Sarah intercepted her. "That guy from the Men's Ward? He asked me to give you this." Sarah handed Cosi a small wooden box. "It doesn't open or anything. I tried."

Cosi recognized it immediately as a puzzle box. Her father had given each of his children one when they were small. Little Ange threw hers in a drawer and Nino put his in his Lincoln Logs canister, but Cosi managed to figure out how to open hers, and proudly showed her father the dollar bill inside.

Cosi thanked Sarah and walked quickly down the hall, working furtively on the box. She could feel the sides sliding back and forth, up and down, but this one was more complicated than the one she had as a child. Finally, she managed to open it and found a note inside.

Walk outside to the farthest building on the right. Go in the back way and look for a door marked Laundry. I will be working there. I would like to say goodbye.

Cosi followed the instructions carefully, her heart thundering in her ears. She found the building, squinting as she walked through the back door into the darkened hallway, until her eyes adjusted and she could spot the laundry sign on a non-descript gray door. She slowly opened it.

Rico stood inside a steamy room with machinery that hissed and thrummed behind him. He wore a plain white t-shirt and a pair of jeans. He had obviously been working, sorting clothes, and she took in the sweat on his brow, the t-shirt clinging to his chest.

"Come in," he said, shutting the door behind her.

They stood facing each other. Cosi shifted apprehensively, but the frisson of danger, mixed with his raw sensuality, acted like an aphrodisiac. Despite all good sense, she decided there and then she would kiss him. Her long years of suppressed desire, coupled with the thought of never seeing Rico again, overcame whatever reticence she had left. She grabbed his shirt and kissed him as urgently as he had once kissed her. Rico reacted with surprise.

"Don't do this," he said. Her hands moved down his chest. "I won't be able to stop you."

"Then don't," Cosi said.

Psychiatric patients cannot wear belts, so it was a simple matter of popping the snap and unzipping his jeans. He was more than ready for her. He lifted her black school uniform and tugged off her panties in two swift motions. He picked her up and, with her back against one of the industrial-sized dryers, entered her. She gasped. He thrust a few times, and it was over.

"Sorry," he said. "It's been a long time."

That was it? Sex, the thing she obsessed about, worried about all these years, was over in 15 seconds. Like so many things in life, reality was a poor second to her vivid imagination.

She pulled up her panties and smoothed her skirt. He bent and kissed the top of her head, pulled her close, and took a deep breath. "Listen. I haven't stopped thinking about our conversation at the basketball court. Tell me you decided to come with me to Brooklyn."

"I'm sorry…" she said, and his face fell. "It's just…I feel rushed. Too many choices…."

"Cosi, I've been in here 10 long years. You say things have changed. I have no idea what to expect when I get out. You could help me, and others, by helping Reverend Taylor. You say you believe in social justice for people like me. What better opportunity will you have?"

Cosi could feel herself wavering. "You're right. But let's do this. When they release you, buy a postcard with Niagara Falls on the front, and write, 'Wish you were here, love Marty' on the back." She pulled out a slip of paper and a ballpoint pen from her purse. "Here's my address, include yours on the post card. Give me time to think it over, and I'll send you my decision."

Rico looked at her. "Marty?"

"Long story," she said. "Please don't call me on the phone. My mother won't react well."

THE night before graduation, Big Ange knocked on Cosi's bedroom door. They had not spoken since Cosi slammed the door of the Infant of Prague Shop in her mother's face.

"I'm coming to Kleinhans for the graduation tomorrow," her mother said through the door. "I want to see what I paid for."

"Suit yourself." Cosi heard her mother walk away and felt ashamed. What right did she have to judge her mother so harshly? Hadn't she just had sex with Rico?

Shame on me, Cosi decided. *I'm guilty of old thinking too. My mother should be able to have sex whenever she wants.*

The Holy Martyrs graduation ceremony was held in elegant, drum-shaped Kleinhans Music Hall, while the setting sun shimmered in its reflecting pool. Candles bathed the large auditorium in a pale light and sprays of white lilies lined the aisles. The graduates, dressed in white caps and gowns, filed down the middle aisle and found seats in front of the stage.

Cosi fidgeted and began to sweat under the polyester fabric. High school was finally over, but she had no idea what she would do next. Gabby had a job and was already making plans to move into the group house on Richmond Avenue. Sister Claire was pressuring her to apply to colleges. And then, there was Rico.

Cosi turned and looked quickly behind her at the audience. She saw her mother sitting with Aunt Franny and Aunt Rosa, all three looking at the printed program. When they announced the names of the students who would begin their postulancy immediately after graduation, Cosi glanced nervously back at her mother, worried she might make a scene when Cosi's name was not on the list. But Big Ange looked straight ahead. When they announced the names of the students who won Regents Scholarships, Cosi looked back again and saw the look of surprise on her mother's face. Big Ange looked directly at Cosi, smiled, and burst into tears. Cosi shook her head. The woman would always be a puzzle to her.

After the ceremony, Gabby ran up and gave Cosi a hug. "We're done!" she whooped, "We're free! I start at the Casa di Pizza on Monday and I'll keep an eye out for you. They're always hiring waitresses, the manager told me."

"That's great, Gabby." Cosi looked over her shoulder, stalling for time. "I think my mother's searching for me. I'll call you tomorrow, OK?"

Cosi hurried up the aisle but not toward her mother. She headed out a side door and began to walk down Porter Avenue toward Fargo. She pulled off her uncomfortable dress shoes and began to run shoeless, the sidewalk surprisingly cool on this mild June evening. She hurried up the steps to the Catalfanos' front door and rang the doorbell.

Mrs. Catalfano looked sadder than usual when she eyed Cosi's cap, gown, and pantyhose-covered feet. "Well, congratulations are in order, Cosi. But if you're looking for Joey, I'm afraid he's not here. Joey and his father got into a terrible fight a month ago. He got on his motorcycle and left without saying goodbye."

Cosi mumbled her thanks and went up to her empty flat. She sat in her dark room, more anxious than ever about the future, and began to sort through her choices. The thought of working as a waitress at a pizza joint depressed her. The idea of going to college terrified her. What did that leave? Rico. She looked at her statue of the Virgin Mary. "If you have any advice, now would be the time." The statue stood silent, glistening in the moonlight.

CHAPTER THIRTY-SEVEN: LONG LONELY NIGHTS

WITH HIGH SCHOOL FINISHED, the days passed slowly. Cosi walked down to the box on the front porch to get the mail each morning, trying hard not to look for a postcard from Rico. In early July, her mother came home with a bag of bread dough from the bakery and dropped a stack of mail on the kitchen table. "Mailman came late today. Something in there from Marty."

Numb with anticipation, Cosi deliberately thumbed slowly through the stack before she picked up the "Greetings from Niagara Falls!" postcard, and waited until her mother was busy to read it.

"Wish you were here, love Marty" it said. Looking more closely she could see, upside down and in tiny letters along the bottom of the card, an address: P.O. Box 515, Buffalo, NY. Now she could write to Rico without fear. Cosi glanced at her mother, who was absorbed in punching down her bread dough.

Cosi went to her room and wrote Rico a long letter. She told him she missed him and hoped he was enjoying his freedom. She had given it a lot of thought, and yes, she thought she could help him. Would he like to get together to talk? She mailed the letter and waited.

It was two weeks before she got a response; this time a sealed envelope from "Marty" with a single sheet of paper inside containing four words: "Brooklyn yes, or no?" So, this was it. Decision time. If she said no, or didn't write back, she would never hear from him again.

She tossed and turned all night, trying to make up her mind, and finally asked herself the question he posed: *What's keeping me here? I have no job or boyfriend. My whole family is gone, except for Mama, and we barely talk. Joey's gone too. All that's here are bad memories.*

In Brooklyn, she decided, she could start fresh. She could live with Aunt Mari, go to college, help Rico at the Baptist Church on weekends. *Who knows, after a time, we might just find out that we really are in love.*

Cosi wrote back: *Yes, I will go with you and do everything I can to help you! I can't wait to see you again. In a week or so, you should come by my house, late at night, after Mama is asleep. I will be out on the top front porch waiting for you, suitcase packed and ready to go.*

She mailed the letter and waited for his response. She wondered what clothes she should bring. She heard they dressed very fashionably in New York City. She counted her babysitting money—$34 —enough to buy a few new outfits at Norban's.

While she waited to hear from him, Cosi tried not to think about all the things she would be leaving behind. She had never been away from home before, and the thought of parting with her West Side neighborhood and the dream of owning a home there one day, hurt her heart. She would miss the neighbors, the family gatherings, and her many relatives, even her obnoxious cousin Rory, who along with the rest of Uncle Danny's family and most of working-class Buffalo, faced a very uncertain future. She thought about Gabby and wondered if they could be long-distance friends.

She knew she would miss Joey terribly, and that she would probably be making a different choice if only he'd given her some sign that he cared for her as much as she cared for him. She knew now that was just a childish dream. Something happened to Joey that she couldn't fathom; he seemed so broken, and she felt powerless in the face of it. Probably better that she wouldn't have a chance to see to him before she left for Brooklyn.

Cosi hated to admit it, but the person she would miss most of all was her mother. Despite all of her lying and conniving, her horrific temper and bad behavior, Cosi knew her mother loved her ferociously. Yet here she was, about to do the same thing Little Ange did—abandon her mother without warning because she was too afraid to face her.

On Friday, when a week had passed, Cosi paced the floor nervously. *Rico might come tonight,* she told herself. *I told him a week or so, but I'm not sure when he got my letter. I'll wait on the porch, just in case.* Around midnight she got out of bed, edgy and anxious, and stood outside Big Ange's door, listening for her mother's snoring. Satisfied she was asleep, Cosi moved quietly to the top porch and slipped outside. She opened one of the folding chairs and put it close to the railing so she would have a good view of the street below.

It was sometime close to 4 a.m. when she decided Rico was not coming. Cosi went to her bedroom, disappointed, and opened her window wide, to be sure she could hear, just in case he came in the early morning hours. She listened to the sound of an occasional car coming down Fargo Avenue, jumped up once or twice, certain she heard someone parking outside. Finally, just before sunrise, she could stay awake no longer and fell into a troubled sleep.

It was the same on Saturday and Sunday night. Cosi dragged herself through each day, weary from lack of sleep. She repacked her suitcase, carefully folding and refolding the new clothes from Norban's, first putting them at the bottom of the suitcase, and then moving them to the top. She decided she would wear her new blue jumpsuit when he came to pick her up. She put it on each evening before she went out to the porch to wait.

Another week passed before Cosi started to worry. *What if he never received my letter?* He would think she changed her mind. She sent another letter, telling him she was waiting on the porch every evening, ready to leave. *Please come as soon as possible*, she wrote.

It was another week before she started crying. She would walk out to the porch and sit there, sometimes in the rain, inventing little games to entertain herself. The tears would start around 3 a.m., of exhaustion or disappointment, she could not say which, and before she would see the first rays of the sun, she would head back to her room and cry herself to sleep.

By the end of July, Cosi decided something had gone terribly wrong. Maybe Rico had gone back to his old neighborhood and gotten into trouble. Maybe he had a psychotic episode and ended up back in the hospital. There was one other possibility, but she would not consider it. He would not have changed his mind, or left without her. She was sure of that.

On the first day of August, she slept through her midnight alarm and for the first time in weeks had a full night's rest. When she awoke to hear the birds chirping, she lay listlessly on her bed, admonishing herself for putting her faith in someone once again.

She let Gabby help her get a job at the Casa di Pizza and decided to get back into running. She would talk to herself as her feet moved in the old, familiar rhythm. *Move on. Forget Joey. Forget Rico. Forget men. Move on. Forget Joey. Forget Rico. Forget men.* The return to running was more difficult than she expected. She seemed to tire so easily now.

On a steamy, late August evening just before midnight, Cosi opened her bedroom window. The rain had stopped, and hot, moist air blew in from the river. She glanced out at the dark street, bathed in the watery light of the streetlamp, and went back to bed, listening to the sand flies hitting the window screen.

Cosi threw off the blankets and lay spread-eagled on the damp bed. Still hot, she threw off her nightgown too. Looking down at her naked body and the tiny pool of sweat between her breasts, she considered how much she had changed. She was a woman now, almost 17. No reason to hitch her wagon to some lying, useless man. There were so many more opportunities for women these days. Tomorrow, she promised herself, she would start to apply to colleges....

Suddenly, Cosi sat bolt upright in bed. She thought she heard something outside. She picked up her nightgown and held it in front of her chest while she tiptoed toward the window and peered out. It was difficult to see anything in the steamy blackness below but she thought she saw someone moving slowly, just below her window. She pulled on her nightgown, pressed her face against the screen, and saw the familiar outline of Rico's head, silhouetted by the streetlight.

Cosi ran around her room in a frenzy, pulling on her blue jumpsuit, looking frantically for her shoes, grabbing the suitcase from under the bed. She was just about to shut her bedroom door when she heard a bang. At first, she thought it might be a blown tire. That happened from time-to-time on the street below. Yet somehow her feet were rooted to the floor and she was unable to move until she heard her mother's bed creaking, and footsteps moving to the door.

"What the hell was that?" called her mother. "It sounded like a gunshot."

Her mother ran past her toward the front door. Cosi tried to make words come out of her mouth, to tell her mother, *do not go down there*, but her mother kept moving. Minutes later, Big Ange reappeared, flushed and panting.

"Call the police. A man was shot trying to break into our house."

Cosi tried to process what she was hearing. *It must have been someone else. It must have been a burglar, someone trying to break in.* Even as she was telling herself this, she remembered. In her neighbors' eyes, Rico was an outsider, a black man, a threat. He was in her driveway in the middle of the night and no one knew him. *How could I be so incredibly stupid?*

Cosi was running then, down the stairs and out the door, into the driveway. She saw him lying, twisted, a dark pool forming under his head. His eyes were glassy as she bent over him. He did not look at her as she whispered his name.

"Rico…Rico…don't die…I'm sorry. I'm so sorry."

Granny Archer was standing in her window, gun still in her hand. Big Ange hurried up to her. "What happened?"

"Heard a noise. Saw him sneaking up your driveway. Got him on the first shot."

Cosi heard her and started screaming, "You old witch! You killed him! You killed an innocent man!" Granny looked at her, bewildered. Cosi knelt by Rico and pulled his bloody head onto her lap, put her hand on his cheek. He was still warm. "Stay with me," she whispered.

Big Ange stared at her daughter, taking in the new jumpsuit. "Cosi, you know this man?"

"Yes, I know him." Cosi glared at her mother. "His name is Rico. We were going to leave here tonight. Together."

Sirens wailed in the distance. Uncle Danny's family and most of the neighbors came out and gathered in small knots. While the ambulance drivers lifted Rico onto the stretcher, Big Ange reached down and picked up a slip of paper on the blood-spattered driveway. It had Cosi's name and address on it, in Cosi's handwriting. Big Ange shoved it in her pocket.

Cosi clung to Rico until the ambulance drivers roughly pushed her away.

She began to shake violently when they covered his head and placed him in the back of the vehicle. The ambulance moved slowly down the street; its siren stilled.

Big Ange put an arm around Cosi, pulling her back toward the house. "You had a shock. You don't know that man. Come with me. Let the police take care of this."

Cosi shook her off. "No! I'm telling the police Granny killed him. She's a murderer. She has to pay."

Big Ange grabbed her by the arm. "You're talking crazy. You come with me."

"Get your hands off me," Cosi snarled. The police had started questioning the neighbors.

"He's dead," Big Ange hissed. "Forget him. Nothing can bring him back. Keep your mouth shut and let Granny tell her story."

Cosi pulled her arm away. "Don't you dare tell me what to do. I'm telling the police the truth. I loved Rico. We were going to Brooklyn together."

Cosi never saw the slap coming and it knocked her to the ground. Her mother stood over her, furious. "You little *puttana*. Just like your worthless sister. You're dead to me, too."

Cosi jumped up and spat at her. Big Ange lifted her hand to strike again, when a police officer came over and separated them. Cosi tried to slow her breath, to calmly tell the officer about Rico, how they planned to leave together, and that she had arranged for him to pick her up at night. The crowd standing on the sidewalk strained to listen.

"So, you were planning to leave for Brooklyn in the middle of the night with this man? How old are you?" asked the officer. He licked his pencil tip and began writing in his notebook.

"Hey Joe," called the officer talking to Granny Archer on her front porch. "This is the lady who shot him. She's the one we need to interview." They deliberately ignored Cosi after that, though she tried several times to interject.

"I think we got enough," said the one named Joe. "Looks like self-defense to me."

When the police drove away, Cosi could feel the whole neighborhood looking at her. While a few remaining lab technicians took pictures of the blood-spattered driveway, Big Ange told neighbors her version of the story. "She's upset. She thought maybe she knew him, but thanks to God, she does not."

Cosi ran into the alley behind the garage. She crouched in the dark, not praying or thinking. She was there when the first rays of the sun inched over the horizon.

In the dim light, Cosi caught a glimpse of something half-buried in the trash-strewn alley. Nino's shoes, sitting there like an accusation. She must have dropped them when she collapsed in the snow last Christmas. She picked up the shoes and held them to her chest, but she did not cry. She had no tears left.

Chapter Thirty-Eight: In Search of Peace

THE ARTICLE DID NOT make the front page of the *Buffalo Evening News*. Cosi found it buried in the Metro section, recounting how a man named Ricardo Gonzalez was shot and killed while attempting to break into a home on Fargo Avenue. The article mentioned that the man, until recently a patient at the psychiatric hospital, had a history of violence. The quote from Mrs. Claymore, a hospital official, stated that the hospital released Mr. Gonzalez as part of an experimental program.

"The jury's still out," Mrs. Claymore was quoted as saying. "Obviously our community takes a big chance when it releases such patients." The article noted that Margaret Archer, 72, an alert neighbor, had shot the man, fearing for her safety and that of her neighbors.

In the story, Police Chief Jerry Gugliamo commended Mrs. Archer on her actions. "The police cannot be everywhere at all times. Citizens like Mrs. Archer, willing to act when they see a dangerous situation, help maintain the safety of our urban neighborhoods." At the end of the article was a quote from an anonymous source, describing how the deceased reportedly knew a teen-aged girl who lived in the house, and had attempted to molest her in the past.

From behind her locked bedroom door, Cosi could hear the phone ringing all day. She heard her mother talking from time to time, but could make out only snippets of conversation.

"No, we're OK. Just shook up. No, we don't need anything. Thanks. We'll be fine."

Cosi could always tell when it was one of the relatives. The conversations were longer and her mother lowered her voice. "Yeah, I guess she used to see him when she worked at that hospital. He musta come looking for her when he got out. Thanks to God, Granny Archer had that gun. I appreciate your prayers, Franny."

Cosi stayed in her room for days, leaving only to go to the bathroom. One night, when the chilly September winds rattled the leaves outside, she lay face down on her bed, looking at Nino's shoes lying on the floor. She thought about the time she lay in this bed after the death of her father, convinced that the Virgin Mary spared her life so she could embark on a holy mission to save others. Cosi laughed bitterly. What a joke. She had no mission. No reason to live, really.

She stood up and walked to her dresser, put Rico's wooden box and the Shakespeare poem in one pocket, and an old joint unwittingly left behind by Little Ange, in the other. She patted the wooden cross Rico had given her to make sure it was there, and bent down to tie Nino's shoe laces together. She hung the shoes around her neck, like an albatross.

Cosi walked out of the flat to the end of Fargo Avenue. When she reached the corner of Niagara Street, she lit the joint and inhaled deeply, coughed once or twice and took another drag. The stone railing on the Peace Bridge was a little higher than waist height, she remembered. It should be a simple matter of hoisting her butt up, flipping her legs over and around the other side. It would be over in seconds.

She took another hit on the joint, letting the smoke burn deeply into her lungs, and like something out of a bad movie, thought she heard an approaching motorcycle. She turned as Joey roared up beside her. He pulled up to the curb and let the bike idle, full-throated, while he looked at her messy hair, the joint, Nino's shoes hanging around her neck.

"Get on," he commanded.

Cosi climbed on and pressed her face against his back as the bike roared off. They pulled into the empty lot near the lighthouse, got off and climbed silently towards the top.

Joey turned to her midway up. "What the hell is going on?"

The pot was taking effect. "Going to the Peace Bridge," Cosi mumbled, "to find peace."

She leaned against the circular wall and slid slowly down, like sap oozing from a tree. She began to sob. Joey picked her up and carried her the rest of the way, set her on her feet and held her tightly in his arms.

"I read about what happened in the papers. I've been talking to your mother and she called me when she saw you walking out the door. She was worried. I came as soon as I could."

It was a long time before Cosi was able to speak, but eventually the story began to spill out. She told Joey about Rico and her plan to help him. Her foolish belief that it would be safe to secretly meet in her driveway. The weariness she felt, the guilt and hopelessness, and her decision to jump off the Peace Bridge.

Joey let go of her and spit on the floor. "You were gonna off yourself? That's weak. I thought you were tougher than that." He began pacing in a circle, not looking at her. "When I came back from 'Nam, strung out on heroin, wanting to die, who was the one person who came to the house, who made me want to get my shit together? You."

She blinked. "Heroin?"

He ignored her question. "You think people died because of stupid mistakes you made. Well, same here. What do you think happened on Hamburger Hill?" He was agitated now, cracking his knuckles and shaking his head while he paced. "My dad wanted me to go off and come back a big war hero like him. But war heroes don't accidently kill their own guys."

He was crying then, wracking sobs that came from somewhere deep and terrible. "You thought you could save this Rico? Save me? What makes you think you can rescue everyone, Cosi? You can't, you know. Some people are just doomed, as a result of circumstances they did not create, and no miracle from on high will save them. But you can save yourself."

Tears filled her own eyes. She loved him more than ever, this man who carried the burden of a terrible mistake, not unlike her own. They had both been to hell and back, had teetered on the brink of destroying themselves— yet they were both still here. There must be something they were hanging onto.

"Do you love me, Joey?"

He looked at her. "Why ask me that? I got really messed up in 'Nam."

"But…do you love me?"

"What does it matter?" He ran his fingers through his hair. "Why make me say it?"

Cosi went to him then, stroked his chin, and made him look her in the eyes. "Because I love you, Joey. I have always loved you, but I was convinced you didn't love me. Now that I know what you've been struggling with…."

He cut her off. "I'm damaged, Cosi. All I can do is look out for you, make sure you're safe. I can't do anything more than that."

His words triggered a dim memory. "You were the one who carried me in and kept me warm after Nino died. That was you, wasn't it?"

He shrugged. "*You* could have died. You needed me."

"I need you now. I need a reason to live."

Cosi could see the pain in Joey's eyes, the torment in his face. "I can't be your reason to live, Cosi. I wish to God I could be, but I can't."

She laid her hand gently against his cheek. "Whether you like it or not, *you* are my reason to live, whether you're capable of loving me or not. While you're still breathing, I can hope."

"And I promise you, until you draw your last breath, I will be there for you."

They held each other then, knowing they had made the only commitment two lost souls could make to each other; not to die, so the other had the will to keep living.

Off in the distance, lights were twinkling in the town of Fort Erie, Canada. Joey kissed the top of her head. "They should fix up this old lighthouse," he said, turning toward the river so she couldn't see his face.

"It's an important part of Buffalo's history, isn't it?" Cosi said softly. "Why doesn't anyone care that it's falling apart?"

"Haven't you noticed? The whole city is falling apart. Shit, the whole damn *country* is falling apart."

Cosi looked south toward the lake, at her father's beloved steel plant, at the other factories along the waterfront that planned to lay off workers, and considered the hardships that would inevitably come. Was there really a future here? Although she loved her city, Joey was right. Like the lighthouse, everything in Buffalo was falling apart. Her hometown seemed to be in a death spiral. She could either leave, or stay and watch it die.

"Let's get out of here." Cosi turned and headed down the stairs.

They climbed onto the Harley and headed down Niagara Street, but instead of taking her home, Joey pulled the motorcycle into the church parking lot at Saint Michael's.

"Why are we here?" Cosi looked up at the tall spire, confused. She followed Joey in, past the holy water font, into the last pew. He sat down, knees spread and arms folded across his chest. He neither bowed his head nor prayed, but looked steadily at the altar. She knelt, unsure what he was doing, and waited.

The church was dark and nearly empty. A few elderly women scattered throughout the pews looked surreptitiously at the muscular man in the leather jacket. Votive candles twinkled like fireflies at a side altar and Father Mario walked in front of the main altar, genuflected, and shuffled through papers on the lectern. Joey stiffened.

"What's wrong?" whispered Cosi.

"We got a history, me and him." Joey stood up and, without a word, left the church. They got on the motorcycle, and when he pulled the bike in front of her house and shut it off, she looked at him.

"What was that all about?"

"What? Me and Mario? Some other time." He pulled out a pack of cigarettes and offered her one. Cosi took it.

He looked contemplative. "I like to sit in the church when it's quiet and I got something heavy to figure out." He lit her cigarette. "You should try it."

Cosi was incredulous. "You still believe in God and all that religious mumbo jumbo—after all you've been through?"

Joey shrugged. "I like an empty church. It calms me."

Cosi looked up at the family flat, at the light on in her mother's bedroom. "I don't want to live here anymore," she said suddenly, the words coming in a rush. "I want to leave."

He took a drag on his cigarette. "And go where?"

"New York City. My aunt and sister live there. Maybe I'll use my scholarship and try to go to college. I hear they have good schools."

Joey sighed. "That's a big move, Stretch. Go upstairs and sleep on it. I'll come by to check on you in the morning."

Cosi managed to slip in and avoid her mother. Lying on her bed, she turned the radio on low. The late-night disc jockey was talking in hushed tones about the feud between John Lennon and Paul McCartney after the release of John's latest album. According to the DJ, John had written nasty lyrics about Paul in several of the songs. Cosi rolled her eyes. It was hard to believe there was a time when things like this were important to her.

"Well, we'll just have to wait to hear Paul's response, won't we?" the DJ chuckled. "In the meantime, let's hear from Paul during happier times, from the album, *Let it Be.*"

Cosi rolled on her side and listened. She let the words of the song wash over her and felt something raw and wounded begin to heal. She got up and hugged the statue of the Blessed Virgin to her chest. Whether the Virgin had spoken to her, or even existed, didn't matter. For a while, at least, she had felt special. The vision, or dream, or whatever it was, had given her strength and a sense of purpose, indeed had changed her life. Maybe that's all there is to faith, she thought. A simple recognition that there is something bigger and more important in life than yourself. Maybe it was time to stop overthinking it. Let it Be..

Holding her statue, Cosi crawled into bed and fell asleep.

Chapter Thirty-Nine: Such Sweet Sorrow

Cosi was up before dawn the next morning, filling a small knapsack with the things she could not leave behind. She had already buried the bloody jumpsuit near the broken Infants of Prague, her way of laying Rico to rest. She shoved a few t-shirts, an extra pair of jeans, and all of her underwear into the bottom of the knapsack, along with her statue of the Virgin Mary, the family photo of the five of them, the letter from Sister Barbara, the wooden box, and the lines from Shakespeare given to her by Rico, whose wooden cross still hung on her neck. She threw her diary in for good measure, hoping she might have a future to write about. She looked at Nino's shoes and carried them into his bedroom. "Don't worry," she whispered to the empty room. "I won't forget you, Nino, but I have to let you go."

Cosi was waiting on the top porch when she spotted Joey's motorcycle. She went inside to collect her things and found herself face-to-face with her mother. Big Ange stood in her worn, chenille bathrobe, her eyes puffy, traces of Pond's cold cream lining the roots of her hair. She looked thinner now, and much older than her 37 years.

"I'm leaving, Mama," Cosi said, shouldering the knapsack, "for good."

Her mother nodded slightly. "Call me on Sundays. No matter what you think of me, I'm the only mother you got."

Cosi turned away, fighting back tears she was determined not to shed. Her feelings for her mother were so complicated it was impossible to make sense of them. Her mother was a liar and manipulator who clung to old superstitions, and was stubbornly ill-equipped to deal with the modern world and how to teach her daughters to thrive in it. She was also a broken woman who had lost everything she held dear. She had been trapped, by society and financial circumstances, and forced to live like a feral animal that had to rely on its instincts to survive. She had schemed and scraped to hold her family together, but in the end, it was not enough.

Dear Joey, Cosi had written in her diary the night before, *it's good to be writing again and I don't care if this entry bleeds over into next year's. What I've learned over the past four years is that all grownups lie, including parents, but the truth does not always set you free. It sometimes comes with a cost, so maybe they lie for a reason. Now I say, 'let lying dogs lie,' and keep your damn secrets to yourself.*

When Cosi came walking down the front stairs, Joey looked at the knapsack, then at her face. "You sure you want to do this?"

A tiny tear trickled down to the corner of her mouth. "I have to go. But I'm not leaving Buffalo. It'll always live deep in my soul because it's part of who I am." She swiped the tear away. "Let's go. West Siders are tough, so whatever comes, I'll deal with it." She confidently swung her leg over the seat of Joey's motorcycle and settled in. "And you? What will you do?"

Joey pulled the helmet over his head and revved the engine. "Me? Look for good roads and avoid the gravel." They laughed then, loudly and genuinely, and the sound surprised and delighted them both.

Cosi took one last look down Fargo Avenue. The curling leaves of the dying elm trees hung on tenaciously while the young, sturdy maples swayed confidently in the autumn breeze. Perhaps she would come back one day and find the maples tall and majestic, giving Buffalo a new look. A new life.

They took off as the sun was just beginning to peek over the houses, cradling the neighborhood in a soft pink blanket. She sighed. Buffalo had never looked so beautiful.

The End

Afterword and Acknowledgements

Virgin Snow is a work of historical fiction. All of the characters and the things that happen to them were entirely made up by the author, with the exception of famous historical figures like Dr. Martin Luther King, Jr. and Robert F. Kennedy, who are factually described in the context of the times. That said, I spent many hours researching the larger historical events that form the backdrop of the story, and tried to chronologically represent the times and events that would have affected people on the West Side of Buffalo, New York, in the late 1960s and early 1970s, as accurately as possible. As a result, I owe a great debt of gratitude to the wonderful librarians in both the Erie County Public Library in Buffalo, and the Buffalo History Museum, and especially to Cynthia Van Ness, the museum's Director of Library & Archives, for her invaluable research assistance.

The very first words of *Virgin Snow* found their way onto a blank sheet of paper in late 2015, as a "first chapter" submission necessary to compete for selection in the Novel Year 2016 Program at The Writer's Center in Bethesda, Maryland. Once selected, I worked throughout the year alongside nine other authors, under the skillful guidance of our coach and mentor, author Amin Ahmad. Many, many thanks go to Amin and my fellow Novel Year writers: Ginny Fite, Frank Joseph, Cathy Baker, John Lubetkin, Stan Whatley, Lauren Woods, Michael Barron, Kenny Robinson, and Janis Villadiego. As we worked to complete the first drafts of our novels, and read and critiqued each other's work, their thoughtful suggestions and encouragement helped breathe life into this book.

Thanks also goes to my first readers, Dorothy Z. Gallagher, Kathy Gallagher, and Doreen Regan. Each gave me food for thought about what women readers most appreciate in fictional stories about the characters and cultures of Western New York. A most heartfelt thanks also goes out to Kathryn Johnson, bestselling author of over 40 internationally published books, for her careful reading of the manuscript and her words of encouragement at a time when I most needed them. I would also like to thank Arleen Seed for her patience while working diligently on the cover concept, and Mark Pogodzinski at NFB Publishing for his assistance in bringing this book to fruition.

Finally, I owe a great debt of gratitude to my husband, my most assiduous reader, proof-reader, editor, and enthusiastic promoter of *Virgin Snow*. Without his steadfast support, this book would have remained a manuscript, buried deep in a drawer somewhere.

ABOUT THE AUTHOR

"Moxie Gardiner" is the pen name of a writer, blogger, traveler, Master Gardener and (soon to be) Master Naturalist. The name "Moxie" was first bestowed upon her during a rare visit to an upscale bar late one night in her native Buffalo, NY, as a back-handed compliment by the posh regulars attempting to politely describe her rather rough West Side edges (which she still wears proudly to this day). She does have a soft side, too, however. She loves the smell of warm wood, the sound of insects in the evening, islands too small for cruise ships, and the underbellies of airplanes when they fly over the setting sun.

After graduating from Buff State, she moved to Washington, DC to pursue a career in journalism. She has written more than 100 speeches, authored and edited countless magazine articles, and faithfully scribbled in her personal journals for the past 21 years. To date, she has traveled to 46 countries and all 50 states, and still has a lengthy bucket list of places to see and things to do, including books to write. *Virgin Snow* is her first novel.

Made in United States
North Haven, CT
14 August 2023

40287014R00163